# The Digital Pill

# The Digital Pill: What Everyone Should Know about the Future of Our Healthcare System

**ELGAR FLEISCH**
*ETH Zurich & University of St. Gallen (HSG), Switzerland*

**CHRISTOPH FRANZ**
*F. Hoffmann-La Roche & University of St. Gallen (HSG), Switzerland*

**ANDREAS HERRMANN**
*University of St. Gallen (HSG), Switzerland*

United Kingdom – North America – Japan – India – Malaysia – China

Emerald Publishing Limited
Howard House, Wagon Lane, Bingley BD16 1WA, UK

First edition 2021

**British Library Cataloguing in Publication Data**
A catalogue record for this book is available from the British Library

ISBN: 978-1-78756-676-7 (Print)
ISBN: 978-1-78756-675-0 (Online)
ISBN: 978-1-78756-677-4 (Epub)

ISOQAR certified
Management System,
awarded to Emerald
for adherence to
Environmental
standard
ISO 14001:2004.

Certificate Number 1985
ISO 14001

INVESTOR IN PEOPLE

# Acknowledgments

All graphics were produced on behalf of the authors by Frey Graphic Recording |Bergstraße 91, 61118 Bad Vilbel, Germany |www.graphic-recording.org

To Carmen, Isabelle, and Michaela

# Contents

# About the Authors

**Elgar Fleisch** is a Professor of Information and Technology Management at ETH Zurich and University of St. Gallen (HSG) and Director at the Institute of Technology Management.

His research interests focus on the current fusion of the physical and the digital world into an Internet of Things. His current largest lab, the Center for Digital Health Interventions, investigates how digital technologies are changing our healthcare system. Elgar Fleisch and his team have published their results in over 600 scientific papers.

Elgar Fleisch is a co-founder of several university spin-offs and serves as a member of multiple academic steering committees as well as supervisory boards including Robert Bosch, Mobiliar Insurance Group and Uniqa Insurance Group.

Born 1968 in Bregenz, Austria, Elgar Fleisch was trained in mechanical engineering, computer science and business administration. He received his PhD in Artificial Intelligence in 1993 and devoted his postdoc time to the "networked enterprise". 2002 he was appointed full professor at University of St. Gallen (HSG), 2004 also at ETH Zürich. Elgar Fleisch spent his sabbaticals at MIT and Dartmouth College, both USA.

**Christoph Franz** is Chairman of Roche Holding AG. Prior to this, he served as CEO of Lufthansa as well as Swiss International Air Lines. Prior to joining Swiss Air, he spent nine years in top management positions with Deutsche Bahn, the German national railway, later becoming a Member of Executive Management in charge of passenger transport. Born in 1960 in Frankfurt, Germany, he studied business and engineering at Technical University of Darmstadt and at École Centrale de Lyon, finishing up with a PhD in Darmstadt and a postdoc at UC Berkeley.

Further mandates include the boards of Stadler Rail AG and Zurich Insurance Company Ltd. He is a Member of the Board of Trustees of Ernst Goehner Foundation, the Advisory Board of University of St. Gallen (HSG) and Member of the Assembly and Counsel of the International Committee of the Red Cross, Geneva. Moreover, he was appointed Honorary Professor for Business Administration at HSG in May 2017.

**Andreas Herrmann** is a Professor of Marketing at the University of St. Gallen (HSG) and Visiting Professor at the London School of Economics (LSE Cities).

His research interests focus on consumer behavior, market research, and product development. He has set up several labs, each collaborating with companies and international organizations. He has published extensively, more than 250 scientific papers and 15 books.

Born in 1964 in Germany, he graduated from Koblenz School of Corporate Management and completed his doctoral thesis in the field of consumer decision-making 1991. After his habilitation on the subject of means end chain analysis at University of Mannheim he was appointed as Full Professor to University of Mainz in 1997. In 2002 he moved to the University of St. Gallen.

# Foreword

Writing a book about the opportunities that digital technologies bring to the healthcare sector is a particular sort of challenge. Every day and everywhere across the globe, new health apps are created, as well as innovative approaches for using patient data to develop new treatments. They have the power to redefine the roles of patients and doctors, supplement drug-based treatments with digital ones, and facilitate a shift from curative to preventive medicine. There is also a tremendous opportunity to alleviate the burden on healthcare systems which, in many countries, are underfunded and already operating at their limits, and to provide proper medical care to many more people than in the past.

It is not possible to provide an overview of all these technological developments, to fully explore them, or to conclusively evaluate them at this point. So this book does not provide an exhaustive outline of digital technologies in the healthcare sector, but is more like a diary kept along a journey that is still ongoing. At the same time, it seems worthwhile to embark on this journey, because we currently have a unique opportunity to completely rethink our healthcare system and to actually reshape it as well. The time has come bring these digital options in the healthcare sector onto the stage of public discourse, and thereby help change all of our lives for the better. Which is why this book is written for laypeople, who are interested in the subject rather than as a purely academic treatise or textbook. It is focused more on the patient and less on the processes in hospitals or doctors' offices.

Exploring this topic has moved and captivated us as authors, too, because only at first glance is it merely about technology, apps, algorithms, data, and sensors. Much more fascinating are the stories behind it, the new opportunities that the digital world is opening up to humankind. In addition to all these opportunities, we are particularly moved by the further awareness that we are currently far from being able to provide each and every individual with access to the best medical care. With the help of apps, digital physician assistants, automated mini-clinics, telemedicine, etc., going forward many more people – regardless of where they live and what financial means are at their disposal – could have access to affordable and effective medical care. Digital technologies thus contribute to the democratization of the healthcare sector, which is an important step in offering people the hope of a brighter future, especially in developing countries.

The pandemic of 2020 has opened our eyes in many ways. It has also showed us the importance of digitalization in the healthcare sector, of keeping things up and running in times of physical distancing and of quickly and reliably collecting and consolidating data when public health is at risk. In addition, the last months have shown us how much we as a society are capable of changing when it comes to moving toward digitalization.

For all our enthusiasm for digital technologies, they are never an end unto themselves, but always an important means of improving medical care for humankind. Which is why this book is not simply intended to paint a picture of the course taken by the healthcare system or to illustrate digital applications using the examples of current startups and established corporations and organizations in the healthcare sector. Rather, our aim is – based on these technological opportunities – to identify and explore the principal response patterns and pillars of a new healthcare system. We offer these for discussion in the conviction that by implementing them, we could change people's medical care for the better. With the 25 patterns and five pillars of the healthcare system of tomorrow, we hope to stimulate debate, question the status quo, and even stir up controversy, invite criticism and meet with agreement – but, even more importantly, to point the way to a more effective and efficient healthcare system.

The image of a broad-leaved tree perhaps most clearly illustrates the goal we are pursuing with this book. We are not simply out to collect examples of digitalization from all over the world and pile them up like a colorful heap of leaves. Rather, we want to use the examples to depict the tree that carries the leaves– complete with its roots, trunk, sturdy branches, and slender twigs. These are what give the tree its structure and its strength, making it a thing that lasts for decades, yet is constantly growing and renewing itself, creating new shoots and letting old ones fall. The leaves come and go every year; the roots, trunk, and branches remain.

This book focuses in the five most important non-communicable diseases (NCD) – cardiovascular diseases, respiratory illnesses, diabetes, cancer, and mental disorders such as depression. These diseases cause great suffering among patients and negatively impact on the quality of life of many people. As they become more widespread, they are pushing the healthcare systems of many countries to their limits. The good news, however, is that NCD can be prevented or at least mitigated through lifestyle changes and preventive medicine. This is precisely where digital technologies come into play. They can be used to modify lifestyles, improve prevention and medical care, and develop innovative treatments. If we succeed here, we will not only be able to alleviate people's suffering, but also lighten the load on our healthcare systems. We use the example of NCD to illustrate the digital patterns of the healthcare sector, because they are responsible for the greatest global suffering and the greatest social costs. However, most patterns apply just as well to acute and contagious illnesses.

We have organized this book in three sections. Each can be read and understood separately without the information contained in the other sections. Readers who are interested in the development and consequences of NCD should start with Part I. If you would like to jump straight to the 25 patterns of digitalization, you can begin with Part II. And Part III brings together the lessons learned in the first two sections to form the five pillars of the healthcare system of tomorrow.

"Digitization" simply means the transformation of analog information into a digital, machine-readable format. In this book, we are talking instead about "digitalization": digital transformation in the sense of using of all manner of information technologies to create new products, services, customer experiences, forms of collaboration, and business models. And what exactly do we mean by the book's title, "The Digital Pill"? We are not using this juxtaposition of terms, which is almost paradoxical and therefore thought-provoking, to simply mean a tablet or treatment containing bits and bytes, but any use of digital technologies that changes our healthcare system, accelerates medical progress, or creates new therapeutic or preventive options.

This book never could have been written without the inspiring, critical, and illuminating conversations with many people who are working to develop digital technologies for the healthcare sector and test them on the market. Troy Cox, Doug Hirsch, Andrew Thompson, Nat Turner, Zach Weinberg, Frank Westermann, Thorsten Wirkes, and many others will all shape our approach to digital therapeutics in the coming years with their medical experience, pioneering spirit, and entrepreneurial mindset. Through their expertise, they are making a significant contribution to ensuring that apps, innovative data analyses, and more will find their way into the healthcare sector. We thank them for taking the time to share their insights and their passion with us.

Many physicians, employees, colleagues, and experts, as well as prominent figures from medicine, government, business, and society, contributed their suggestions and feedback. Our thanks go to them all for their willingness to share their knowledge and experience. Among them were Lisa Marsch, Gerald Fleisch, David Gorgan, Tobias Kowatsch, Tim Jäger, Joseph Kvedar, Dave Kotz, Sandy Pentland, Florian von Wangenheim, Florian Wirth, and Felix Wortmann. The detailed, critical reviews, notes, and comments provided by Martin Brutsche, Thierry Carrel, Steffi Gassmann, and Christoph Stettler were particularly valuable, as were those of Daniel Grotzky. He was involved in the creation of this book from the very beginning and continuously sought the advice of his medical colleagues at F. Hoffmann-La Roche AG wherever there was uncertainty. A special thanks goes to Annette Mönninghoff. She took care that we never lost track on this exciting journey. Her inputs were most valuable and extremely helpful. Working with her was a great pleasure!

We particularly wish to thank Niall Kennedy of Emerald-Verlag and Patrik Ludwig of Campus-Verlag for their support. They have shown their enthusiasm for this project from the very start.

We hope we have produced a book that incorporates many different perspectives and contributes to an open, honest, multifaceted, and nuanced discussion of digital applications in the healthcare sector. As authors, we have been tremendously inspired by the potential of digitalization. And we have also been moved by the questions and challenges that have emerged in this context and which are addressed in this book.

Elgar Fleisch
Christoph Franz
Andreas Herrmann

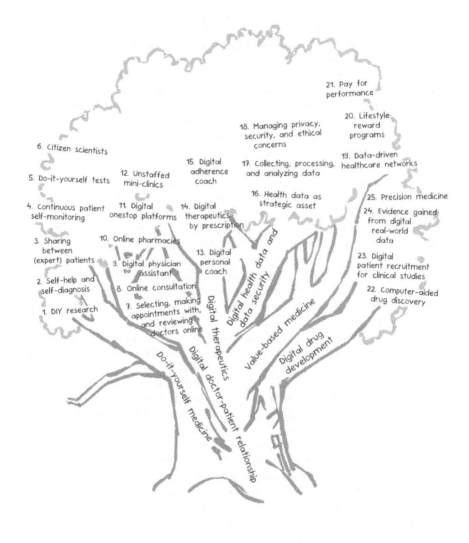

# Preface

Thanks to the successes of modern medicine, the healthcare systems of this world are being pushed to their limits – the one-sided cost spiral is increasingly jeopardizing the access of disadvantaged populations to healthcare and, consequently, endangering the social order as well. Can the "digital pill" generate the veritable quantum leap that will cure our society?

Generally speaking, every healthcare system is under considerable pressure to change and digitalize. A lot could already be done today. However, many service providers are digitizing their paper-based processes in an inward-focused manner, squandering the opportunities of a real partnership-based digital transformation. Rarely do new applications result in more time for hands-on work with patients – for the most part, computer work is becoming more and more of a priority. At the same time, too much is at stake for the individuals concerned in the change process – fears of reduced income, loss of employment, or potentially less interesting work are dominating the discourse. So across the globe, money is being thrown away on unsustainable IT silo solutions. The slow grind of legislation, the strong segmentation of the healthcare market, the inertia of regulatory authorities, and, finally, the widespread fear of change on all sides also contribute to the preservation of the status quo. It must be remembered that changes in healthcare systems affect not only the employees working in the healthcare market, but, at a fundamental level, every citizen – and therefore every one of us. Maintaining each individual's right to privacy demands the highest standards of ethics, processes, and technology, and gives rise to the question of who should own the data, who manages it, and who earns money from it. Although the individual right to privacy must remain intact, each individual can make an important contribution to public health by contributing their anonymized health data, whatever the source. Here, it is the volume of data that is important – the more complete the data is, the larger in quantity and the better in quality, the greater is the potential that can be mined by artificial intelligence. The necessary sociopolitical effort that is required, at least in Western style democracies, to establish such a data alliance, is comparable to the push that led to the creation of essential social services in twentieth century Europe. The logical conclusion is that the proceeds must belong to the innovators in the healthcare market, but primarily to the individual and to society as a whole. In truth, the hurdles posed by these challenges and expectations seem insurmountably high. Digital transformation requires time for cultural change to take place and social solidarity to arise.

In many countries, healthcare systems are governed by financial considerations. We might say that medicine is dependent on the infusion of money. An ungodly, supposedly "free" healthcare market reigns supreme, one that responds to financial incentives. Often enough, this is not governed by medical criteria, but, in a compartmentalized healthcare system, is subject to the special interests of the service providers and professional groups. This results in an inherent risk that the shifts generated by new incentives will lead to further distortions in the healthcare market that are not sufficiently focused on patient benefit. As long as there are enough resources available within the system, there is little pressure for revolutionary change. Popular wisdom tells us that "necessity is the mother of invention." Healthcare systems, however, will steer the economies of many nations into dire straits in the foreseeable future, so that this state of necessity will slowly but surely spread across the globe – with poorer regions of the world never even progressing beyond this status in the first place. In other words, change will come – so let us approach it in a timely and controlled manner.

The Covid-19 pandemic in early 2020 gave the world a time-lapse demonstration of how this could work. Suddenly, medical concepts had to be rolled out in a matter of days. Medical knowledge evolved sometimes in a matter of hours – even health professionals were entirely dependent on information from the internet. During the lockdown, in many countries there was a minor revolution in the way we work. Working from home, virtual meetings, and remote training became widespread and widely accepted. Following the initial cancelation of all events, within weeks digital offerings were created to take their place and have now come to be seen as more than just a substitute and earned themselves a permanent place. Within days, consultations via video calls suddenly became billable, popular, and appreciated. The anticipated benefits from the use of contact-tracing apps suddenly seemed more important than the absolute right to privacy of the individual citizen – a new phenomenon, at least for Europe. So change is possible.

Digital transformation requires cultural change, a bird's eye view, an outside perspective. Which is what makes this book a seam of gold that is well worth mining. Following strictly Hegelian dialectics, it maps the current state of the world's healthcare systems in language that is easy to read and understand. It considers their current capacity for meeting the challenge of the prevention, treatment, and costs of the increasing number of cases of NCD in the context of the changing demographics of our aging population. This book outlines the immense, as yet unleveraged potential of digitalization in the areas of health maintenance and therapeutics, from which, like a phoenix from the ashes, ultimately rises a realistic and positive picture of how to arrive at a healthcare system that can master the challenges. It is richly and colorfully illustrated with vivid and touching examples from different corners of the world. The authors communicate 25 practical problem-solving approaches, which the book calls "response patterns," that when combined, improve the resilience, fitness, and agility of healthcare systems, allowing positive outcomes for patients to materialize. Due mention is made of the extremely creative and pioneering global startup scene in the field of digital health and medicine. The potential risks associated with the new technologies are also given sufficient attention. After all, new developments invariably entail not only positive effects but negative ones as well. The latter must be countered with appropriate measures. The risks of digital transformation must also be weighed against the risks of delayed action – as well as those of not pursuing it at all.

We must and will succeed in using digital medicine to consolidate forward-looking healthcare systems that are able to meet the challenges of the increasing number of non-communicable diseases in an aging society – through an increased commitment of resources to the areas of health maintenance, smart treatments and care models, digitally supported research, and innovation. Thanks to the scalability of digital care and medicine, all social classes, groups, regions, and even countries of this world can be granted access to an affordable healthcare system.

Martin Brutsche
Professor and Doctor of Medicine, Chief Physician,
Clinic for Pulmonology and Sleep Medicine, KSSG,
and President of the Swiss Society for Pulmonology (until 2018)
May 2020

Part I

# Will the Healthcare System Become a Victim of its Own Success?

*Chapters*

1. Medical Progress is a Success Story that Comes with Consequences.
2. Non-communicable Diseases are Straining Our Healthcare System.
3. Digitalization Will Be a Key Success Factor for the Healthcare System of the Future.

Chapter 1

# Medical Progress is a Success Story that Comes with Consequences

*The main theses of this chapter:*

- The medical progress of the past 100 years is the investment of the century. In the space of only 100 years, our life expectancy has doubled.
- Antibiotics and vaccines played a decisive role in the battle against infectious diseases.
- As life expectancy has increased, however, this hasn't always meant improved quality of life in old age. The years we gain are often accompanied by chronic illnesses. Today we are better equipped to survive diseases such as heart attacks or cancer but as a result, we more and more frequently have to live with these illnesses.
- Without the mutual support provided by those with health insurance or the support of taxpayers (in the case of state-funded systems), medical progress does not reach everyone.
- More than half of all Americans who file for personal bankruptcy do so as a result of medical debt.

Let's start with some good news: In only 100 years, our life expectancy has doubled. And not just in wealthy, developed nations. As the twentieth century began, a human being could expect to live about 40–46 years. In the meantime, average global life expectancy has risen to 72 years. In India today, people actually live three times as long as their ancestors did 100 years ago; life expectancy in that nation has increased from 24 years at the beginning of the twentieth century to all of 69 years [1, 2]. These numbers stand for billions of human lives – people who now enjoy more wealth, education, and longevity than any other generation that ever lived on our planet. If we consider that human beings have been around for more than 150,000 years, this amount of progress in only one century is nothing less than spectacular.

What made this amazing success story possible? Of course it doesn't just come down to medical advancements. Growing prosperity, improved nutrition,

The Digital Pill: What Everyone Should Know about the Future of
Our Healthcare System, 3–10
Copyright © 2021 by Emerald Publishing Limited
All rights of reproduction in any form reserved
doi:10.1108/978-1-78756-675-020211001

and better hygiene – clean drinking water, regular waste, and wastewater disposal – as well as the peace that spread across Europe and other parts of the globe following the two world wars have all played a part. However, the primary reason for the increase in life expectancy is the progress made in combating infectious diseases. Until a few centuries ago, such illnesses were the most common cause of human mortality. Becoming infected was often a death sentence, one that robbed many of life during infancy. At the beginning of the twentieth century, one in 10 children in the United States still died before their first birthday. Back then the most common causes of death in young children were pneumonia, influenza, tuberculosis, and gastroenteritis [3].

But then the tide turned. More than any others, two medical innovations have proven to be particularly effective weapons in the fight against infectious diseases and therefore responsible for the increase in human life expectancy: antibiotics and vaccines. The story of the discovery of penicillin, the first antibiotic, has become a modern legend that most of us learn at school. Bacteriologist Alexander Fleming returned to his laboratory in London after a long summer vacation with his family. He had a reputation as an excellent researcher but an untidy one. Before leaving town, Fleming had started some bacteria cultures in Petri dishes. When he went to examine them upon his return, he saw that one of the cultures was contaminated and mold was growing in the Petri dish. When he looked more closely, Fleming noticed that the bacteria culture was not growing in the area surrounding the mold. So he started studying it, and discovered it belonged to the genus of Penicillium. This was why he named the new substance he went on to develop "penicillin." It was to become the most effective substance available for fighting bacterial infections at the time.

Fleming's discovery marked the start of the age of antibiotics. "When I woke up just after dawn on September 28, 1928, I certainly didn't plan to revolutionize all medicine by discovering the world's first antibiotic, or bacteria killer. But I suppose that was exactly what I did," as Fleming would later say [4, p. 366]. Antibiotics like penicillin have saved hundreds of millions of human lives. Exact estimates are difficult to make – but the antibiotics produced by the pharmaceutical companies Pfizer, GlaxoSmithKline, and Roche alone have been prescribed billions of times since their approval. In addition, it is hard to imagine that medical advances like organ transplants would ever have been possible without antibiotics.

Alongside antibiotics, the development of vaccines played a major role in raising human life expectancy. The amazing success of vaccines becomes particularly clear when we look at the first viral disease – a disease caused by a virus – for which one was developed: smallpox. Wolfgang Amadeus Mozart suffered from it, as did Abraham Lincoln and Josef Stalin. These three men survived, although some bore considerable scars for life. Smallpox is one of the most dangerous and deadly diseases ever to affect the human race – every third person who contracts it will die as a result. Even in the twentieth century, more than 300 million people died of smallpox before it was finally declared eradicated in 1980 [5].

And what made this possible? The development and distribution of the smallpox vaccine.

When a healthy person is vaccinated, they are given a weakened form of the virus to stimulate the production of antibodies in the immune system. If the vaccinated person later comes into contact with the actual pathogen, their immune system is prepared and can fight and destroy the virus.

Edward Jenner, a country doctor from England, is considered one of the fathers of the widespread immunization that we know today. Many of his patients were milkmaids, who often became ill from cowpox, a milder form of the poxvirus. And Jenner noticed that none of the milkmaids caught the dangerous and often deadly form of the human virus. Based on this observation, he developed a method in which he inoculated healthy individuals, including his own son, with the secretion from cowpox blisters. The subjects then experienced a mild form of the infection. Later Jenner infected the same individuals with the dangerous smallpox virus – and miraculously, they remained unaffected. This marked the birth of mass immunization, which even today is still called "vaccination" – revealing the origin of the practice. Because "vacca" is nothing other than the Latin word for "cow" [6].

These victories don't mean we can rest on our laurels. Keeping infectious diseases in check is an ongoing battle, as the recent painful experience of the coronavirus pandemic shows. We need to keep developing new generations of virostatic agents and vaccines; novel viruses and bacteria have to be countered with good pandemic preparedness. Skepticism about vaccines among some segments of the population and the resulting insufficient vaccination rates, has caused a

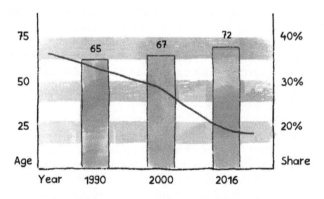

**Fig. 1.1.** *We Live Longer and Die Less Frequently of Infectious Diseases: Life Expectancy and Percentage of Deaths Caused by Infectious Diseases.* **Source:** *Institute for Health Metrics and Evaluation, University of Washington (2019). Share of death from infectious disease of total deaths, Worldwide, All Genders; Life Expectancy in Years.*

resurgence of almost forgotten diseases like measles. So intervention and education are important here as well. But one thing is certain: vaccines and antibiotics have turned the tide in our fight against communicable diseases, resulting in a fundamental change in our understanding of human health. In 1990, one in three people still died of infectious diseases; today it's only one in five. These advances also meant an increase in life expectancy, most recently from 65 years in 1950 to 72 years today (Fig. 1.1). This development bears witness to the success of medical progress but is also the source of new challenges.

### More Years – To Suffer Ill Health?

For the most part, more years of life also mean better quality of life. In the past, it was normal for every family to have at least one child who died young. It was rare to live to see your great-grandchildren. Between 1950 and 2000 life expectancy in Germany, for example, rose from 64.6 years for men and 68.5 years for women to 78.4 and 83.4 years, respectively [7]. But these longer lives also presented society and individuals with new problems.

Medical advancements have not only led to a decrease in infectious diseases, but also enabled us to successfully treat many non-infectious diseases that would almost certainly have proved fatal a hundred years ago, like cardiovascular disease and cancer. However, there is a fundamental difference here to our fight against viruses and bacteria – because unlike infectious diseases, non-communicable diseases (NCDs) often cannot be cured, but only halted or slowed. A study by the University of Southern California shows that we are not "heathier" per se and therefore live longer. Instead, thanks to medical progress, today we are better equipped to *survive* diseases such as heart attacks or cancer – but as a result, we more and more frequently have to live with these illnesses [8].

Before the medical innovations of the twentieth century, a disease usually ended in either recovery or death. Today many of the years of life we have gained are frequently also years, in which an individual will endure one or multiple diseases. This can mean substantial suffering for the patient and their family, and poses new challenges for healthcare systems.

Health economists came up with an indicator for this in the late 1990s, which they called "years lost to disability," or YLD. This means years that the person missed out on because they were severely impaired by their illness. Sometimes the indicator is expressed as "years lived with disability," which paints a somewhat gentler picture. The World Health Organization (WHO) calculates this figure by multiplying the percentage of people affected by the average duration of a disease and a weighting factor [9]. The weighting factor indicates the health impairment caused by a disease, so it is lower for diabetes, for instance, than for cancer (Fig. 1.2).

If we examine the trend, we see a steep increase – by somewhat more than one-quarter since the turn of the millennium – in the number of years in which people are affected by illnesses. In other words, more and more people worldwide are living with a serious disease. Many suffer for years, sometimes unable to work and

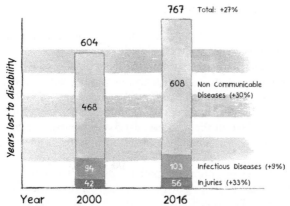

**Fig. 1.2.**    *We Live with Disease for Many Years: Years Affected by Disease in Millions.* **Source:** *World Health Organization (2017). Includes maternal, perinatal, and nutritional cases.*

severely restricted in their daily lives. In 2016, this came to a total of 767 million years of illness worldwide. This trend has been driven by non-infectious chronic illnesses, commonly known as NCDs. The increase in mental illnesses has been particularly strong in recent years. We will discuss NCDs in more detail later in this book.

Length and quality of life don't always go hand in hand. Just because we more frequently "survive" diseases today doesn't mean that human suffering has decreased.

This initial examination shows that medical progress has been a success story – people are living longer and longer lives. However, we also live much longer with illnesses, and this often causes a lot of human suffering, for patients and their families alike.

### Medical Progress also Means New Challenges

In addition to vaccines and antibiotics, the last 100 years have seen medical advances such as new diagnostic and treatment methods that make it easier to fight disease. Blood tests and imaging methods such as computer tomography, ultrasound, and X-ray help physicians diagnose diseases. Cancer can be treated with radiation, surgery, and chemotherapy, and dialysis machines filter the blood in the event of kidney failure. The list of advancements is long and significant.

But what are the consequences of this progress? We live longer and longer, we live in greater prosperity, and we can more frequently declare victory in the battle against disease. More and more grandparents not only live to see their grandchildren born, but also how they thrive and grow, finish school, get married, and start their own families. In the past, this was the exception rather than the rule. But these gains also bring new challenges.

### Economic Consequences

This progress literally comes at a price: it has made medical care more and more expensive in recent years. Treatment-related costs have been rising substantially for years. Take kidney failure, for example: Being diagnosed with kidney failure was once tantamount to a death sentence, but today, with the help of dialysis and kidney transplants, patients can live for many years. In Germany, to name but one example, dialysis treatments cost more than 25,000 euros per patient and year [10]. So where in the past no costs were incurred, today hundreds of thousands of euros are needed. This raises an important question: Who pays the bill?

Historically, it was of course the patients and their families who footed the bill. That was until the beginning of the twentieth century, when health insurance companies began selling policies that let the insured spread the risk, or state-financed healthcare systems distributed the costs among taxpayers. In practice, in most countries today, we find a mix of these three forms of financing.

Because even now, medical costs are not always borne entirely or even mostly by the public or private systems. For many people, illness means economic insecurity. In countries without mandatory universal health insurance, in particular – such as the United States, most African countries, and some Asian nations – falling ill often leads to the loss of hard-earned prosperity gains. While in nations such as Germany or Switzerland people seldom have to dip deep into their personal reserves to treat a serious disease, an estimated 11 million people in Africa fall into the poverty trap every year, because they are forced to rely on credit to cover the costs of medical treatment, which they then are unable to repay [11]. In India, patients pay 62% of all medical expenses out of their own pocket. Which means that many live in fear, not only of the disease itself, but above all of the resulting debt that could ruin their lives [12].

Many people in the United States find themselves in a peculiar situation. In almost no other nation is the contrast between the enormous achievements of medical progress and the challenges confronting the healthcare system more striking. In no other nation is more medical research conducted or new medications approved more quickly; nowhere else are there as many top-notch hospitals and pharmaceutical or biotech companies. But at the same time, in some areas, the country has long been facing real challenges in supplying all segments of its population with modern medical care.

The financial plight of Americans without health insurance is clearly evident when you look at the GoFundMe crowdfunding platform. This website lets people launch appeals for donations, which can then spread virally over the internet. Most of the time, hundreds of people donate small sums of 5–50 USD. The stories behind these calls for assistance are often heartbreaking. On the platform you'll find mothers and fathers who can no longer support their families, because they have cancer, as well as parents of young, gravely ill children who are overwhelmed with the heavy financial burden of medical costs. How must it feel not to be able to obtain the best possible medical treatment for your child because you don't have the money?

Almost a third of the requests for donations on GoFundMe are medical in nature. Every year some 250,000 desperate Americans turn to their fellow citizens, because they are unable to pay their medical bills. And every year, more than 650 million USD are raised in this manner, money that sometimes saves lives [13].

Anamaria Markle, a woman from New Jersey, eventually found her medical costs prohibitive. The British newspaper *The Guardian* reported on her tragic case [14]. At the age of 50, Anamaria was diagnosed with ovarian cancer. She lost her job shortly thereafter and, one year later, her health insurance. She simply could not afford the cost of private insurance. The bills for surgery, chemotherapy, and drugs began to pile up. Anamaria Markle died of cancer at the age of 52, because she could no longer afford to pay for further treatment. She was survived by two daughters.

The fate suffered by people like Anamaria show that medical progress does not automatically benefit everyone. In countries without universal health coverage, it leads to a two-tier healthcare system, in which the rich have access to modern medicine but poorer people can no longer keep up. It is a system that lacks compassion, as one statistic shows only too well: What is the most common cause of personal bankruptcy in the United States? Medical bills [15].

But there are also glimmers of hope – like in Asia, where some governments are trying to alleviate the negative economic consequences of disease.

China is currently making huge efforts to reform its healthcare system as well as provide its citizens with innovative, state-of-the-art medicine. Since 2009, the Chinese government has more than quadrupled its healthcare spending – albeit starting from a very low baseline – revamped its hospital system and accelerated approvals and reimbursements for new medications [16].

Thailand launched a universal health insurance system in 2002. Prior to that, only one in four Thai citizens had health insurance. Today, thanks to the publicly funded system, poorer people too have access to health care [11].

India also introduced health insurance in 2018, aimed at opening the door to medical care for less affluent segments of its population. Under the program called *Ayushman Bharat,* 500 million people can sign up for coverage. *The Guardian* reported on the story of Rajiv Gupta, a tailor whose mother urgently needed an artificial hip. She was no longer able to walk due to severe pain [12]. The cost of the operation was more than 2,000 euros, which was beyond Rajiv's financial means. But the new health insurance program allowed his mother to finally receive a new hip. Thailand and India are impressive examples of how even emerging countries can provide their entire populations with primary health care.

## Demographic Consequences

Medical progress has led to significant demographic change, which has also played a role in driving up healthcare costs. Today we live twice as long as people did one hundred years ago. At the same time, particularly in the highly developed industrialized nations, we have fewer children. Aided by growing

prosperity, sex education, and the availability of contraceptives, the birth rate has fallen by half since 1950, from five births per woman to an average of only 2.5. The consequences of this drop can already be seen. A study by a Singapore research team predicts that by 2050, one in five people will be over 80 years old. In wealthy, economically developed counties, almost one in three will be over 80 [15].

This will have serious impacts on our healthcare system. As we age we become more vulnerable to disease, our bodies grow frailer, and our immune systems and organs get weaker. The older we become, the higher our risk for developing cancer. In the United States, medical costs for people over 65 are four times as high as for those aged between 20 and 45 years [17]. And we see a similar pattern in Europe. In Switzerland, healthcare costs also increase exponentially after the age of 65 years; an individual over the age of 80 incurs medical costs twice as high as a 60 years old [18]. What does the aging of a society mean for its healthcare costs, and who is going to pay them?

The success of the healthcare system brings new problems of its own: We are finding more and more ingenious ways to fight diseases and we live longer and longer, often with a high quality of life. At the same time, for many of us the number of years in which we live while suffering from disease is increasing. As individuals and as a society, we are reaching the limits of what we can afford. The healthcare system risks running off the rails – precisely because it is so effective.

Chapter 2

# Non-communicable Diseases are Straining Our Healthcare System

*The main theses of this chapter:*

- Non-communicable diseases (NCDs) are the new major challenge facing the healthcare sector. Billions of people around the world suffer from cancer, diabetes, cardiovascular and respiratory diseases, and mental disorders.
- Diabetes is becoming a risk to the Chinese economy and society. Today, every second person there has elevated blood sugar levels.
- Developing countries in Asia and Africa are shouldering a double burden. While still fighting infectious diseases and infant mortality, they are also facing an epidemic of NCDs.
- Patients with NCDs live with their illness for decades. Few are cured, and many suffer. Caring for sick relatives will soon have the same social status as childcare.

For many years, David Maldonado lived the American dream. Together with his nine siblings, he came from Mexico to the United States as a child and prospered in his new home. He got married, found a good job as a salesman, and soon was earning more than 100,000 USD per year. That was enough to give him a comfortable, safe life in a suburb of Dallas, Texas. His two children were diligent students, and David's wife Maribel took care of the family and worked as a hairdresser on the side. A happy family – until they were confronted with an unexpected diagnosis.

Doctors discovered that Maribel had breast cancer and prescribed a double mastectomy. After that, everything changed for the Maldonados. Not just because of Maribel's diagnosis, but largely because of the American healthcare system. The Bloomberg news agency caused quite a stir when they reported on the fate of the Maldonado family as part a series on the pitfalls of that system [1]. The report showed how illnesses can now destroy the life of a middle-class family overnight – because the American health insurance system does not offer them sufficient protection.

The Digital Pill: What Everyone Should Know about the Future of
Our Healthcare System, 11–23
Copyright © 2021 by Emerald Publishing Limited
All rights of reproduction in any form reserved
doi:10.1108/978-1-78756-675-020211002

Even basic mandatory insurance is not part of the US healthcare system; most Americans are insured through their employers. This was the case with the Maldonado family, who had health insurance thanks to David's job. David paid a monthly insurance contribution of 260 USD as well as a co-payment for medical treatments and prescriptions. The costs for Maribel's operation and follow-up treatments were covered by his insurance. But after the worst was over, David and his coworkers were called into their boss' office. He told them that the company could no longer cover the rapidly increasing health insurance premiums for its employees. Their jobs were safe, but the company would no longer offer health insurance benefits. As a result, the Maldonados' life quickly spun out of control.

David received a letter from the insurance company stating that his monthly premium would increase from 260 to 1,375 USD. A year later the price rose again, to 1,900 USD. At that time, his son Cristian was planning to go to college. David realized that he could no longer pay for it all, even though the family had already given up vacations and many other creature comforts. He decided to cancel the policies for himself and his son and to insure only his wife and daughter. This reduced his monthly payment to 750 USD. But the solution was short-lived.

The following year he received another letter from his insurance company raising his premium to 1,060 USD. Since then David's daughter Alexa has also been uninsured, even though she has suffered from asthma since childhood.

The United States is a particularly extreme example of the impacts of inefficient healthcare investments. Because although the country's healthcare expenditure is among the highest in the world and as a result a very large share of medical innovations originate there, in 2017 average life expectancy was around 78 years – not only lower than in Switzerland (84 years) and Germany (81) [2]. Not surprisingly, 87% of people in Switzerland and 77% in Germany are satisfied with their healthcare system, compared to only 52% in the United States [3–5].

The greatest share of health expenditures go to inpatient and outpatient care. Together, these two areas make up almost two-thirds of total healthcare costs, and include the remuneration of doctors and nursing staff in practices and hospitals, as well as hospital operations. Around 20% of healthcare costs are incurred for medications and other medical supplies. The remaining costs are generated by long-term care for elderly or seriously ill people, as well other services. In particular, spending on long-term care has been growing substantially in recent years due to the rise in life expectancy across the globe (Fig. 2.1).

However, the healthcare costs have risen sharply in recent decades not only in the United States, but across the globe as well. This is not only because specific treatments cost more, but also because insurance companies are covering more and more treatments. In 2016, a total of 7,800 billion USD were spent on healthcare worldwide [6]. We can view this in a positive light – after all, this sum is five times greater than global military expenditure and

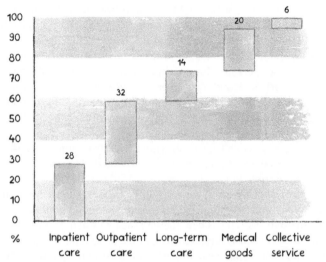

**Fig. 2.1.** *Health Spending by Type of Care OECD Average in 2017.*
*Source: Based on OECD (2019), Health at a Glance 2019: OECD Indicators (p 163).*

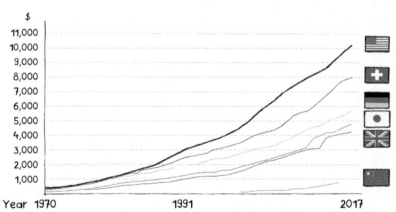

**Fig. 2.2.** *Health is Becoming Expensive: Per Capita Health Spending in USD, 1970–2017.* ***Source:*** *OECD (2019): Health at a Glance: OECD indicators.*

approximately equivalent to the combined gross domestic product (GDP) of France, the United Kingdom, and Italy. It shows that society values human health. On a global level, healthcare costs account for about ten% of GDP – a percentage that has more than doubled in the last 50 years. But the sheer size of this expenditure requires careful scrutiny of how effectively resources are used.

The United States, where David Maldonado lives, is by far the leader in per capita health expenditure, spending more than 10,000 USD per year. In the last 50 years, this amount has increased thirtyfold. If we exclude inflation, costs have still increased twentyfold after this adjustment. In 1970, annual costs were only around 320 USD per person. Measured per capita, at 8,000 USD per year Switzerland has the world's second most expensive healthcare system. Medical costs in Switzerland are 18 times higher than military spending [7]. In Germany, it's around 6,000 USD per capita; in Canada and Australia, about 5,000; in China, only 700 (Fig. 2.2).

While Switzerland needn't start worrying about its national defense, it is clear that such growth in expenditure cannot be sustained. The cost of health insurance policies has doubled in the last 20 years, while at the same time wages have only increased by slightly more than 20% [9]. In fact, the costs of the healthcare system are significantly higher than that of the total amount paid in health insurance contributions. This is why the healthcare system in Switzerland too is partly financed by the state. Despite this, people are having to pay for more and more themselves. The rising costs impact families and people with low incomes in particular. For middle-income families, healthcare costs can total up to 25% of disposable income. So it's no surprise to find that surveys show that rising costs in the health sector are one of the greatest areas of concern among the Swiss [8, 9].

In Germany too, healthcare expenditure has continued to rise in recent years. In 2000, the German Federal Statistical Office recorded healthcare expenditure of 214 billion euros. In 2017, it was 375 billion [10]. And the picture looks much the same in many other parts of the world. Wealthy nations such as Switzerland and Germany may still be able to bear these rising costs. Other countries, however, will soon encounter much greater problems. Insurance no longer works like it used to; the state has to step in and people are having to pay for more and more medical examinations, treatments, and medications themselves – in whole or in part.

The precarious nature of the situation becomes clear when we compare the growth in healthcare costs with GDP. Around the world, the cost of health care is rising significantly faster than that of GDP. As a result, families are having to spend a greater and greater share of their disposable income on health care (Fig. 2.3).

In the UK, medical costs have increased thirtyfold in the last 50 years, whereby about half of the increase is due to inflation. The British have a publicly financed health system, the National Health Service. It is funded exclusively from state budgets and not ring-fenced contributions from employers and employees. For this reason, during budgetary squeezes, sometimes less money is available than in insurance-based systems like those in the United States, France, and Germany. The consequences for patients are in some cases very long waiting times for operations, a limited choice of doctors, and a growing share of costs that must be borne by the patients themselves.

To keep their insurance costs down, many Americans are choosing policies with extremely high deductibles. In recent years, the amount of money individuals have

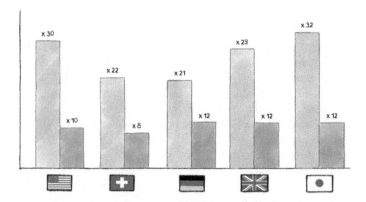

■ Growth per capita healthcare spending 1970-2017
■ Growth per capita GDP 1970-2017

(Comment: Data in current prices, no corrections for inflation were made)

**Fig. 2.3.** *Disproportionate Increase in Health Expenditure: Growth in Health Spending and GDP 1970–2017.* **Source:** *OECD (2019): Health expenditure and financing database: Health expenditure indicators.*

had to pay themselves for health care has more than doubled, while wages have only risen by 26% over the same period [11]. And in the United States, as already mentioned, there is no mandatory universal health coverage. Most recently, about 9% of Americans, or some 28 million individuals, were without health insurance. Of those under 35, one in five does not buy health insurance [12], even though they know that falling ill could mean financial ruin.

But anyone who thinks that growing healthcare costs are a strictly Western phenomenon can think again. Medical costs in China quadrupled between 2006 and 2016 [13]. In recent years, the government has stepped up its efforts to modernize the healthcare sector, increase its focus on NCDs, approve new drugs more quickly, and extend health insurance and services to broader swaths of the population. The reforms initiated by the Chinese government and its willingness to spend more money on health are showing results: From 2001 to 2016, the share of medical costs covered by patients themselves fell from 60% to 29% [14].

Developing countries in Asia and Africa are in a more difficult position than an economic powerhouse like China. They are often still battling infectious diseases (like HIV in South Africa) and have high maternal and infant mortality rates. For example, infant mortality in the Asia-Pacific region is eight times as high as in the OECD nations [15]. The healthcare systems of these countries have long faced challenges such as a lack of public health infrastructure, which require major investment. And now non-communicable, chronic illnesses are added to the list of challenges – NCDs are increasing sharply in developing countries as well. The number of overweight people in the Asia-Pacific region has grown to almost 60%

of the population, for instance [15]. Diabetes and cardiovascular diseases are on the rise not only in China, but also in Singapore, Indonesia, Thailand, and Pakistan. In South Africa, healthcare costs have increased 11.4% on average per year in the last 10 years. This is about five percentage points higher than that of the general inflation rate.

Independent of the question of affordability, we need to ascertain whether this enormous health spending is invested efficiently. Life expectancy is a useful indicator here. After all, statistics show that the life expectancy of a country's population is related to its health expenditure. So basically, the more money there is in the health system, the longer people live.

The price of ever-rising life expectancy will become a challenge for many countries if they do not rein in the costs associated with the NCDs that are becoming more widespread with increasing age (Fig. 2.4).

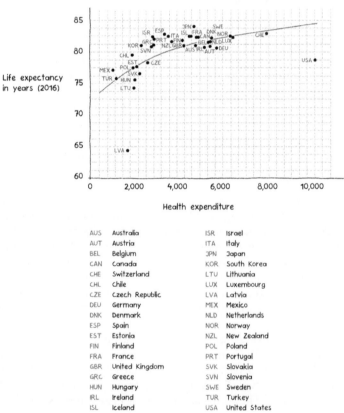

| AUS | Australia | ISR | Israel |
| AUT | Austria | ITA | Italy |
| BEL | Belgium | JPN | Japan |
| CAN | Canada | KOR | South Korea |
| CHE | Switzerland | LTU | Lithuania |
| CHL | Chile | LUX | Luxembourg |
| CZE | Czech Republic | LVA | Latvia |
| DEU | Germany | MEX | Mexico |
| DNK | Denmark | NLD | Netherlands |
| ESP | Spain | NOR | Norway |
| EST | Estonia | NZL | New Zealand |
| FIN | Finland | POL | Poland |
| FRA | France | PRT | Portugal |
| GBR | United Kingdom | SVK | Slovakia |
| GRC | Greece | SVN | Slovenia |
| HUN | Hungary | SWE | Sweden |
| IRL | Ireland | TUR | Turkey |
| ISL | Iceland | USA | United States |

**Fig. 2.4.**   *Life Expectancy and Health Expenditure (USD) Per Capita and Year.*
**Source:** *OECD (2019): Health expenditure and financing database:*
*Health expenditure indicators; United Nations (2017): World population*
*prosepcts.*

### Non-communicable Diseases: Human Suffering and High Costs

Earlier we became acquainted with the Maldonado family of Dallas, Texas, who are struggling with the sort of diseases that cause the greatest amount of concern and problems in modern societies. The mother has cancer and the daughter has asthma – both of which are examples of chronic, NCDs.

And all the data show that NCDs are on the rise. According to WHO, in 2060 twice as many people will be affected as today. What medical conditions count among the five most important NCDs? Cardiovascular diseases, that is, diseases of the heart and circulatory system, followed by cancer, chronic respiratory diseases such as asthma, diabetes, and mental disorders (Table 2.1). These are the illnesses affecting large segments of the population today. In almost every family across the globe, we can find someone suffering from such a condition. We all are aware of the human suffering that they can cause.

What makes NCDs so insidious is that people are often forced to live with them for many years. A study published in the journal *Annals of Family Medicine* looked at the average age of diagnosis of American diabetes patients. In the 1990s, it was still over 50 years old; by 2000 it had dropped to 46 years [16]. The authors attribute this to improved early detection of diabetes. This is known as "lead-time bias" – because patients are examined earlier for elevated blood sugar levels, diagnoses can also be arrived at earlier. In addition, overweight and lack of exercise contribute to the early diagnoses. In the United States, experts now recommend screening all patients over the age of 45 for diabetes.

But what does it mean to already have diabetes at the age of 46? What does it mean to suffer from a chronic illness relatively early in life?

Unlike for infectious diseases, there is only seldom a drug that can bring about a quick cure for chronic diseases. When it comes to diabetes, it is necessary to distinguish between different types of disease: Type 1 diabetes usually appears in childhood or adolescence and is caused in part by genetic factors. Type 2 diabetes accounts for about 90% of all diabetes cases and, in addition to genetic factors, is largely caused by the lifestyle of individual patients. Type 2 diabetes, like all other chronic diseases, develops gradually and usually over a period of many years. Overweight and lack of exercise contribute to this form of diabetes. In diabetics, too much sugar accumulates in the blood because the regulation of their blood sugar levels is impaired. Over time, this hyperglycemia can seriously damage the blood vessels and the organs they supply. Left untreated, diabetes can lead to very serious complications such as kidney damage, heart disease, and blindness, which shows that this disease is in no way a harmless illness. Patients must constantly monitor their diet and blood sugar levels. Daily medication is usually necessary. And they often live with these constraints for decades. If they are not able to regulate their blood sugar levels, they live in constant danger of artery and kidney damage. Sores and wounds also heal more slowly, so if their diabetes treatment is sub-optimal, diabetics can suffer from ulcers on their feet and legs. Relatives of people with NCDs suffer as well, because caring for a family member for many years is also a strain. If your father has an open sore on his foot, he will probably need help putting on his clothes and dressing the wound, won't be able to walk long distances or drive, and will have other significant limitations. Family members often have to cut back on their working hours to help with care. Mental disorders, which also count as NCDs, also have a significant impact on the lives of relatives. Individuals suffering from burnout or depression are often unable to work and also lack the drive to help much around the house. So the others have to shoulder not only the paid work to support the family, but some of the household labor as well.

The treatment of NCDs takes an enormous economic toll. In the United States, they represent 86% of healthcare costs; in Switzerland, 80% [17, 18]. The share of overall costs is so high not only because chronic diseases affect so many people, but also because the costs continue to be incurred for many decades. According to estimates by the World Economic Forum and the Harvard School of Public Health, in 2010 NCDs were responsible for global expenditure of around 6,300 billion USD. This is roughly equivalent to the combined GDP of Japan and South Korea. When calculating such expenditure, both direct and indirect treatment costs as well as loss of income due to disease are taken into account. Estimates show that by 2030, the global cost of treating NCDs will have more than doubled to 13,000 billion USD. Which means it will already have caught up to the GDP of China, the second largest economy in the world [19].

Medicine may have been focused on fighting infectious diseases in the nineteenth century, but in the twenty-first century, a new enemy has been declared. NCDs are now the most common cause of death worldwide – killing around 41 million people per year by 2016. This amounts to half the deaths caused by the entire Second World War. In the United States, one in two individuals is already affected by NCDs. And in 2010, China already overtook America as the country with the most diabetes cases (Table 2.1).

### Diabetes Epidemic in China

Mary Shi exemplifies the new, young generation of diabetics in China. In her early thirties, she is a very well-educated software engineer with bright prospects, living in Shanghai. Within Mary's lifetime, China has transformed itself from a developing country to the world's second largest economy, which has led to major changes in society as well. For people with money, Shanghai offers everything the heart could desire. Not just cool cars, but the entire Western lifestyle. There are more than 600 Starbucks coffee shops in the city, a sign of the country's globalization. The entire spectrum of Western fast food chains is available to anyone who wishes.

But there is a dark side to this lifestyle. Since she was 18, Mary has been living with type 2 diabetes – a form of the disease that could have been prevented or at least delayed by a healthy lifestyle. She had spent months studying for the *gaokao*, China's notoriously grueling college entrance exam. One day she

Table 2.1.   Top Five Chronic Non-Communicable Diseases (NCDs).

| Cardiovascular Diseases | Cancer |
| --- | --- |
| Cardiovascular diseases are the collective designation for a number of conditions, in which either the heart or the blood vessels are affected. Around 500 million people worldwide suffer from some form of cardiovascular disease. According to WHO, every year around 18 million people die of cardiovascular diseases, three quarters of them in developing and emerging nations [20] One example of cardiovascular disease is coronary heart disease, which can lead to a heart attack, stroke as a result of arteriosclerosis or arrhythmia, and heart valve disease as a result of age-related wear and tear. Other major diseases that fall within this spectrum include cardiac insufficiency, pulmonary embolism, deep vein thrombosis, and inflammatory blood vessel diseases. There are many additional cardiovascular disorders that largely occur due to various degenerative, inflammatory, infectious, or genetic conditions | Across the globe, 17 million new cases of cancer are diagnosed annually – and the number is expected to rise to 27.5 million by 2040. Nine million people die of cancer every year. It is now possible to identify more than 250 types of cancer, each with a different genetic composition What all cancers have in common is the uncontrolled division of cells due to genetic mutations in the genome. It is thought that purely hereditary cancers account for only about 5–10% of cases; the majority are caused by a combination of genetic and environmental factors, including smoking, alcohol consumption, obesity, and a poor diet Today many forms of cancer are treatable, and some can be cured if diagnosed at an early enough stage. Because of the genetic particularities of different types of cancer, personalized medicine – in which treatments are tailored to the genetic profile of a tumor – has been an important development in this field |
| Several cardiovascular diseases and other NCDs are caused by preventable factors, including tobacco use, alcohol abuse, unhealthy diet, obesity, and lack of exercise. Besides prevention, the early detection and treatment of risk factors such as high blood pressure, diabetes, and high cholesterol are also essential in the fight against cardiovascular diseases. Depending on the underlying condition, most treatment options aim either to improve lipid metabolism, control inflammation, or prevent unwanted blood clotting | |

Table 2.1.    (*Continued*)

| Chronic Respiratory Diseases | Diabetes |
|---|---|
| According to WHO, every year almost 4 million people die of chronic respiratory diseases, the most common of which include chronic obstructive pulmonary disease and asthma. Two hundred and thirty-five million people suffer from asthma alone | Diabetes is a complex metabolic disorder characterized by altered glucose and insulin metabolism, which can manifest in different ways depending on the type of diabetes. Current figures place the number of people who suffer from diabetes worldwide at around 425 million. It is estimated that on average today, one person dies every seven seconds from diabetes and associated complications like heart attack, stroke, and kidney failure. And by 2045, the number of people with diabetes is expected to reach more than 630 million |
| In addition to tobacco smoke, other risk factors include air pollution, workplace chemicals and dust, and frequent lower respiratory tract infections during childhood. Chronic respiratory diseases are not considered curable. However, various forms of treatment are available to facilitate breathing, prevent a worsening of the condition, and help alleviate shortness of breath | Type 1 diabetes, also known as juvenile diabetes, is a genetic form of the disease in which the pancreas produces very little or no insulin, which leads to hyperglycemia |
| | But more far more common – affecting more than 90% of those diagnosed – is type 2 diabetes. It is characterized by high blood sugar levels, insulin resistance, and relative insulin deficiency. The primary causes of type 2 diabetes are overweight and obesity, lack of exercise, and genetic predisposition. If diabetes is detected early enough, complications can be prevented through monitoring and controlling of blood sugar levels, a balanced diet, and increased exercise. Treatments for both types of diabetes are readily available but administering them is time-consuming, because it requires frequent blood glucose monitoring. It is also important to diagnose the disease early through regular screening |

*Mental Disorders and Neurodegenerative Diseases*

Mental disorders include depression, bipolar disorders, schizophrenia, and other forms of psychosis. Examples of neurodegenerative diseases are dementia and autism. These typically place a heavy burden on both sufferers and their family members. The Institute for Health Metrics and Evaluation estimates that around 500 million people around the world suffer from mental disorders like depression and anxiety disorders that can affect quality of life, daily routines, and ability to work. Despite this, mental disorders and neurodegenerative diseases often remain hidden. They frequently go undiagnosed due to social stigmatization, and their impacts on the economy and society as a whole continue to be greatly underestimated. Although treatments are available for many of these illnesses, there is still an unmet need for better interventions for most of them collapsed, and everyone assumed it was due to stress. But the doctor had a different diagnosis: diabetes. The psychological toll of the disease and the social discrimination she has experienced since then have been far worse than the daily medications, as Mary told the online portal Quartz when they asked her to share her story.

For several years, China has been experiencing nothing less than a diabetes epidemic [21]. Mary Shi was unusually young when she was diagnosed with type 2 diabetes, but she is one of an increasing number of young diabetics in China. Compared to other countries, the proportion of young people with diabetes is high and growing rapidly. Over the last 40 years, the number of diabetics has risen from 1% to more than 11% of the total population. In other words, one in 10 Chinese now suffers from diabetes. A third of the world's diabetics live in China. Of course, this is due in part to the changing lifestyle there, driven by growing prosperity (Fig. 2.5). As a result, there has been a rise in the number of overweight and obese people, with more than 40% of the population now considered overweight. Genetic factors also play a role in the rapid spread of diabetes in China: Asians develop diabetes at a much lower body mass index and at a younger age than Caucasians or Blacks.

This presents the Chinese healthcare system with a major challenge. Long lines in front of hospitals are not infrequent occurrences. Access to health care is particularly difficult in rural areas, with people often having to travel long distances to reach the nearest physician – which is why digital medical solutions such as telemedicine are particularly important in the People's Republic. Poor access makes it much harder to treat those suffering from a chronic disease like diabetes, which requires constant monitoring and regular visits to the doctor. Studies show that only 70% of diabetics in China are even aware of their condition, while only 25% receive treatment for it. Health has become a luxury that not everyone can afford. Estimates show that Chinese families with a diabetic member spend 24%

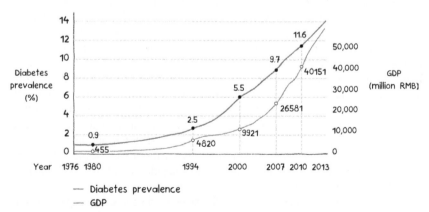

**Fig. 2.5.** *China's Economic Boom has also Brought Problems: Diabetes Prevalence in Percent and Economic Output in Millions of RMB.*
*Source: Chan, Zhang, and Ning (2004).*

of their income on medication [22]. New and innovative medications, in particular, still have to be paid out of pocket, so it's no wonder that poorer families cannot afford them. Mary is lucky that she earns enough to pay for advanced treatment.

### Cardiovascular Disease in Mexico

The dramatic scale of NCDs and the human suffering that they cause can also be observed in Mexico. This nation of more than 123 million inhabitants is the most populous country in the Americas after the United States and Brazil, and is plagued by cardiovascular diseases. While the risk of dying from cardiovascular diseases has fallen by almost 50% in OECD countries since 1990, in Mexico it remains high [23].

Diet plays a key role, with more than 70% of the population considered overweight or obese and more than 30% suffering from high blood pressure [24]. Mexico is a prime example of the new eating habits affecting many developing countries. In recent years, natural, whole foods have been replaced by highly processed, high-calorie equivalents. They are often less perishable and more affordable than the traditional foods. Take carbonated and milk-based beverages, for example. In Mexico, the consumption of high-calorie drinks doubled between 1999 and 2006. At 163 liters per person and year, in no other nation are as many soft drinks consumed. This is 40% higher than even in the United States, where soda pop was invented [25]. Mexicans' love of sugary drinks goes so far that an estimated 10% of all infants have been fed with sweet soft drinks by the age of six months [25]. Sometimes the high consumption of soft drinks is also attributed to the poor quality of the tap water in Mexico.

In Mérida, a city in the province of Yucatán, if you go to one of the *pulperías* – the small shops that can be found on many corners – you won't usually find any bottled water on the shelves. However, the refrigerators are full of colorful fizzy drinks, which are often less expensive than water. This has serious consequences. For a report on Mexicans' soft drink addiction, reporters from *BBC News* visited a woman named Silvia Segura in a poor district of Mérida. On the walls of her home were hooks for the hammocks, in which the family members slept because it was more comfortable and cooler than sleeping in beds. In the living room, however, there was a double bed – after she had become too ill to climb into a hammock, Silvia's mother had slept there until her death. A short time before the reporter's visit, she had succumbed to complications of type 2 diabetes. Until the very end, according to Silvia, her mother never lost her appetite for sugary drinks. "My entire family drinks Coca-Cola," said Silvia. "My mother, may she rest in peace, was a real *cocacolera* – she couldn't live without Coca-Cola" [25]. When her mother was in the hospital, Silvia would smuggle the soft drink in when she visited and give her a few sips.

It is only a few short steps from a diagnosis of diabetes, like Silvia's mother received, to diseases of the heart and circulatory system. Diabetics have twice as high a risk of developing cardiovascular diseases as non-diabetics. Studies show that less than half of patients suffering from high blood pressure in Mexico even know about the disease. And in many cases, those who are aware of it still have no idea what can be done to fight it. Only half of the country's inhabitants have health insurance and even those with coverage have to pay half of the medical costs themselves. Health economists predict that, taking account of both direct (treatment and drug costs) and indirect costs (reduced labor productivity), by 2030 the cost of cardiovascular diseases in Mexico will rise to 25 billion USD per year [26].

Starting in 2004, per capita healthcare expenditure was increased sharply in Mexico with the aim of giving more people access to health care and improving the quality of care [27]. However, despite this considerable investment, the healthcare system remains under pressure as the rapid increase in NCDs forces it to shoulder an enormous burden. In 2014, the government tried to pull the emergency brake. It decided to impose a tax on sugary drinks and non-essential high-calorie foods like potato chips and chocolate bars. This made such products around 10% more expensive. Studies show that the tax has helped to slow consumption of these sweet soft drinks. But cultural eating habits are slow to change, and it takes a long time for interventions of this sort to bear fruit. To date, no significant reduction in cardiovascular diseases has been observed [28]. Perhaps this should come as no surprise in a country where many supermarkets are painted in the colors of the Coca Cola logo and soft drinks can be purchased on every street corner.

What is eminently clear is that NCDs are a global phenomenon that affects billions. More and more people are suffering from diabetes, cancer, mental disorders, or heart disease. Across the globe, this is placing enormous cost pressure on healthcare systems – or driving people without insurance coverage to financial ruin. The majority of countries have yet to find a sustainable way out of this dilemma.

Chapter 3

# Digitalization Will Be a Key Success Factor for the Healthcare System of the Future

*The main theses of this chapter:*

- Not enough emphasis is placed on prevention. Less than 3% of all healthcare costs are spent on preventive medicine.
- Our current healthcare system is not worthy of its name: we treat disease instead of safeguarding health.
- We take better care of our cars than of our own health. We adhere strictly to the vehicle maintenance schedule, but rarely go in for our recommended check-ups and screenings.
- We cause about 50% of our own illnesses. About half of the risk of developing a non-communicable disease (NCD) can be boiled down to four factors: We eat too much and the wrong things, don't exercise enough, smoke too much, and drink too much alcohol.
- Digital technologies help strengthen our knowledge of our own health and the related consequences. They aid us in changing our behaviors and lifestyle, making them a form of medicine.
- Digital technologies make us more aware of our personal responsibility. They act as a kind of global positioning system for our health.
- Digitalization is an important key to mastering the challenges facing our healthcare system. It helps make health accessible and better for everyone, and serves as a check to rising costs.
- Correctly applied, digitalization makes the healthcare system more efficient. Because financial resources are limited everywhere, these efficiency gains have a therapeutic effect.

NCDs affect almost every one of us. Either we suffer from them ourselves, or we know someone in our circle of family and friends who has diabetes, high blood pressure, or even cancer. We have already shared the stories of several such individuals – Anamaria Markle and David Maldonado from the United States, Mary Shi from China, and Silvia and her mother from Mexico. NCDs can pose

The Digital Pill: What Everyone Should Know about the Future of
Our Healthcare System, 25–38
Copyright © 2021 by Emerald Publishing Limited
All rights of reproduction in any form reserved
doi:10.1108/978-1-78756-675-020211003

a particular financial and psychological burden for families. In many developed countries, health insurance companies do cover the direct costs of the illness. However, enormous indirect costs are also incurred, especially for the care of relatives. Even in wealthy countries, a NCD can often mean an enormous struggle for the affected families.

In Switzerland, a four-person, middle-income family spends up to 25% of its income on health care [1]. In a study in South Korea, almost 70% of the families who were caring for relatives with cancer stated that they had to spend the majority of their savings. One in five persons in the study had moved into a smaller home to cope with the financial burden of care [2].

What can be done to alleviate the burden on these families? One of the most famous quotations from Goethe's *Faust* sums up the situation perfectly: "I hear the message, but my faith fails me." We have to understand that NCDs cannot entirely be considered an act of fate. To a large extent, whether or not we develop such a disease lies in our own hands. This message is not only communicated to patients by their doctors, but can also be read in the popular media. Today many people know that they should attach more importance to exercise and a healthy diet. But too many of us still too often close our eyes to this uncomfortable truth.

The World Health Organization (WHO) assumes that half of NCD risk can be controlled by individuals. In the case of cardiovascular diseases, 80% of the risk is considered preventable. Even when it comes to cancer, 30–50% of the risk can be mitigated through changes in lifestyle [3, 5]. So prevention is the strategy through which we can get the NCD and cost crisis under control.

WHO has identified four individual factors by which we can lower our risk of developing an NCD: first, a healthy diet, second, sufficient exercise, third, abstinence from smoking, and fourth, moderate alcohol consumption. In other words, we know how we could reduce our risk of illness – but all too often, we don't take responsibility for our own health (Table 3.1).

In collaboration with the member states of the United Nations, WHO published a comprehensive report on the NCD epidemic in 2010 [5]. The goals of the report were to document the current global situation and to develop a strategy for reining in chronic, NCDs. Two years later, the member states published nine global NCD reduction goals as well as a standardized approach for measuring progress in the fight against these disorders, focusing on both the number of cases and the prevalence of risk factors. Among these global goals are cutting tobacco and salt consumption by 30%, lowering excessive alcohol consumption by 10%, and reducing the number of people who don't get enough exercise by 10%. The aim was to reach these goals by 2025, but unfortunately things are not looking good. In an interim report in 2017, the WHO warned that not enough progress had been made, and the improvements that had been achieved were very unevenly distributed among the different countries [8, p. 5].

Although there are well-defined goals and preventive measures (like higher taxes on tobacco and alcohol, as well as stricter food guidelines), they have been rolled out very slowly or not at all. Far too little importance is placed on prevention and screening in our current healthcare system. If we leave the responsibility

Table 3.1.   Individual Risk Factors.

| *Unhealthy Diet* | *Smoking* |
| --- | --- |
| In recent decades, the standard of living has improved dramatically in many developing countries. This has meant that people's diets have changed at a fundamental level, including higher calorie density, increased consumption of fat and sugar, and foods containing added sugar and less fiber [4]. In the last 30 years, the consumption of fat has risen by almost 50% worldwide. WHO recommends cutting salt consumption to 5 grams per day; saturated fatty acids (e.g., meat and milk) should be reduced and replaced by unsaturated fatty acids (e.g., olives and nuts). It also advises people to eat at least. 400 grams of fruit and vegetables per day. An unhealthy diet leads to an increased risk of cardiovascular disease as well as of bowel or stomach cancer [5]. | Using tobacco increases a person's risk of developing a lung tumor, respiratory disorders, and cardiovascular diseases. According to WHO guidelines, even one cigarette is one too many – smoking should be avoided completely. While tobacco consumption has fallen sharply since the 1970s in Western Europe and North America, it remains high in Asia and the states of the former Soviet Union. In Indonesia, three out of four men smoke; in China, one in two. More than 70% of all cases of lung cancer are caused by smoking, as well as 42% of all chronic respiratory diseases and 10% of all cardiovascular diseases. The global health costs of smoking are calculated at 2,100 billion USD. This is equivalent to the cost of damage caused by armed conflict [5]. |

Table 3.1.    *(Continued)*

*Excessive Alcohol Consumption*

Alcohol is part of our culture. A glass of prosecco at a gallery opening, maybe even a bottle of champagne for your birthday, a happy-hour beer with your colleagues, mulled wine at the Christmas market. When was the last time you went out for a meal and didn't drink alcohol? Try it sometime, and your dinner companions will probably ask you if everything is okay – or are you may be coming down with something? And many people continue to drink by themselves, often in the belief that it helps them cope better with their lives

Unlike smoking, where one cigarette is one too many and there is a threat of direct health consequences, there is a quantity of alcohol that is defined as "low risk." But experts still cannot agree on what this amount is – there is no global benchmark. In Germany, the upper limit set by health authorities is about two small glasses of beer or wine for men and one small glass of beer or wine for women per day. This is the equivalent of 24 or 12 grams of pure alcohol. And people should refrain from drinking any alcohol at all on at least two days of the week. Because it's not just the amount of alcohol consumed that is relevant, but also the regularity with which it is consumed [6]

In wealthy countries in particular, people tend to drink too much alcohol. Europe tops the statistical rankings, with fatal results. Alcohol has a cytotoxic effect, which can lead to tumors of the esophagus, stomach, and intestines as well as to cardiovascular diseases and cirrhosis of the liver. In addition, studies show that alcohol consumption has negative effects on the brain and contributes to dementia. This results in billions in costs for the healthcare system, as well as major negative impacts on workplace productivity. And the suffering caused to alcoholics and their families is immeasurable

*Not Enough Exercise*

Going for a walk or bike ride every now and then is not nearly enough. Lack of exercise is defined as when an adult exercises less than 150 minutes per week at moderate intensity or less than 75 minutes at high intensity. A brisk walk or using the vacuum cleaner already qualifies as moderate activity, while jogging, playing soccer, or an aerobics class count as high intensity

Almost one in four people are not active enough. The situation is even more critical among young people – WHO recommends that children and adolescents exercise for 60 minutes a day. This can include, for instance, running around on the playground or cycling to school. Only 20% of all children and adolescents are sufficiently physically active, with one in four adolescents not getting enough exercise. These statistics are frightening, because physical activity is so important to our health. Regular exercise reduces our risk of cardiac arrhythmia, stroke, diabetes, and breast and colon cancer. Statistics show that a couch-potato lifestyle can lower life expectancy by four years, a considerable amount. Furthermore, exercise is also good for our mental health [5]

In developed countries, the high standard of living leads people into inactivity, as illustrated by the contrasting example of Uganda, one of the poorest countries in the world. Ninety-five percent of Ugandans get enough exercise – a top score not achieved by any other nation on earth. The situation is particularly dire in the oil-rich nations of the world, where even the shortest stretches are covered by car. The frontrunner in this sedentary lifestyle is Kuwait, where 67% of the population gets far too little exercise [7] for solving the NCD epidemic to each individual, we will fall short. We also need to rethink our healthcare system as a whole – and maybe even completely restructure it. We need a dialog on responsibility for health in relation to the freedom of the individual. At the moment, we are living with the greatest possible degree of individual liberty, but shouldering the resulting costs as a group.

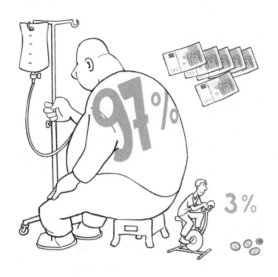

Historically speaking, our Western healthcare systems are designed to handle acute, infectious diseases. Ninety-seven percent of the total costs are incurred for the treatment of diseases, only 3% for preventive medicine. Following the global recession of 2008, the percentage spent on prevention got even smaller. The consequences are devastating – because unlike infectious diseases, which require urgent but short-lived treatment, NCDs often generate costs over decades [9].

There are major disparities in spending on preventive medicine among OECD countries. Canada and the UK spend almost twice the OECD average, for instance, while Greece devotes only slightly more than 1.3% of healthcare expenditure to prevention [9]. Why is it so hard for us to spend money on preventive medicine?

If we look at other areas of life, effective mechanisms for prevention are commonplace. In Germany, for example, there are clear regulations defining how many kilometers a car can be driven before it has to go in for servicing. They also govern what functions of a vehicle must be checked at what intervals. Of course road safety is a valuable asset – but shouldn't that also apply to our health? A study shows that only about half of Germans go for screening, with women taking slightly more care of their health than men [10]. If a car has to go in for inspection every two years or else have its registration revoked, why don't we have our bodies checked regularly as well?

In many cases, by the time a condition like diabetes is diagnosed, irreparable damage has already occurred. Think of the kidney failure, amputations, or blindness that can result from diabetes. But even if such worst-case scenarios do not occur immediately, we should try to prevent NCDs so that we have to spend less money on treating them for decades. We know the risk factors; we know how to prevent them. Every one of us has a responsibility – and so do governments. Early detection can also help prevent the suffering and costs of diseases and complications.

Take overweight as an example. It impacts young people in particular, yet in many schools little is taught about healthy eating or the importance of physical activity. How can it be that 80% of our children do not get enough exercise? Why is it so hard to integrate an hour of physical activity into the school day when evidence clearly shows that this will make our children more fit for the future – both literally and figuratively? In many countries, there are still no laws regulating the consumption of alcohol and tobacco although we know they pose significant health risks. In some respects, medicine was much more advanced in the past. Consider the wisdom of Mary Shi's ancestors here: As an ancient Chinese saying tells us: "Healing an illness is like waiting until you are thirsty before you start digging a well" [11].

### *Preventive Health Care in Ancient China – A Historic Model*

Health care in ancient China was fundamentally different from our systems today. They would always take a holistic view of health, focusing on harmony between the body, mind, and spirit. When we speak of health today, we usually mean the absence of disease. In ancient China, this definition would have been much too narrow. It was not the symptom-free person who was considered healthy, but the one in whom body, mind, and soul were in balance. A Taiwanese proverb sums up this idea well: "A bad doctor treats symptoms, an average doctor treats the disease, a good doctor cures the whole person" [11].

So it makes sense that physicians operated under an entirely different incentive system than today. Our healthcare system pays doctors for the treatments they administer. The more sick people doctors treat and the more complex the treatments are, the more money they earn. In ancient China, physicians were paid for maintaining good health, not for treating disease. A doctor received a monthly payment as long as his patients remained healthy. If they became ill, the payments stopped until they were restored to health. It was considered scandalous to take money from sick people, who were already suffering and not able to manage their daily affairs on their own. The system was geared toward prevention. Doctors helped people live good lives. They advised them on correct nutrition, healthy exercise, and spiritual balance [11, 12].

### *Preventive Dental Medicine in Sweden – A Contemporary Model*

Another good example of prevention in medicine comes from dental care in Sweden. While even in wealthy countries like Switzerland, people have to pay out of pocket for every visit to the dentist if they don't have a supplemented dental plan. Sweden has been taking a different approach for 50 years now.

Regular dental check-ups are free of charge in Sweden for children and adolescents up to 23 years of age, so they are not dependent on their parents' ability to pay [13]. Going to the dentist becomes routine for every young person. Dental care is also heavily subsidized for older or disabled persons. Dentists provide information about proper dental hygiene and also explain the importance of fluoride toothpaste. And good dental hygiene is also taught in schools and preschools.

The success of the preventive system can be seen in the health statistics. The majority of children today show no signs at all of cavities or tooth decay. The number of children without cavities tripled between 1985 and 2005. In 1985, four out of five young people between the ages of 12 and 19 years had cavities; today that number is only two in five [14]. Preventing disease instead of treating it not only keeps individuals from having to suffer – it also cuts costs. And that is exactly what is necessary to save our healthcare systems.

### Health Promotion Board in Singapore

Singapore is Asia's poster child for health. This city-state and island country places great importance on preventive health care. To this end, the government founded the Health Promotion Board (HPB) about 20 years ago. The HPB is a governmental organization that aims to empower people in Singapore to take charge of their own health [15].

Why is preventive public health so important in Singapore? As HPB Chairman Philipp Lee explained,

> it is estimated that the average lifespan of Singapore's population will rise to third-highest by 2040. We will therefore need to support Singaporeans in living their life in good health, so that they not only live long but live well. [15, p. 4]

Compared to other nations across the globe, Singapore spends relatively little on health. Somewhat less than 5% of its GDP goes to health care. The focus on prevention can help keep costs low despite the aging of the population.

The measures that HPB supports are very wide-ranging: subsidized screening for people over 40, healthy meals and nutrition education in schools and preschools, dental visits in schools, national sports programs, raising awareness of the importance of healthy sleep habits, and mental health programs for children, parents, managers, and employees. And these are only a few examples.

In 2018, free sport and exercise programs were offered in 820 locations in the island nation, from shopping centers to city parks. In addition, the state is offering digital encouragement to get its citizens moving. Five years ago, it launched the Healthy 365 App, which almost half the population has downloaded. The app lets users take part in the annual National Steps Challenge. Participants get a free fitness tracker and collect points based on the number of steps they take each day. The points can be redeemed in a variety of shops. And at the end of the challenge, there's a large prize-drawing where people can win airline tickets and other prizes.

The HPB's programs have been well-received, as this schoolgirl's statement shows:

> My weight and my diet have changed, and so have my taste buds!
> I eat less salty food and I am very conscious of my food choices.
> I also dance and take swimming lessons. I feel lighter and much
> better. [15, p. 22]

However, despite all these efforts, Singapore is not immune to the NCD epidemic. A study shows that the number of diabetics in Singapore will rise to 15% of the population by 2050 [16]. The reasons given by the study for the increase will sound familiar: the aging of society and the increasing obesity rate.

### Healthy Diet and Preventive General Medicine in Spain

Spain also seems to be a role model in many respects. In Bloomberg's latest health index, Spain clearly outperformed Italy, which had been the leader for many years. Next come four further European nations – Iceland, Switzerland, Sweden, and Norway. Japan is the healthiest Asian country, followed by Singapore; Australia and Israel are also in the top 10. The index rates countries using several variables including life expectancy, subtracting points for risks such as tobacco and alcohol consumption and obesity. It also considers environmental factors such as access to clean water and hygiene [17].

According to the Washington Institute for Health Metrics and Evaluation, people in Spain will have a life expectancy of 86 years by 2040. An important reason for this high figure is the medical care provided in Spain, especially by the very well-trained primary care physicians. They encourage their patients to take preventive health measures, which has an especially positive impact on the development of secondary diseases. Thanks in part to this focus on prevention, the number of cases of cardiovascular disease and cancer has been reduced in the last decade. The eating habits of people in the Mediterranean countries also play a role in this trend. The consumption of olives and nuts alone helps prevent cardiovascular disorders.

The discussion concerning prevention and NCDs shows that better health care does not necessarily have to mean higher costs. The key to a better life lies in the will and the ability of all of us to rethink our choices and habits and elevate the position of prevention within our healthcare systems. In addition, policy-makers have to provide incentives for a healthy lifestyle without placing excessive restrictions on individual liberties. It's time for smart ideas, clever incentives, and bold action.

### Digitalization is Essential to Tomorrow's Medicine

Digitalization, or the switch from analog data on paper to digitally stored information, is not a new phenomenon. Computers and smartphones are everywhere. And the internet is by no means a new invention. If you watch the movie "You've Got Mail" starring Tom Hanks and Meg Ryan today, it is obvious that the technology has been around for a while. The first commercial emails were sent around 30 years ago. The generations growing up today have no memory of a time before the internet. For Generation Z – young people born after 1995 – there is nothing more natural than shopping on their smartphones, connecting with friends in chats and on social media, and getting their news online. They check WhatsApp every few minutes, but rarely look in the mailbox.

The medical sector, on the other hand, is only slowly entering the digital age. The fax machine is still the most important means of communication for self-employed general practitioners [18]. In most countries, communication between physicians still takes place through patient referral letters, which often arrive by snail mail weeks after the patient was treated. If patients switch doctors, in most cases the new doctor has no access to their medical history and records. And if patients want to look at their own records, they can – if they are lucky – request hard copies of their medical reports and lab results. However, since these reports are usually not sent to patients but only to the physicians treating them, even this is often a hopeless endeavor. As a result, many diagnostic tests have to be repeated, which is a waste of money – and valuable time.

But digitalization is also making advances in the medical sector. In the United States, it is standard practice to send prescriptions digitally from the doctor's office to the pharmacy. Estonia is a pioneer in the world of digital medicine. For more than 10 years now, it has had uniform digital medical records for all citizens. Telemedicine, electronically documented medication schedules, and digital prescriptions have all become routine [19].

Even if the digitalization of the medical sector is progressing only slowly, it can no longer be halted – it must and will happen. Which is reason enough to take a close look at how it will transform medicine. What opportunities does the digital revolution have in store for health care? How can it help meet the challenges of demographic change, the NCD epidemic, and steadily growing medical costs? And where do we also need to be cautious with regard to digitalization?

We have identified five potential levers of change that can allow digitalization to play a key role in the healthcare world of the future. Taken individually, none of the five levers seem revolutionary. Rather, they support and accelerate changes that have long been underway, facilitated by medical progress. Taken together, however, these digital levers could bring about a positive revolution in the world of healthcare, from research to prevention, diagnosis, treatment, and probably even remuneration and administration (Fig. 3.1).

### Digitalization Supports Behavioral Change

Everybody knows how hard it is to stick to New Year's resolutions. How often have we sworn we would get rid of the annoying extra kilos we put on last year? But we rarely achieve lasting success. It takes a lot of strength to change our habits.

Digital technologies can help us track healthy behavior over the long term. We all know that our personal lifestyle choices have a considerable impact on our health. Digitalization can help us apply this knowledge. Examples of this particular lever include digital fitness trackers, digital scales, and medication-management apps, which remind patients to take their pills on time and how many they need.

### Digitalization Boosts Efficiency

Growing medical costs are a major challenge for our healthcare systems. While some cost drivers like demographic change are unavoidable, there are others that are caused by inefficiency and waste within the system. Digitalization can play a decisive role in reducing or preventing inefficiencies, which in turn can alleviate some of the cost pressure being experienced by our healthcare system.

According to a study by the New England Healthcare Institute, 30% of the medical costs incurred in the United States are unnecessary – in other words, they could be eliminated without having a negative impact on the quality of the healthcare system. This could save 700 billion USD annually [20].

There are many areas where treatment is inefficient. Emergency rooms are one such example. Statistics show that when people come to hospital emergency departments, in 71% of cases it is medically unnecessary or could have been avoided [21]. Twenty-four percent of the visits were not actually urgent, 41% of the cases could have been treated by a primary care physician, and 10% of the emergency cases could have been prevented. In the United States, the most common reasons for emergency room visits include headaches, back pain, and urinary tract infections. On average, a visit to the emergency room costs 1,233 USD [22].

People go there because they are not sure where else to go or because they need assistance outside of regular office hours. This trend is especially strong in urban areas, where many people no longer have a primary care physician. In the United States, there is the additional problem that people who are sick but have no health insurance often go to hospital emergency departments, because these facilities are required to see all patients. The costs of unnecessary emergency room visits in the United States are estimated at 38 billion USD per year [20].

Digitalization can help make sure that only people who actually need urgent medical attention go to the emergency room. In the second part of this book, we will report on the innovative Oscar insurance, whose chatbot has proven to be effective in guiding patients to the right medical care. Patients who originally wanted to go to the emergency room because they were suffering from a urinary tract infection on a Saturday evening – outside of their primary care physician's office hours – instead received a recommendation from the Oscar chatbot that they use telemedicine to communicate with a doctor who could write them a prescription immediately. This is just one example of how digitalization leads to more efficient solutions.

### Digitalization Democratizes Medicine

The NCD epidemic is presenting the medical sector with new challenges. More and more patients with longer and longer lasting illnesses are crippling the system. Lines in front of medical practices are not limited to the developing world. In the United States too, it is becoming increasingly difficult to get an appointment with a doctor. One study showed that the waiting time for a doctor's appointment increased by 30% from 2014 to 2017 [23].

Once you have finally obtained an appointment, the doctor will only give you a few minutes of their time. Researchers from several European universities investigated how much time general practitioners in 67 countries spend with patients on average [24]. They found that in one third of the countries, general practitioners spend less than five minutes with patients. In China, it is only two minutes. In Germany, Singapore, and Israel, it is less than 10 minutes. The United States and Switzerland do better: in these nations, doctors have more than 20 and more than 15 minutes, respectively. The time shortage is easily explained: much too much administrative work. Statistics show that depending on the country, doctors spend up to 50% of their time on administrative tasks [25, 26].

Other parts of the world are so sparsely populated, far from healthcare facilities, or economically underdeveloped that the people living there hardly have access to medical care. In regions such as this, digitalization can help make health care more easily available. This is not only relevant on the savannahs of Africa, but also in thinly populated areas of the American Midwest and in parts of eastern Germany, where many doctor's offices are closing. Patients in these locations could receive medical consultations by video chat, and digital mail-order pharmacies could supply medications based on electronic prescriptions.

Digitalization has already radically transformed and democratized many sectors, making access to services and products easier and cheaper. One good example is the home video industry, which has completely reinvented itself in the last 10 years. Only recently, it was normal to rent a DVD from the local video store for a weekend family movie night. In sparsely populated areas, there were often no such stores, so people had to watch whatever movies were being shown on television. Today it is almost impossible to find a video rental store. The largest rental chain in the United States, Blockbuster Video, finally closed its doors in 2010. The home video industry went completely digital in a very short period of time. Netflix, Hulu, Apple, and Amazon Prime have emerged as the winners of this transformation – all companies who were new to the game. Movies are no longer rented but rather "streamed" – or transmitted over the internet. In 2018, Netflix had acquired some 140 million subscribers with this business model, posting revenues of almost 15 billion USD [27].

But the customers profit as well. The video rental store might have locked its doors at 10 p.m., but today no one has to worry about closing time. Regions with weaker infrastructure benefit the most – as long as they have internet access. In the past, they were cut off from the supply chain. Today people can enjoy content that they can access around the clock, no matter where they live. Streaming services are not only available at any time, they also offer customers personalized recommendations. The changes in the video industry show how people can benefit from digitalization, receiving a broader selection at often lower prices. This concept can be applied to the medical sector as well.

### Digitalization Improves Quality

In addition to demographic transition, the epidemic of NCDs, and rapidly increasing costs, our healthcare systems are being hit with another wave of change as medical knowledge expands exponentially.

Well into the 1950s, the rule of thumb was that it always took half a century for our store of medical knowledge to double. Now experts estimate that in 2020, this knowledge will double every 70 days. This means complexity and a flood of innovation that can no longer be mastered by human beings alone [28]. Even with intensive continuing education, many doctors can no longer keep pace with the sheer volume and depth of medical information and the speed with which this knowledge is growing.

Digitalization facilitates personalized, case-specific access to the burgeoning knowledge of the medical sector. Modern databases with search functions make it easier for physicians to find relevant publications on specific medical topics. In addition, digitalization can help establish certain quality standards on a broad scale and gradually enhance them. Digital decision-making tools can provide assistance in making optimal treatment decisions based on the latest available medical knowledge and guidelines. Moreover, digital communication simplifies coordination between different doctors. This will benefit not only the top professionals, but above all the doctors who work in small private practices or hospitals in rural areas. These physicians almost never encounter rare diseases. So telemedicine can help them obtain a second opinion in such cases. Or a digital assistant can use image recognition to evaluate a symptom, aiding in the diagnosis and decision on appropriate treatment.

### Digitalization Accelerates Medical Research

Medical progress in recent decades has also led to an exponential increase in the complexity of medical research. The decoding of the human genome has been of particular significance, yielding enormous masses of data that could scarcely have been processed without the power of digital computing.

The new field of gene therapy, whether applied in oncology or the fight against genetic diseases, simply would not have been possible without the digital revolution. In other words, digitalization both facilitates and accelerates the progress of medicine. The field of personalized medicine, in which treatments are tailored to the needs of small groups of patients and in some cases even of individuals, would have been unthinkable without digitalization. Up to now, personalized medicine has only been applied in a small percentage of treatments, but the potential is great.

One expression of the skyrocketing complexity of medicine has been the significant increase in the costs of drug development. The average amount spent on the development of a new medication in the 1970s was 179 million USD; by the 1980s this figure had already doubled. At present, a staggering 2.5 billion USD are invested on average to take a drug from in vitro evaluation to approval [29]. The use of new digital technologies in research – like health databases, algorithms, and artificial intelligence – could help reduce these costs going forward.

Digitalization is already revolutionizing the world of healthcare today. And it will have an even greater impact in the future. It is an important key to mastering the challenges facing our current healthcare system. At the same time, the new digital healthcare world also raises new questions: How do we protect the medical privacy of individuals? How do we protect medical data from unauthorized access? In a costly healthcare system, how do we sustain health insurance based on solidarity despite having increased transparency about patients? How do we maintain individuals' freedom to make medical decisions about their own bodies and lifestyles in a world, in which all kinds of data about them are constantly being compiled, stored, and made available as medical information?

In the second part of this book, we take a closer look at these questions and illustrate the changes in the healthcare system with the help of 25 response patterns, divided into six chapters. In the context of each pattern, we introduce exciting startups and established companies that apply them in their business models. We try to provide meaningful examples of these trends by describing actual innovations and technologies. Not all of these technologies are currently widely available or approved all over the world, and many are not being applied on a large scale. The examples presented here are by no means intended as recommendations or advertisement, but serve only to illustrate the trends more vividly and encourage reflection on the future of medicine.

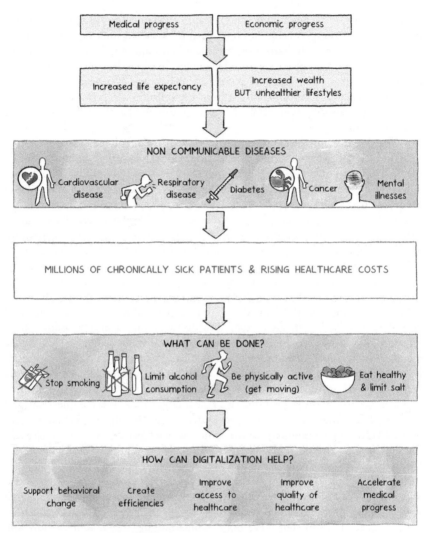

**Fig. 3.1.**    *Medical Progress and its Consequences.*

# Part II

# Digital Technologies are Changing Patients and Healthcare Systems

In Part I, we described the incredible progress that medicine has made in the last 100 years and why, in the area of non-communicable diseases (NCD), it has become the victim of its own success. We showed what massive burdens NCD place on every family and every healthcare system. But at least half of this burden is not ordained by fate. It is the result of the lifestyle we have chosen, a lack of knowledge, a lack of preventive care, and a lack of willingness to change our behavior.

Digitalization has already shaken up many industries and overturned their underlying principles. We only have to consider the advertising industry, the retail sector, and the music industry. The internet in particular has always been most successful, where there are long-term relationships involving many touchpoints between customers and service providers, where customers have been willing or able to take on many tasks themselves, and where a lot of data are generated in the course of these interactions that can be used to improve the service.

Against this somewhat dry and analytical backdrop, it seems clear that the internet, smartphones, omnipresent sensors, and intelligent algorithms can be the components that make up a tool called digitalization, which we can wield in the fight against NCD. Such diseases extend over long periods of time and require the active participation of the patient. These ongoing interactions generate infinite volumes of valuable data – for the patient, the doctor, and the healthcare system.

So we wanted to examine *how* the internet can combine with other information technologies to help alleviate the major burden imposed by many diseases. How did we do that? We looked at hundreds of companies and organizations, from patient associations to startups to large corporations, and for each case study, identified how they are using IT to change the healthcare system. In the process, we encountered an almost overwhelming variety of approaches. The case studies showed us that

- There are not only organizations that are focused on performing a single task as perfectly as possible (e.g., a digital coach for the very easy, inexpensive, confidential, or even anonymous treatment of depression) as well as those that offer a very broad spectrum (e.g., the all-inclusive approach of tomorrow's health insurers).
- Most companies evolve from one year to the next – for example, their offerings become broader, they focus on new customer groups, or successful technology firms are purchased by other players.

- The traditional lines between service providers, health insurance companies, employers, pharmaceutical companies, and technology firms are blurring, meaning that players from different sectors are re-imagining and offering one and the same services based on digital technology.
- Independent of the products and services they offer, all companies are drawing on the same broad set of new digital technologies and developing them even further. These core technologies include the internet of medical things, genomic data science, and machine learning.

We quickly realized that a simple description of technologies and companies would not suffice to show ourselves and our readers these ongoing changes in a tangible and applicable form. So we decided to use the case studies to identify those processes, tasks, or other relevant aspects of the business model that have been massively reshaped or made possible by digital technologies. Over the course of many small steps, a list of 25 response patterns of the digital healthcare sector emerged.

Every actor in the future healthcare sector – from healthy citizens to pharmaceutical companies – will use one or more of these IT-driven patterns in their daily work. Companies, whether new or long-established, will assemble their business models from these patterns. In other words, the patterns are like Lego bricks that will be used to build the new healthcare sector. The patterns follow the precept of usefulness. They focus on the patient and not, for example, on the internal processes of the hospital. They draw on different phenomena, operate at different levels of detail, are not without overlaps and, above all, make no claim to being exhaustive.

Part II of this book summarizes the 25 behavior patterns, which are listed below, in six chapters and describes each one individually. For better readability, each chapter begins with a list of its main theses. The chapters do not necessarily have to be read in any particular order.

| Chapters | The 25 Patterns of the Digital Healthcare Sector |
|---|---|
| *4. Do-it-Yourself Medicine* | 1. DIY research |
| | 2. Self-help and self-diagnosis |
| | 3. Sharing between (expert) patients |
| | 4. Continuous patient self-monitoring |
| | 5. Do-it-yourself tests |
| | 6. Citizen scientists |
| *5. The Digital Doctor– Patient Relationship* | 7. Selecting, making appointments with, and reviewing doctors online |
| | 8. Online consultation |
| | 9. Digital physician assistant |
| | 10. Online pharmacies |
| | 11. Digital one-stop platforms |
| | 12. Unstaffed mini-clinics |

| Chapters | The 25 Patterns of the Digital Healthcare Sector |
|---|---|
| *6. Digital Therapeutics* | 13. The digital personal coach |
| | 14. Digital therapeutics by prescription |
| | 15. Digital adherence coach |
| *7. Digital Health Data and Data Security* | 16. Health data as a strategic asset |
| | 17. Collecting, processing, and analyzing data |
| | 18. Managing privacy, security, and ethical concerns |
| *8. Value-based Medicine* | 19. Data-driven healthcare networks |
| | 20. Lifestyle reward programs |
| | 21. Pay for performance |
| *9. Digital Drug Development* | 22. Computer-aided drug discovery |
| | 23. Digital patient recruitment for clinical studies |
| | 24. Evidence gained from digital real-world data |
| | 25. Precision medicine |

Chapter 4

# Do-it-Yourself Medicine

*The main theses of this chapter:*

- In every field, the internet is leading to a rise in self-service – and the healthcare sector is no exception. Patients want to take a more active role whenever possible. And the internet gives them the tools they need.
- Patients do online research before and after each doctor's appointment and seek advice from artificial intelligence (AI)-based chatbots and expert patients. The internet is the first source consulted by many patients – and in their eyes at least, almost as good a resource as their doctor.
- As a result, cyberchondria, a type of hypochondria exacerbated by internet research, is increasingly becoming a diagnosis in its own right.
- Health literacy means good health. Tell me what you know about health and I'll tell you how healthy you are. Health literacy is as important to having a good life as reading and writing.
- An examination by an excellent physician will still be the best thing for a patient for a long time to come. But triage, in this case an initial assessment of the urgency of a case performed by a chatbot is accessible to everyone and is increasingly superior in quality to an examination by a substandard doctor.
- This digital self-triage is quickly becoming a key process offered by health insurance companies and healthcare providers. It marks the beginning of a guided patient process.
- Granular, incorruptible data measured over time by the patients themselves will be a factor in every visit to the doctor, preventive measure, diagnosis, treatment, and behavioral modification. Because anything we cannot measure, we cannot target and control.
- Over the course of time, the do-it-yourself (DIY) laboratory test will increasingly supplement the lab test ordered by the physician, or even replace parts of it. This will lead to a further logical decoupling of consultation, examination, and the generation of data – and specifically of laboratory results.
- Patients and healthy individuals are prepared to do their part to improve the healthcare sector – whether as expert patients in peer-to-peer networks, citizen scientists, or data collectors.

The Digital Pill: What Everyone Should Know about the Future of
Our Healthcare System, 43–62
Copyright © 2021 by Emerald Publishing Limited
All rights of reproduction in any form reserved
doi:10.1108/978-1-78756-675-020211004

- The internet is changing medicine like the printing press changed the Christian church. The physician's image is shifting from one of demigod to esteemed peer – just as engineers lost their status as miracle workers at the end of the twentieth century, but at the same time became more important. The same thing is now happening in health care. Many aspects of medicine are becoming as comprehensible to laypeople as driving a car or uploading YouTube videos.
- The word "patient" is increasingly a misnomer. The patient of tomorrow is more likely to be a healthy individual who wants to stay that way. The terms "patient," "consumer," and "producer" are overlapping more and more. Modern citizens do not just generate their own electricity at home, but their own health data as well.

The appeal of DIY has thus far mainly manifested itself in people tiling bathrooms, digging garden ponds, and repairing bicycles. Home improvement is more popular than ever, with the various chains' slogans achieving cult status: "How doers get more done." "Do it right for less." "Ace is the Place." DIY is considered a good way to get back to the roots and regain a sense of autonomy in an increasingly digitalized, specialized, and often alienating world.

What traditionalists say is that, if used wisely, digitalization too offers people an opportunity to reclaim their independence – especially when it comes to answering questions about health. Many people are still hesitant to engage with their own health, whether out of a sense of complacency, respect for the supposed omniscience of the doctor, or fear of an unpleasant diagnosis. On the other hand, many others are now driving themselves and their doctors crazy by diagnosing themselves – usually with cancer – on the basis of information they find online. As always, the goal should instead be a happy medium: a relationship of trust between physician and patient, but with recourse to the many advantages that modern technology offers.

One thing seems clear: With the help of all kinds of digital assistants, patients will be able to handle more and more aspects of prevention, diagnosis, treatment, and after-care themselves – depending, of course, on their skills and inclination. And they will take on increasingly more responsibility, perhaps even the leading role, in the healthcare system. Indeed, a historic upheaval is in the offing. This will probably be hard to bear for those who still hold onto the classic cliché of "gods in white coats," but on the other hand it could be a boon for doctors who are genuinely interested in their patients and therefore quite happy to be relieved of routine tasks, collecting information, and red tape.

## DIY Research

Who hasn't been there? When something seems off with our health, nowadays our immediate instinct is no longer to reach for the phone to make a doctor's appointment. Instead, the first step is to grab our smartphone and consult Dr Google. On the internet, we can find a disease to match any symptom. The most popular sources are Wikipedia and other online encyclopedias, followed by the homepages of health insurance companies and the many health-related websites of independent patient or self-help organizations, along with online medical consultations.

Companies such as WebMD, MedicalNewsToday, Harvard Health Blog, Healthline, Ottonova, Oscar, and Outcome Health offer curated, quality-checked medical expertise in the form of articles, images, and videos – including tips and tricks for relief and prevention that can be applied in all kinds of situations. The contents reflect the state of the art in medicine and are easy to understand, entertainingly written, and well laid out. And they usually manage to steer clear of medical jargon. The medical information is tailored to the everyday needs of the patients.

Depending on the country and region, some 50–80% of all patients regularly search for medical advice on the internet. They are not only interested in learning the facts, but also hope to share comfort and discuss experiences with other patients – or sometimes simply want a diversion. A study by the Bertelsmann Foundation in Germany shows that 58% of patients gather information on the internet before consulting a physician, and 62% google their doctor's diagnosis after the appointment [1]. They doublecheck the information provided by the doctor, research alternative treatment methods, and seek dialog with other patients as well as emotional support. More than half are very happy with the results of their searches, while another 40% are somewhat satisfied. During the two-hour, in-depth interviews, not a single respondent indicated that they were dissatisfied with the findings of their own research.

Patients regard the internet as a valuable source of information, even though two out of three respondents said it was virtually impossible to judge its accuracy. In addition, half of the respondents admitted they found the sheer amount of available information confusing. And the study found that many patients are too quick to trust the internet. They do not pay attention to whether or not the information they have discovered is actually based on scientific fact, but rather on how often it appears online. Terms we have come to know from the political sphere, like "fake news" and "alternative facts," can also apply to the healthcare sector. But from the users' point of view Dr Google has some major advantages, just like many products of the digital economy – it has unlimited amounts of time, safeguards the anonymity of the patient, is available anywhere and at any time, costs nothing, and never leaves you in the lurch. This is not always for the good, however.

Unfortunately, the constant availability of Dr Google can also lead a patient to develop "Google syndrome," the obsessive use of internet health sites to find a diagnosis, also known as "cyberchondria," a term coined by American psychiatrist

Brian Fallon [2]. For cyberchondriacs, the internet is a treasure trove of information that fuels their anxiety about their health. They surf for hours, often drawing false conclusions, exaggerating their symptoms, and, in the end, drawing wild conclusions without ever consulting a doctor. Driven by their excessive fear of illness, they continue to investigate their often-harmless symptoms – like headaches or stomachaches – until they end up at brain tumors or pancreatic cancer. That is because they are falling prey to confirmation bias, the inherent urge of the human mind to seek and favor information that confirms its preconceived ideas. Contradictory evidence is systematically ignored.

This confirmation bias is put to perfect technical use by search algorithms, which are programmed by their creators to pursue economic goals. For example, the term "chest pain" results in an extremely high number of hits related to heart attacks, although chest pain is only rarely evidence of a heart attack or other very dangerous conditions. Or as Stephan Hofmeister of the National Association of Statutory Health Insurance Physicians in Germany says,

> At the end of the day, on the internet it is always cancer – that's the problem. You can always google your way there, depending on how much of a hypochondriac you are and how easily and quickly you get scared. [3]

Four-fifths of all hypochondriacs are cyberchondriacs. They have more detailed knowledge than the "analog" hypochondriac. They visit their doctors with stacks of printouts of medical articles and resist all attempts at reassurance. And if the doctor does not go along with their diagnosis, they simply switch to another practitioner. Physicians have to invest an enormous amount of time and energy to get such patients back on the right track. Fallon believes that cyberchondria generates many billions in unnecessary treatment costs across the globe.

Regardless of whether Dr Google should be viewed as a net positive or negative, today's reality is that patients mine the internet intensively for information. It is now part and parcel of every modern doctor-patient relationship. So doctors would be well advised to actively recommend accurate sources of information such as apps, health insurance sites, or healthcare portals to their patients. At the same time, patients should put all their cards – the information they have found – on the table. Transparency and communication are the key to building trust within the doctor-patient relationship. Unfortunately, according to the study quoted above, today one in three patients occasionally withholds information that they have found on the internet out of fear of offending their doctor [1]. But four out of five doctors actually see it as positive that patients are looking for information online. After all, health literacy leads to better overall health.

People can only be healthy when they are able to take control of factors that affect their health. And this first and foremost includes knowledge about health and illness. Health literacy is the ability to locate, understand, evaluate, and apply information about health so we have the capacity to make good decisions in our daily lives. The importance of this ability is illustrated by the fact that, according to surveys, health literacy is a better predictor of a person's state of health than their income, employment status, education, or ethnic origin [4]. As we stated earlier: Tell me what you know about health and I'll tell you how healthy you are.

Health literacy is an especially important factor when it comes to the prevention of non-communicable diseases (NCD). Cancer, heart disease, and diabetes are associated with many risk factors, in particular behavioral factors such as lack of exercise, poor eating habits, smoking, and alcohol consumption. A European study showed that the higher a person's health literacy level, the greater the importance they attach to physical exercise [4].

That is why every self-respecting health coach will try to boost the health literacy of their clients. And World Health Organization recommends the intensification of measures to increase health literacy with the aim of preventing the most common diseases on a large scale. To put it simply, people should know more about their bodies and take better care of them, because this will also lower their risk of heart attacks, diabetes, cancer, back pain, and mental illness. This requires, among other things, that even complex subjects are explained to laypeople in a simple and easy-to-understand manner. In this context, it is worth mentioning the rise of plain language initiatives, which aim to keep medical language as uncomplicated as possible.

## Self-help and Self-diagnosis

### *Babylon Health*

It was a Friday afternoon. Mary came home from work and rushed to look at herself in the mirror. The pea-sized bump that had recently appeared on her neck was still there. It didn't seem any smaller – or had it even gotten bigger? Mary was starting to get seriously worried. She hesitated, but then she called a surgical outpatient clinic in London. After several minutes on hold, she spoke to a receptionist who offered her the next available appointment – in three weeks' time.

Three more weeks of uncertainty? But it might be cancer! Looking for instant reassurance, Mary ended up on all sorts of internet sites. But none of them seemed to offer her an answer to the question about her neck. After a few hours of searching, she came across the Babylon Health app. Mary answered a few standard questions and then decided to request a consultation with a general practitioner. By the time the doctor contacted her 30 minutes later, she had learned that he was from India and had studied medicine in England. He looked at the pictures that Mary had sent of the growth on her skin, discussed it with her, and arrived at his diagnosis: a harmless cyst. Mary was relieved.

The symptom checker offered by Babylon Health, a London-based company with offices from New York to Rwanda to Malaysia and Singapore, is a perfect example of a digital triage tool. The term "triage" refers to a process that assesses and classifies the medical urgency of a particular symptom. Are my fatigue, fever, loss of appetite, and cough simply symptoms of the common cold or signs that I have pneumonia? Should I sit back and wait for it to get better on its own, or go to the doctor – or even the hospital – immediately?

Ali Parsa, who founded Babylon Health in 2013, says his company is all about the democratization of health care. He believes that every person should have fast, affordable, and reliable access to the healthcare system. This might still be feasible in the UK, but not in Rwanda, for instance, where there are only several hundred physicians for twelve million inhabitants.

Accessible and affordable health care begins with a triage tool that anyone can use anywhere, anytime, and at no cost through an app or internet browser. Like a flesh-and-blood doctor, a chatbot asks about symptoms and continues to probe until it is clear to the Babylon system whether the patient can take care of themselves or should seek out a physician immediately.

Babylon uses a proprietary pool of knowledge as its database; according to the company, it is one of the world's largest structured medical knowledge bases. This database records human knowledge of modern medicine in such a way that machines can work with it. Modern AI methods are used to arrive at diagnoses based on patient histories. Furthermore, the algorithms analyze the latest medical literature and feed these digital findings into the knowledge base, which learns continuously. So over the course of time it acquires literally "superhuman" abilities, at least when it comes to not forgetting, processing massive amounts of information, and staying permanently up to date.

But where does it all lead?

Digital consultation and triage runs entirely in self-service mode, which is particularly convenient and cost-effective for patients. In mid-2019, six years after its founding, Babylon was reporting 4,000 clinical consultations per day. With every patient interaction, the database and software get a little bit better. The quality of the diagnoses, triage, and treatment recommendations is constantly improving. Over time, it will almost inevitably become higher than the quality an average doctor can offer, at least for simple illnesses. The future of triage, then, is the self-learning chatbot, which can give patients peace of mind at any time of the day or night, or, in complicated cases, immediately connect them to a flesh-and-blood doctor on demand.

In a comparison with the human triage service provided by the UK's National Health Service, the NHS 111 helpline, the Babylon symptom checker scored significantly better. It correctly placed about the same number of patients in the emergency category as NHS 111 (23% versus 21%), but – equally correctly – asked many more patients to care for themselves (40% vs. 14%) and sent significantly fewer patients to their family doctor or primary care physician (29% vs. 60%). This spares them a lot of worry and saves an incredible amount of labor and money. A study examining the performance of online triage in dealing with potential heart attack patients came to a similar conclusion. It also showed that online triage led to fewer false alarms [5].

So does that mean that physicians will soon become superfluous? Not at all. First, we are only talking about a small fraction of a doctor's responsibilities and decisions. Second, this tool shoulders some of the routine and administrative work that physicians perform, freeing them up to concentrate on their patients. Eric Topol, a leading US expert in digital medicine, believes that AI like that of Babylon could liberate doctors from their fate as "glorified data clerks" and enable them to devote more time to the people who need their help [6]. According to Topol, many studies show that the better the personal relationship between doctor and patient, the more effective the treatment.

But the question remains – why did the team of passionate scientists, clinicians, mathematicians, and engineers choose to name their creation after the ancient city of Babylon? Because almost 2,500 years ago, citizens of the bustling metropolis who needed medical advice often gathered in a public square to pool their knowledge about the treatment of illnesses. This is one of the first examples of the democratization of health care – and since the Babylonians had the longest life expectancy in the ancient world, the founders of Babylon Health were inspired by their story.

There has been repeated public debate about whether Babylon Health's automated system really delivers a better diagnosis and treatment for patients than the conventional method of consulting a doctor in person. Whatever the conclusion of such comparisons, they apply not only to Babylon Health, but also to other platforms and services. Given the steadily growing volume of data, over time the accuracy of diagnoses and treatment recommendations can be expected to increase significantly. And the rapid advances being made in AI will accelerate this development as well.

Babylon Health is only one of hundreds of companies that are leveraging AI-based self-diagnosis and triage. Others include technology startups such as K Health, Buoy Health, Your.MD, and Health Tap, as well as a rapidly growing number of health insurance companies, hospital chains, established technology companies, and healthcare organizations across the globe that are seeking to empower their citizens, customers, and patients by offering a free symptom-checking service.

In addition to the general triage tools that are being used for a wide range of common illnesses, countless tools have been developed in recent years that specialize in providing guidance on specific types of symptoms – not least in the field of dermatology. People who discover a new mole on their arm do not, as in Mary's case described above, have to turn to Babylon. They can also take a picture of the mole from inside the Swiss Online Doctor app, add a description of their symptoms, and receive advice from a medical specialist within 48 hours – for a small fee. Over the course of time, an extremely valuable trove of quality-tested data comprising millions of images, descriptions, and corresponding medical assessments is being created – and algorithms can use it to learn to preform triage. We are at the very beginning of this process, which is one of evolution rather than revolution.

## Sharing Between (Expert) Patients

When it comes to complicated, long-lasting, and rare diseases, the automated consultants soon reach the limits of their capabilities. So in such cases, millions of people reach for the next tool that the internet has put in the hands of the health-care sector and millions of empowered patients: online forums in which they can share information with people in similar situations.

### *PatientsLikeMe*

In his book *What Would Google Do?*, American journalist Jeff Jarvis called the attention of millions of people to the PatientsLikeMe platform. As he wrote in the book, he had tweeted about his atrial fibrillation – abnormal heart rhythm – and written about this heart condition in his blog. This prompted other patients to reach out to him and point him to the platform, where sufferers could talk about their problems and concerns and offer each other encouragement. They also share their experiences of hospitals, physicians, and medications. Jarvis wrote that he found this dialog especially valuable. He no longer felt alone with his disease.

PatientsLikeMe was founded in 1999 by Jamie and Ben Heywood after their brother Stephen was diagnosed with a chronic degenerative disease of the central nervous system. Twelve years later, the platform was expanded to include all illnesses. Today more than 600,000 patients use it to share information about more than 2,700 diseases and health conditions. With topics ranging from diabetes to sleep disorders to cancer, its more than 40 different forums are considered particularly helpful. This is where patients go to rate treatments, recommend physicians and hospitals, and talk about health insurance providers. And they also try to boost each other's morale [7].

There are millions and millions of data, patients, treatments, and drugs recorded on the platform, corresponding to the different diseases. This information can all be made available to users, along the lines of: "Patients suffering from disease X generally have very good experience with drug Y."

In addition, PatientsLikeMe works with companies from the health care and pharmaceutical sectors to develop better treatment options on the basis of the data. One example is the partnership with iCarbonX, a Chinese biotech firm, aimed at achieving a better understanding of the origin and progression of diseases. PatientsLikeMe is also working with the American pharmacy chain Walgreens to analyze patient reports about the side effects of medications.

Every user of PatientsLikeMe has access to clinical studies and can read about the prognoses, side effects, and possible applications associated with new drugs. And they can find information about the active ingredients contained in the medication so they can assess its compatibility. If a patient is interested in participating in a clinical study, there is an entry form with an option to sign up.

There are already many additional platforms of this type, like HealthUnlocked, Medhelp, and Braintalk that serve as points of contact for millions of patients with life-altering diseases. The patients can use the platforms to talk about their experiences and find other patients with similar demographic patterns and clinical conditions. All of these platforms share the goal of helping patients find the answer to the question: "Given my state of health, what is the best possible outcome I can achieve for myself and how do I get there?"

What do patients like the most about such platforms? They learn to understand the symptoms of their illness. They meet people who tell them what it's like to begin a certain treatment, to start or stop taking a medication or change the dosage. Participating in these online communities increases their sense of well-being, their feeling of being in control of their own particular disease, their overall personal ability to deal with the disease, and their medical knowledge.

The more familiar patients are with such a platform, the more information they share. The more active they are, the more they benefit. This is why such patient communities grow into goldmines of information – from the corporate point of view as well. This explains the enormous interest of large, established healthcare players in these mostly fledgling and financially precarious digital startups. In 2019, PatientsLikeMe was purchased by US corporation UnitedHealth, while

Medhelp was bought by StayWell, a company in turn owned by pharmaceutical giant Merck.

## Health Unlocked

It didn't seem all that serious at first. Britta occasionally felt short of breath, coughed more often, and sometimes had pain in her chest. Her primary care physician diagnosed asthma, and Britta didn't consult a specialist until she started experiencing shortness of breath during physical activity. After several examinations came the diagnosis: lymphangioleiomyomatosis (LAM), a rare lung disease affecting about one in 160,000 women between the ages of 20 and 50 years. Britta was shocked, and her doctors weren't really sure how to proceed. What was for sure, however, was that the disease destroys lung tissue – which meant she might require a lung transplant one day.

Britta wanted to find out as much as possible about LAM and spent hours searching the internet until she happened upon the website of Health Unlocked, a platform for people to share information on their illnesses, including especially rare diseases. Britta found other patients suffering from the same extremely uncommon lung condition, which almost exclusively affects women. They talked about their daily struggles, and reported on the medications and treatments they tried. And most importantly, they gave her hope. Britta learned that her disease was genetic. In patients with LAM, the TSC1 and TSC2 genes mutate and lose their function. This leads to uncontrolled growth of cysts in the lung tissue, which causes a progressive deterioration of lung function. While there is no cure for Britta's disease, at least there are several different medications that can stabilize the decline of lung function. The life expectancy of patients with LAM is increasing steadily. Britta's heavy burden was lightened somewhat when she no longer felt like she had to bear it alone. The other LAM patients took on the role of experts on the disease – more so than the general practitioner who had diagnosed her with asthma.

The Health Unlocked platform was founded in 2010 by Jorge Armanet and Matt Jameson Evans, bringing together patients, health insurance providers, pharmaceutical companies, and medical doctors. Today it has four million registered users and more than 40 million annual visitors who can use its more than 700 forums to report on their health problems and concerns with a wide range of diseases such as multiple sclerosis, anxiety, and depression. Health organizations also participate in many of these forums.

On the platform, patients share information about the symptoms and progression of their diseases and discuss their experiences of doctors, hospitals, medications, and treatments. Studies show many people find this communication with others to be valuable and helpful in itself. In addition, it boosts the users' motivation to actively combat their disease and to consult with physicians, care services, and hospitals – rather than simply resigning themselves to their fate. The platform also provides a multitude of facts, figures, diagrams, and graphs about new medications and treatments and offers pharmaceutical companies a chance to provide information about specific diseases.

## Continuous Patient Self-monitoring

### *AliveCor*

One fall afternoon, Andrea and her father John went for a walk together as they so often did. They had not gone far when John noticed a strange feeling in his chest. His heart seemed to be racing and he felt dizzy and disoriented. Andrea was alarmed. She herself had been suffering from heart problems for some time and so always carried a portable Kardia electrocardiogram (ECG) device to measure the electric activity of her heart. Although John was reluctant, she managed to persuade him to perform an ECG with her Kardia app. And 30 seconds later they had an answer. The Kardia app showed that John probably was experiencing atrial fibrillation (A-fib) and should see a doctor immediately. The cardiologist in the hospital confirmed the diagnosis a short time later. He prescribed John drugs to thin his blood and prevent the formation of clots.

This is just one example of how the Kardia app from AliveCor can save lives. In our example, John benefited from the fact that his daughter also continuously monitored her own pulse and could lend him the necessary technical equipment. Atrial fibrillation is very dangerous, because a blood clot may form that can lead to stroke.

The story of AliveCor began in 2011, when David Albert, an experienced doctor and the former clinical director of the cardiology division at General Electric, presented a seemingly normal smartphone cover in a YouTube video. But this was no ordinary phone case. Albert and two colleagues had applied for a patent for wireless data transmission from portable ECG devices. The phone case could record an ECG within seconds and transmit it simultaneously to the cloud and the Kardia app on the smartphone screen. The device caused a sensation at the Consumer Electronics Show in Las Vegas, and shortly thereafter Albert received the first three million USD in venture capital. 2012 saw the market launch of the Kardia smartphone case.

Eight years later, AliveCor has attracted more than 63 million USDs in venture capital and expanded its product portfolio. The case has been replaced by a credit-card-size pad that can also be attached to a keychain. Its electrodes have to be touched with the fingers and then placed on the knee or ankle. This is how the ECG is recorded. Since 2017, the Kardia ECG has been available integrated into a band for the Apple Watch, allowing constant monitoring of the heart's electrical signals. The KardiaBand was the first medical device accessory approved by the US Food and Drug Administration (FDA). In the United States, the KardiaMobile and the KardiaBand are available for 99 USD, an affordable price that has led to more than 30 million ECGs being recorded using Kardia products. AliveCor generates additional revenue with an offer to store personal ECG data for more than one month; the startup charges 10 USD per month for this service. The AliveCor products are currently available in 14 additional countries, including Germany, Switzerland, Australia, Hong Kong, and Canada.

The AliveCor team has also improved the range of features for doctors, who can retrieve and check their patients' ECGs in the KardiaPro system. In the United States, physicians can also bill these remote diagnoses through the regular health insurance providers.

> Utilization of the Kardia device with the KardiaPro monitoring service has proven to be a remarkable improvement in the management of patients with A-fib. Managing non-Kardia A-fib patients feels like navigating a forest with a blindfold,

says well-known American cardiologist Anthony Pearson [8].

There is no question that AliveCor has changed the world of cardiology and will continue to do so going forward. This achievement was honored by the technology magazine *Fast Company*, which named AliveCor the world's most innovative company of 2018 in the field of AI. However, there are also critical voices in American medical circles. "A wearable device should not mean a wearable physician," warns Khaldoun Tarakji of the Cleveland Clinic. In his opinion, the medical community must carefully weigh when and where it applies these new technologies [9].

### Quantified Self

The trend toward digital self-monitoring officially began in 2007, when *Wired* journalists Gary Wolf and Kevin Kelly launched the Quantified Self movement in the San Francisco Bay area. Their aim was to join forces with others to explore their experiences with self-tracking. Today the movement has gone global. Regular meetings of these life-loggers are held in 35 countries. Broadly speaking, their aim is to understand themselves better in personal, health, and fitness-related matters as well as specific habits.

Depending on the problem, they measure anything and everything that can be quantified in some way. A perusal of the movement's homepage, quantifiedself. com, is astonishing. In addition to clinical parameters such as blood pressure, pulse, weight, and blood sugar level, in the site's blogs members share how, why, and with what degree of success they have been measuring their mental abilities and more. They also track their environment, food, location, media consumption, spending habits, moods and emotions, productivity, sleep, social media friends and contacts, emails, phone calls, physical activity, and stress levels. Their credo: Anything we cannot measure, we cannot control.

For more than 15 years, one of the authors of this book has been tracking, among other things, his time spent at work – every day, down to the quarter-hour. He does this voluntarily, in what started as an experiment. The insights gained from this self-experiment, which has long since become a daily routine, are astonishing and demonstrate the power of continuous measurement. If done correctly, the logs reflect the truth. There is no way to cheat. The data must be recorded continuously, that is multiple times per day. If we just sit down on the weekend and think about what we have been doing all week, we end up with a very fuzzy picture. Essential details are lost, wishful thinking prevails over reality, and we tend to record how our time *should* have been allocated rather than where it really went. The same also applies to all patients who, during a routine check-up, are asked by their doctors how often they have exercised in the last four weeks, how high their average blood pressure has been, whether their weight has remained constant and they are sticking more or less to their diet, and if they are taking their pills at the right times.

Over time, self-collected data can reveal patterns that lead to behavioral changes. We might realize that the project we are investing the most time in is not the most successful. Or that day trips are major time wasters, so it is better to stop taking them. Or that in the years we get more exercise and work fewer hours, the number of days we are sick decreases significantly. Or that April and November are invariably the most work-intensive months.

Long before the era of the smartphone and the internet, people such as athletes or sufferers of chronic illnesses measured and documented their vital signs and activities every day, creating a handwritten portrait of themselves out of numbers and notepaper. Connected sensors in the form of scales, step-counters, and the like have automated this tracking process, making it significantly easier. The smartphone – the pocket computer that has supplanted the pocketknife to become the handiest tool in almost every situation – documents the measurements automatically, analyzes them, and presents them in a manner that a layperson can understand.

Experience shows that as soon as something useful also becomes easy to use, it crosses the bridge to mainstream acceptance. In this context, it seems obvious that in the foreseeable future, self-measured vital signs will become a fundamental resource for every visit to the doctor, every treatment, every diagnosis, every preventive measure, and every change in behavior. It also explains why countless new, old, small, and large companies within the digital healthcare sector are seizing on this topic. Apple and Google are merely the most well-known technology firms that are using this angle to enter the healthcare market. They are starting where their skills are best able to mitigate the financial difficulties of the healthcare system: with NCDs and diabetes in particular. And they are doing it through the continuous, patient-centered generation, collection, and processing of data.

No sooner had the FDA certified the ECG function in the new Apple Watch than, Apple moved beyond its lifestyle-centric view of the customer. The

Cupertino-based company developed its HealthKit as a separate, secure storage space for private health data on every iPhone. It not only collects the data captured by its own hardware and software, but also offers space for data from digital patient records as well as third-party apps. This allows Apple users to save – and analyze – all their health-relevant data in a single location. Apple's CareKit makes it easy for healthcare providers to build apps for patient interaction, while its ResearchKit simplifies research collaboration – all dependent on the consent of the user.

The amount of health data that people can continuously and unobtrusively track using hardware and software is amazing: steps, weight, blood pressure, heart rate, pulse wave velocity, body fat, muscle mass, body water, bone density, sleep phases, sleep duration, sleep quality, blood sugar, ECG, and much more. Companies such as Ava, Azumio, Biovotion, Dexcom, Fitbit, Garmin, Healbe, Huawei Misfit, Moov, Samsung, Withings, and Xiaomi provide the necessary technology. And companies such as mysugr, helloheart, onduo, and iCarbonX use it.

Correctly compiled and interpreted, this data provides a much more comprehensive and much better overview of a patient's health than was possible before digitalization. This has three important effects: First, the treatment can be better tailored to the patient, making it more efficient and effective. The quality of the treatment is improved while unnecessary costs are avoided. Second, when presented and applied correctly, these detailed and incorruptible data can help patients identify patterns and change their lifestyle. And third, this patient-measured data, if made available by the patient for this purpose, contributes to an ever-expanding knowledge base for medical research.

## Do-it-yourself Tests

Diagnostics is an often-undervalued area of the healthcare system. Using tests to correctly diagnose an illness is usually the starting point for follow-on treatment by the doctor, identifies whether the patient is suffering from a disease or is at risk of developing one, and nowadays often also determines what medications are prescribed. Up to now, many tests have been performed as follows: The patient goes to the doctor's office or the hospital, where a sample is taken – tissue, blood, urine, stool, or saliva, for example. Often this sample has to be sent to a laboratory for analysis. Several days or weeks later, the patient is notified of any significant findings.

Digitalization speeds up this process in two ways: First, it is becoming increasingly easy to conduct certain tests at home yourself and get a result immediately – like taking a pregnancy test or measuring your blood sugar level. Second, in cases in which you used to have to go to a doctor's office or hospital to give a sample, you can take one yourself at home and send it directly to the service provider. The results are then sent directly to you by email.

Taken together, we can describe this phenomenon as "DIY testing." It is a hybrid service because, like e-commerce, it has a digital and a physical component. In the first, simpler version, the patient orders a test kit and conducts the test all by themselves at home. In the second version, which makes more complex tests possible, the patient orders a medical test over the internet, collects a sample at home, sends the sample in, and receives the result and interpretation via the internet. Tedious, time-consuming, and cost-intensive trips to the doctor or laboratory are no longer necessary; the diagnoses become less expensive and more easily accessible, making it increasingly possible to integrate them into prevention and early-detection strategies.

It is important to note that there is a wide and still cluttered field of providers offering varying medical quality. This trend has given rise to companies such as Viome, 23andme, Color Genomics, Helix, freenome, onlinedoctor, and Healthy. io. But the large, established diagnostics companies such as Siemens Healthineers, Roche, and Abbott are also increasingly relying on digital solutions that connect patients, doctors, and laboratories.

To generate a real advantage, it is essential for self-tests to be not only more convenient or faster, but also add genuine medical value compared to the previous standard. Because even expert patients will not be able to perform complex medical analyses in their own homes without additional resources anytime soon. The necessary laboratory equipment, procedural expertise, and ability to interpret results are still essential to produce medically valid results that can be used in determining the course of treatment.

The examples below illustrate the move toward DIY testing:

### Urine Test by Healthy.io

According to the British Kidney Patient Association, one in eight people in Great Britain suffers from chronic kidney disease. The National Health Service spends spend around two billion pounds annually treating these patients. Undiagnosed chronic kidney disease can lead to kidney failure and give rise to cardiovascular diseases. So it makes sense and is indeed essential to conduct regular urine tests to monitor kidney function – but such tests are typically only done in a doctor's office. Patients often consider such examinations tedious and time-consuming, so many of them only show up sporadically for testing.

With this difficulty in mind, Tel Aviv-based startup Healthy.io developed a urine test that patients can perform at home. All you need are certified testing strips, an app, a color-coded slide, and a great deal of AI. It is easy to use. The patient takes a urine sample, dips the test strip into the urine, waits until the strip changes color, and uses the app to photograph it in front of the slide. Algorithms then check the photo for abnormalities and decide on the next steps.

The benefits to patients are obvious. Taking a urine sample and a snapshot of the dipstick is quick and easy; fitting a drive to the hospital or doctor's office into your busy schedule, on the other hand, is often very difficult. So it's no wonder that in comparison, the Healthy.io urine tests deliver more continuous and therefore better data for monitoring patient health. In the United States, it is estimated that less than 10% of people suffering from chronic kidney disease are actually aware of the fact. Better access to urine tests can help catch kidney diseases at an early stage, preventing the development of secondary diseases.

According to Founder and CEO Jonathan Adiri, Healthy.io is aiming to pioneer the use of computer-based image processing and self-learning machines in order to provide patients access to the best medical advice and care at all times and in all places. In addition to Great Britain, the urine test has been well received in Israel. It is estimated that around 250,000 tests have been carried out so far. The number of customers could increase significantly from 2021 onward, when the startup will begin offering the FDA-approved test in the United States. Today Healthy.io's urine test can detect numerous diseases, infections, and even pregnancy complications, with further applications planned [10].

### Stool Sample Test by Viome and DayTwo

While Healthy.io analyzes urine samples, companies such as Viome and DayTwo offer analysis of the human microbiome based on a pea-sized stool sample. The term "microbiome" stands for the extensive ecosystem of bacteria, viruses, fungi, and single-celled organisms that populate our bodies and especially our guts, invisible to the naked eye. Depending on the source, an average of between 40 and 100 trillion such microorganisms live (or, in the case of viruses, exist in a gray area between living and non-living) in and on a human being, which taken all together are about the size of a football and account for about two kilograms of body weight. This is somewhat heavier than the average human brain. One gram of fecal matter is home to more bacteria than there are people on earth. These microorganisms are made up of three times more cells and 300 times more genes than a human being. Patients interested in finding out about their microbiome can order a test kit, take a stool sample, fill out a form, send in the sample, and receive a recommendation through an app.

Research on the connections between microbiome and health is still in its early days. This means that although such analyses are commercially attractive and interesting to the customers, they do not yet play a role in medical practice or have relevance for the treatment of patients. The major challenge is to identify the cause and effect of specific bacteria and to translate this knowledge into concrete treatment options. The microbiome of the digestive tract is potentially as complex as our genes and has just as much impact on our health. Across the globe, researchers are working to unlock the secrets of the microbiome. They are sequencing the genomes of all the microorganisms, mapping them in a phylogenetic tree, and starting to establish connections between populations of microorganisms and health conditions. Areas of focus include weight, immune function, inflammation, allergies, appetite, digestion, arthritis, multiple sclerosis, colon cancer, breast cancer, depression, anxiety, and other cognitive functions.

Today many companies have entered this field. On its website Viome, headquartered in the United States in Los Alamos, New Mexico, promises to provide a personalized analysis of microbiome and metabolism and corresponding nutritional recommendations to reduce harmful and increase beneficial metabolism. The outcome is said to be increased energy and general well-being. Tel Aviv-based DayTwo offers dietary advice for keeping blood sugar levels in equilibrium as a preventive measure against cardiovascular diseases and type 2 diabetes. If research spending and capital investment can be taken as indicators, then companies in the field of direct-to-consumer microbiome analysis have a bright future. So far, however, there have been no serious studies.

### Genetic Testing by Color Genomics

Imagine that both of your parents develop cancer. Your mother contracts breast cancer, the most common type of cancer for women; your father, colon cancer, one of the most common types for men. Given the high number of cases, this scenario is not improbable. You might logically ask yourself if you have a heightened risk of getting cancer as well. A genetic test could provide important answers, but this kind of analysis can cost up to 5,000 USD. Since health insurance companies in most countries do not usually cover this expense, many people cannot afford such a test.

Color Genomics has stepped in to fill this gap. The company has been offering genetic testing since 2013. For 249 USD, it will analyze around 30 genes in order to assess an individual's risk of developing cancer. In the opinion of Color Genomics founder Othman Laraki, genetic testing should be available to everyone. Like so many entrepreneurs in the healthcare market, he is concerned not only with making a profit, but also with the democratization of medical screening and health care. The company is continuously expanding its portfolio of tests and analyses. Recently a test for breast and ovarian cancer was developed that detects 19 genetic markers. Another test evaluates eleven genetic markers to determine the risk of developing cancer of the skin, stomach, prostate, uterus, and pancreas.

The process is quite simple. Patients have to contact a doctor to sign them up for the test. They then receive a test tube for taking and sending in a saliva sample. And then Color Genomics sets to work analyzing the sample. The result is a prognosis of the genetic risks of developing certain types of cancer over the course of the patient's life. Of course there are other factors besides genetics that play an important role, like their willingness to exercise, eat a healthy diet, and steer clear of cigarettes and alcohol. The company does not try to brush this under the rug. As Othman Laraki repeatedly – and correctly – points out, not enough attention is paid to prevention.

Home DNA testing has definitely become a trend. A lot of people believe it offers them a tool for seizing control of their own fate. Some people are simply trying to learn more about their family trees – what percentage of my ancestry is Vietnamese and what percentage Chinese? But most want to know more about their health today and going forward, and how to modify their behaviors.

It is important, warns Robert Green, medical geneticist at Brigham and Women's Hospital in Boston and director of the Genomes2People research program, that users are aware that DIY DNA tests are not the same as genetic testing in a strict medical context. DIY tests are often not backed up by professional medical advice on what to do with the results. And the quality of the test results is not uniformly assured.

Furthermore, home DNA tests are often rejected in a real professional medical environment, because their methodologies are sometimes disputed. In 2013, the FDA issued a warning to 23andme, one of the major providers of such DIY tests, because it was unable to substantiate its advertising claims through clinical studies [11]. So it is wise to be careful when interpreting the results. People who take DIY genetic tests tend to overestimate their conclusiveness and take negative results too much to heart. And sometimes genetic testing also yields results that we would rather not have known about in retrospect, because there is nothing we can do about them.

### The Limits of Do-it-yourself

Direct-to-consumer laboratory testing, wrote the scientific journal *Annals of Clinical and Laboratory Research* in 2017, has dramatically changed the healthcare system in a very short period of time [12]. The authors of the article, however, concluded that many of these developments are undesirable. The patients and/or customers work directly with the laboratories and do not seek advice from a physician. While this may increase the privacy, convenience, and speed of tests and reduce their costs, it also leads to unnecessary anxiety, misinterpretation, and misdiagnosis – because the safety net of having the results interpreted by a doctor is completely absent in these cases. The authors call for higher standards for the accreditation of DIY laboratories. In their view, the tests must not only be safe and of high quality, but also provide reliable and easy-to-understand guidance on interpreting the results, so that patients will not misunderstand them.

The business of DIY testing is apparently so lucrative that ambitious entrepreneurs are resorting to dubious and possibly criminal methods. The blood-testing company Theranos, founded by Elizabeth Holmes, may be the best-known example of this. Often described as young, charismatic, and smart as a whip, the entrepreneur was celebrated as the female Steve Jobs of the healthcare sector. Her company was worth more than nine billion USD before a journalist uncovered its allegedly fraudulent practices. Theranos apparently did not conduct most of the blood tests on its proprietary, supposedly revolutionary analysis platform, but used modified Siemens equipment. Holmes is suspected of having deceived patients, doctors, insurance companies, and investors for years. Now she is on trial for fraud and fighting to restore her reputation [13].

As we now know, the company uBiome also built its success on shaky scientific foundations. It made grand claims in the marketing of its stool sample analyses and filed dubious health insurance claims. In this manner, uBiome was able to drive its market value up to 600 million USD. That was shortly before the start of investigations into criminal and civil charges that drove the company into bankruptcy.

These examples show that medical products and services are not ordinary consumer goods, even if the internet sometimes presents them in this light. There can be no compromise when it comes to standards of medical quality. That said, if it does become feasible to guarantee this quality, then combined with other information, such as other health data collected from patients on a regular basis, and in the context of ongoing treatment, such services may play an important role in the future.

## Citizen Scientists

One goal of most of the companies named in this book is to expand the existing base of medical data and knowledge. Because with every new data-based finding, our knowledge about people and their health increases.

For example, if a patient with characteristic A takes five milligrams of drug B, their clinical values change by the amount of C. Now imagine if every medication taken, every food consumed, every unit of exercise, every activity of every human being were not only measured, but also immediately stored in a single gigantic global database in machine-readable form. Then all patients could use this database to learn what exactly would work best for them and their health at this particular time. This vision has already been made a reality in a tiny slice of the retail sector – the Amazon recommendation system, which has allowed the company to grow into the largest and most powerful retailer in the Western world. Amazon didn't get big because it offers the best products, but the best buying recommendations.

The expansion of the knowledge base is also the objective of the next development in the digital healthcare sector: turning ordinary individuals into citizen scientists. In their roles as patients, these people do not just try to help themselves, but others as well. They voluntarily compile data by collecting information and by performing small experimental self-tests, which they document in accordance with guidelines and make available to everyone else through the internet – just like someone adding to an entry on Wikipedia.

In the fields of astronomy and ornithology, for instance, lay researchers are already commonplace and widely accepted. In the Western healthcare sector, however, this is not yet the case. The historic distinction between professional researchers and non-professional helpers is considerable. So no one should be surprised that the call for the inclusion of laypeople in research, which is becoming ever louder as digitalization advances, is dismissed by some critics as populist rhetoric.

This is despite the fact that the term "citizen scientist" originally described a sort of partnership between formal medical science and individual patients. Online data contribution platforms, social media, and smartphones are broadening these possibilities and blurring the boundaries between professional and non-professional research [14]. Here are just a few examples: On 100forParkinsons, participants use a smartphone app to collect data for 100 days and share and compare it. The American Gut Project pursues similar aims in the area of the human microbiome; the Kinsey Reporter in the field of sexual behavior.

On the Mark2Cure and Cochrane Crowd platforms, anyone can help search for key information in specific documents to find urgently needed knowledge in thousands of medical texts more quickly. On the Stall Catchers platform, thousands of laypeople search video clips from brain scans for blood clots.

Lay researchers usually participate in observational studies; that is to say they record data about themselves which they share online. Sometimes they are also involved in intervention studies. They carry out experimental self-tests and record the effects in a clear and comprehensible fashion. For example, they might eat a special diet for two weeks, measuring the effects on the microorganisms in the gut and on their well-being. In summary, we can agree that lay researchers play a lot of different roles in actual practice, and there is justified debate about how useful their work is.

Chapter 5

# The Digital Doctor–Patient Relationship

*The main theses of this chapter:*

- Because patients increasingly see themselves as customers and partners, the patient experience and patient satisfaction are becoming increasingly important.
- Patient reviews of physicians are growing exponentially in number and playing an ever-greater role in patient decisions. Certain aspects of the Uber and Tripadvisor experiences are being carried over into the doctor–patient relationship, with all the advantages and disadvantages of such review portals.
- In addition to recommendations from family and friends, digital word of mouth is becoming an important selection criterion. Digital reputation management has become a new challenge facing doctors and other healthcare providers.
- Measured in terms of quantity, online consultations are rapidly overtaking physical consultations for routine medical examinations.
- Digital physician assistants reduce the degree of subjectivity and variability in clinical diagnoses and treatment recommendations, helping prevent errors. With the available store of global knowledge at their fingertips, they are becoming more accurate every day and an indispensable part of every doctor's team.
- Online pharmacies are emerging as competitors to brick-and-mortar pharmacies, with – not always legitimate – offers for seamless, convenient home delivery of medications.
- In the future, there will be providers who can cover all of a patient's healthcare needs in a single stroke. Such one-stop shops will be a mainstay of the healthcare system of tomorrow.
- Unstaffed mini-clinics will boost the accessibility of health services and reduce costs for everyone involved. In the near future, they will become a regular feature of every good shopping mall and university as well as factories, airports, train stations, office buildings, and some highway rest stops.
- Digitalization is the key – maybe even the only way – to provide the 3.4 billion people who earn less than 5.50 USD per day with access to high-quality health care.

**The Digital Pill: What Everyone Should Know about the Future of
Our Healthcare System, 63–79**
Copyright © 2021 by Emerald Publishing Limited
All rights of reproduction in any form reserved
doi:10.1108/978-1-78756-675-020211005

Physicians and their patients are not only the two main actors in the health-care sector, but their relationship is also the key to its success. Traditionally, the relationship between doctor and patient was an unequal one, with the doctor–patient model widely characterized as paternalistic. The knowledge and power gap between doctors and their patients was high. Patients had to almost blindly trust the medical information and treatment recommendations they received from their physicians. The doctors were often considered "gods in white coats," while patients long played a passive role. For about 30 years now, the doctor–patient relationship has been changing more and more, with a growing trend toward a patient-centric model. Professor Teresa Hellín of the University of Alcalá in Madrid describes the ideal physician as follows:

> To attend those who suffer, a physician must possess not only the scientific knowledge and technical abilities, but also an understanding of human nature. The patient is not just a group of symptoms, damaged organs, and altered emotions. The patient is a human being, at the same time worried and hopeful, who is searching for relief, help, and trust. The importance of an intimate relationship between patient and physician can never be overstated because in most cases an accurate diagnosis, as well as an effective treatment, relies directly on the quality of this relationship. [1]

With digitalization, a further wave of change is sweeping over the doctor–patient relationship. How do online review sites impact this relationship? How will doctors and patients engage with each other in a world, in which digital communication increasingly supplements or even replaces personal interactions? How will digital aids change the relationship between doctors and patients? In the following chapter, we present five response patterns.

## Selecting, Making Appointments with, and Reviewing Doctors Online

Imagine you have moved to a new town and are looking for a new dentist. Or you have lived in your town for a while, but need to consult a gynecologist for the first time – and the doctor recommended by your friends is not currently accepting new patients. Or you live in a rural area and urgently need to find a lung specialist as close to you as possible. What do you do? Of course you ask your friends and family and your primary care physician, but their networks also have their limits. This is what happened to Chinese entrepreneur Wang Hang when he was looking for a doctor in 2006. He discovered that it wasn't so easy to find the right one. So he founded the Hao Dai Fu platform, headquartered in Beijing. Today Hao Dai Fu, which basically means "good doctor," is one of the largest health platforms in China [2].

Do-it-yourself patients are used to taking matters into their own hands. This includes their choice of obstetrician, pediatrician, dermatologist, physical therapist, and psychotherapist. And they prefer a format that they are familiar with from their experience with Alibaba, Amazon, or other e-commerce sites. They want all the important information at their fingertips: an online overview of doctors' offices in their area as well as information about each individual doctor, from their area of specialization to their prices for treatment. And they want to see how previous patients have rated the treatment they received. Once they have selected a doctor, of course they also want to book an appointment online.

This of course means that enough doctors have to want and be able to offer such a service, and that they all must have an internet presence that allows for sufficient comparison and makes it possible to leave reviews. And it requires that their offices be in a position to manage their scheduling digitally, because only then can the time slots be booked online.

Companies such as Practo in India, DocPlanner in Poland, RateMDs, and Healthgrades in the United States, Hao Dai Fu in China, and Jameda in Germany have set up platforms to address precisely this problem. Their goal is to provide the largest possible number of patients with the widest possible choice of physicians and to simplify the process of connecting patients with healthcare providers. They use a similar format to Yelp and Tripadvisor. Measured in terms of participating patients, doctors, and reviews posted, their numbers are already high today – and growing rapidly.

Every day thousands of newly written patient reviews are added to these online platforms. And their influence on patients' medical decisions is growing.

### *Practo*

People who fall ill in India and seek medical assistance face a great many challenges. First they have to find a suitable doctor, which can be difficult because there are only an average of 0.7 physicians for every 1,000 of the country's inhabitants.

Patients often also have to take care of the delivery and analysis of samples or arrange for X-rays or MRI scans themselves. And if they are seriously ill, it is not at all easy to arrange to be admitted to a hospital.

Young entrepreneurs Shashank ND and Abhinav Lal have founded a company to help patients overcome all of these hurdles. In essence, Practo consists of a platform on which patients can schedule consultations with physicians and arrange for all the tests and analyses that are necessary to obtain a diagnosis. India offers good conditions for such a service – after all, the country has a very high concentration of mobile phones compared to the rest of the world. Today, the Practo network includes 200,000 doctors, 10,000 hospitals, 4,000 fitness centers, and 8,000 laboratories – located not only in India, but also in Brazil, Indonesia, Singapore, and the Philippines. This allows Practo to set up some 45 million medical consultations and examinations for its customers each year. It also offers a forum where its users can write reviews about their doctors or hospital visits [3].

## *DocPlanner*

This platform lets patients make an appointment with a doctor in their area. The service was founded by Mariusz Gralewski in Poland in 2011, but today can be used in more than 20 countries. The physicians registered with DocPlanner have online appointment books so that patients can reserve a slot. In addition to appointment scheduling, the service also designs websites for doctors, gives pointers on the organization and operation of the office, and helps with setting up telemedical consultations.

DocPlanner has rapidly extended its reach. Some 1.5 million doctor's visits can be arranged each month for its 30 million registered patients and 2 million registered doctors. Three million people visit the website each month. Further services are in the works, like telephone consultations for patients, the provision of information about doctors, hospitals, and health insurance companies, and the creation of forums on specific diseases and treatments [4].

Two trends are driving the growth of online patient reviews: First, consumers are now used to consulting online ratings and comments when making purchase decisions, not to mention reviewing products and services themselves. In this light, it can be said that the healthcare sector is simply catching up to other industries. Second, there is the move toward patient empowerment and self-determination already described in the previous chapter. This is leading to new criteria in the way patients evaluate the quality of health services – with customer experience and satisfaction being transformed here into patient experience and satisfaction.

The majority of patients find such ratings and the simplified process for making appointments very helpful. In surveys, almost seven in 10 Americans indicated that reviews written by patients are important in their selection of doctors, although not as important as recommendations from family and friends [5].

An overwhelming majority of physicians views such ratings critically – and understandably so. They worry that most of the negative reviews are written by dissatisfied patients who are not able to accurately assess the quality of their work. And the doctors in question cannot refute unjustified negative posts because to do so would violate doctor–patient confidentiality. It is also practically impossible to tell whether the comments are really written by actual patients [5].

It is true that there are sometimes reputation-damaging posts that may be entirely made-up or designed for the purpose of blackmail. Companies such as rateMDs use this to their advantage. They sell doctors a package that includes a rating manager. Purchasers can have up to three negative reviews removed. If the doctor stops paying the fee, the negative reviews appear again [6]. On the one hand, this opens the door to what seems a form of blackmail – the cyberbullying of physicians. On the other, proponents of the ratings argue that, just like the customers of all other service providers, patients have the right to freely express their opinions. After all, when customers speak their mind and give feedback on their doctors' work, they are simply keeping up with the times.

Recently, the *Journal of Medical Internet Research* published a study on patient-generated online reviews. It summarized the findings of 63 original studies and came to the conclusion that the majority of the ratings are very positive and the patients said good things about their doctors in their reviews [7]. And online reviews are clearly becoming a source of valuable information. What do the patients find important and what do they rate highly? How can the relationship with patients be improved? Although it is still early days, this much is certain: The purely medical aspects are only one side of the equation.

## Online Consultation

### Doctor on Demand

Maeghan lives in Fort Worth, Texas, and works as an insurance professional in Irving, Texas. "My work is really demanding, and I often have days where I work ten to twelve hours," she writes on the website of the company Doctor on Demand.

Sometimes I don't have the chance to take a lunch break. This makes scheduling a doctor's appointment really tough. With Doctor On Demand I can get help in just a few minutes. [8]

Founded in 2012, Doctor on Demand operates a platform in the United States aimed at putting patients in contact with physicians, psychologists, and therapists. Originally Doctor on Demand focused on the 20 illnesses that are most likely to cause people to go to a hospital emergency room. Mostly they are not dramatic crises, but flu and cold symptoms or rashes. Today the company offers a wide range of consultation services, including telemedical consultations with psychologists and psychiatrists.

Doctor on Demand has also set up a service for companies aimed at cutting their costs for the medical care of employees. Previously, anyone who felt sick had to leave the workplace and go see a doctor. But the Doctor on Demand platform offers the option of consulting a physician on your smartphone – including sending pictures if necessary – and quickly receiving medical advice. The company repeatedly points out that only experienced doctors with a proven track record are permitted to conduct such consultations.

The platform has clearly won Vera over. She tried Doctor on Demand not only for herself, but for her daughter, and gave an enthusiastic review of her experiences in a video that she uploaded to YouTube. She used Doctor on Demand to get a second opinion about an allergic rash she had developed. After only a few minutes in the Doctor on Demand digital waiting room, Vera was able to speak to a physician located in her area. She took a lot of time for Vera and explained that the most common causes for rashes of that sort were food intolerance, an allergic reaction to a medication, or an infection. This explanation helped quell Vera's fear that she was suffering from an immune disorder, because in such a case the rash would not disappear after a few days, but would last for several weeks. Vera's experience in obtaining treatment for her daughter was also positive. The child had a cold, and following the teleconsultation the doctor prescribed her a drug that Vera could pick up at her local pharmacy. That meant she did not have to take her sick and complaining daughter to a doctor's office. So for Vera, the advantages of Doctor on Demand were clear [8].

A lot of people are in the same boat as Vera – they have a packed work schedule or live in areas where there aren't a lot of doctors. It is much more convenient, fast, and affordable if you can talk to a doctor online when you have a minor concern. Companies such as Chunyu Yisheng, Doctor on Demand, Teladoc, MD Live, KRY, Push Doctor, and many more have discovered these advantages and offer digital services, where patients can use a chat, phone, or video call to consult a doctor almost immediately, regardless of location. Instead of using a chatbot as we saw in the 'Do-it-yourself' response pattern, they can talk to a flesh-and-blood doctor – but online rather than in person. Today telemedicine is so popular that it is now part of almost every healthcare program.

The authors of a 2018 study, all of whom are doctors and researchers from India, identified five factors in the strong growth of online medical consultations: greater convenience, a shift toward care-intensive non-communicable diseases (NCD), increased cost efficiency leading to wider accessibility, better privacy, and easy ways to get a second opinion [9].

## Chunyu Yisheng

Since 2011 this Chinese company has offered an app that helps patients get fast and easy medical advice. The application allows users who are suffering from minor illnesses to speak to a doctor directly and immediately. Today some 40 million people use it to access a network of 40,000 physicians. For doctors in China, who are often overworked and underpaid, this consultation service is attractive because it provides a significant additional source of income [10].

The service is based on a freemium business model: The app is available to patients and doctors for free, with payment required only for additional services, such as particularly extensive consultations, arranging face-to-face appointments, or consulting a specialist. Chunyu Yisheng generates further revenues through advertisements for health insurance providers, medications and other medical products, and private hospitals.

In rural areas of China in particular, where medical care is often thin on the ground, telemedicine and consultations over the phone are increasingly important. So Chunyu Yisheng is anticipating further growth, especially since many Chinese are apparently prepared to put aside considerable savings for the use of medical services.

And more and more physicians are being won over to the advantages of online consultations. Take Lydia Campbell-Hill, a 35-year-old doctor from Cornwall in England. In an interview with the *BBC*, she claimed that online consultations had changed her life.

> As a 'part-time' general practitioner working three days a week, I was doing 39 hours or more. I was solo parenting, paying vast amounts on childcare, and not seeing my child much. [11]

After leaving her job in the clinic and starting to primarily work online from her living room or kitchen, she said, "My stress levels dropped and I can fit my hours around school, even working a couple of hours in the evening after my son has gone to bed" [11].

There are other excellent reasons behind the trend toward online consultation. In a lot of cases, the purpose of a doctor's appointment is to discuss lab results or renew prescriptions. Such conversations can easily be taken care of in a teleconsultation. According to Luke Buhl-Nielsen of the Swedish telemedicine company KRY, in Sweden up to 45% of the patients who seek advice from a primary care physician can be dealt with digitally. And such virtual consultations are usually significantly cheaper than in-person visits [11]. In India, an average traditional consultation costs between 1,000 and 1,500 rupees, while an average online consultation costs between 50 and 500 rupees. Patients also no longer have to worry about catching illnesses from other patients in the doctor's waiting room or passing on their communicable disease to others.

Walmart, the world's largest retailer, offers its employees doctor's appointments for four USD, but only when the consultation takes place online. A 15-minute appointment on Skype in a quiet room at work is significantly more cost-effective than the half-day that employees typically have to take off to go see a doctor [11].

The next problem is the global shortage of physicians. In the United States alone, estimates say that by 2030 up to 50,000 fewer doctors than needed will be practicing. This also explains the enormous growth in teleconsultations in countries with low per capita numbers of physicians and an uneven distribution of doctors among regions. Even in the United States, today two in five patients belonging to Generation Y, the first generation of digital natives, use a digital channel to consult physicians. While in 2017 this channel was only used 23 million times, by 2022, 105 million digital meetings are expected to take place in the United States alone [11].

## Digital Physician Assistant

In 2019, David Talby, the Chief Technology Officer of Pacific AI, told the magazine *Forbes* a wonderful story. He described how, as a child, his father took him along on visits to his advisor at the bank. His father ran a business, frequently needed loans, and maintained a good relationship with his bank. After all those years of working together, every banker there knew his father and his business. And based on this knowledge, the banker would decide how big a loan his father could take out and what the terms would be [12].

Today David runs a company and goes to the bank himself. Building, office, business suit, helpful attitude, and the title on the banker's card – it all looks pretty much like it did when he was young. But there is one major difference. David's banker doesn't really make any of the banking decisions anymore. He is not the one who decides on the conditions of David's loan, or if he can even have one. Or what products the bank can offer him. The computer does all that. When it comes down to it, David's banker is simply a friendly and familiar interface to an automated system.

Of course the healthcare sector is very different than the banking industry. However, even many doctors can no longer keep pace with the rapid developments in the realm of medicine. They are unwillingly constrained by tight schedules, in which administrative work takes up far too much of their days. There is sometimes not enough time to question established approaches and try something new. At the same time, the patients' expectations and knowledge are growing – at least in routine situations, they sometimes view themselves more as customers than patients. So it is hardly surprising that digital patterns are emerging which are aimed primarily at assisting physicians and other healthcare providers in their challenging work. Companies such as Wlycloud, Enlitic, Arterys, RADLogics, WeDoctor, Ping An Good Doctor, Merantix Healthcare, and MedScape offer digital services that advise doctors on diagnoses and treatments and assist them in making better and more rapid decisions. Their scope extends from the interpretation of X-ray images to providing a second opinion on a test result or treatment.

Artificial intelligence (AI) is transforming some fields of medicine, especially radiology. While some radiologists fear for their jobs, others see this new technology as an opportunity to make diagnoses faster and more accurately. In addition, algorithms can identify even minute tissue changes which cannot be perceived by the human eye. However, probably the most radical change is that software based on machine learning can acquire the experience and knowledge of a multitude of radiologists. This will mean, for instance, that in the future ultrasound or X-ray images will not just be looked at by one or several specialists, but always through the lens of the global store of knowledge about the disease in question.

## Enlitic

Enlitic was founded in San Francisco in 2014 with the idea of applying AI to the evaluation of medical data. For example, AI would empower radiologists to make diagnoses more rapidly and accurately. In addition, the founders hoped that diseases and other problems could be spotted much earlier on radiographs than is currently the case. To this end, Enlitic needs a large number of radiological images and the corresponding evaluations so that the algorithms can learn to recognize certain patterns from this data.

In 2017, around one billion ultrasound, X-ray, CT, and MRI images were produced. Studies show that in approximately every fifth case, an incorrect diagnosis was given or no disease was found – with consequences for the patient as well as follow-on costs for the healthcare sector [13]. This is precisely where AI offers such advantages. In addition to precision and speed, a system based on machine learning can draw conclusions from all previously performed diagnoses. Ideally, a single database would exist containing as many cases as possible, including all information on the patient and the diagnoses made.

For example, it has been shown that the machine learning software can detect certain masses in the lung much better than even a group of experienced radiologists. Similar results were seen in the identification of the most fine and tiny hairline fractures in bones – the software beat all the specialists. A particular challenge is the detection of very rare types of tissue changes, for example, in the lungs. Here, experts have to rely on pictures in textbooks to identify tumors. AI can prove a significant source of assistance here, because it can draw on a large number of such images for comparison.

Kevin Lyman, CEO of Enlitic, expects AI to create a completely new ecosystem in the healthcare sector. It will be possible to combine data from all kinds of sources to create a holistic picture of a patient's state of health. Even patients in remote regions of Africa that are located far from professional healthcare services could benefit from the advances in medical imaging techniques. All that it would take would be ultrasound images, for instance, which would then be analyzed in the United States, Europe, or China using the requisite algorithms. In a few seconds, the local doctor would have a diagnosis based on the experience gained in the treatment of millions of patients.

## Arterys

Arterys was also founded in San Francisco with a clear mission: The company, which initially focused on cardiovascular diseases in infants and children, is aiming to reduce subjectivity and inaccuracy in clinical diagnosis using AI-based image processing. It now offers a broad set of software-based services that assist physicians in making diagnoses, and which have now also been approved by the US Food and Drug Administration (FDA). Cardiological examinations in particular produce enormous amounts of data that mostly cannot be analyzed on the spot. The Arterys cloud-based software makes it possible to outsource the calculation-intensive parts of the process. It is already foreseeable that the speed and accuracy of diagnoses will be improved with the data of each additional patient. In addition, the selection of treatment is not simply left to a single physician; the doctor can draw on the cumulative experience of many other physicians, as well as the treatment guidelines of various medical associations which are incorporated into the AI.

## RADLogics

RADLogics has developed a software that can give radiologists a preliminary assessment of the symptoms before they even look at the images. In essence, this is a preliminary report that the radiologist receives along with the visual material. The aim is not to replace medical specialists, but to relieve them of often time-consuming and tedious tasks, such as counting pixels. As they were designing the software, the RADLogics programmers observed numerous radiologists in medical facilities and hospitals. Here they noticed that about 80% of their time was spent on the preliminary work ("pixel hunting"). This made it clear that the radiologists had to spend a lot of time working on the diagnosis in order to reduce the risk of misinterpretation. So what was needed was a software that would relieve the radiologists of all this preliminary work. In addition, the patient's digital medical records needed to be available when the images were analyzed so it was possible to draw a comprehensive picture of the person's state of health.

### *Wlycloud*

The Beijing-based startup Wanliyun, or Wlycloud emerged at much the same time. China is facing tremendous obstacles. Since 2010, cancer has been the most common cause of death in the People's Republic, and despite the country's rapid development over the last years, the government is lagging behind when it comes to the prevention of this disease. Half of China's population still smokes. So it is no surprise that lung cancer is the most frequently diagnosed form of cancer. In recent years, the Chinese government has tried to come to grips with the situation with extensive lung screening programs. But they have a massive problem: There are not enough radiologists or oncologists, especially in rural areas.

Wlycloud has stepped up to tackle this problem. Founded in 2009, the company operates radiology centers in rural parts of the country without even having a radiologist on site. The images are uploaded digitally to the company's cloud servers and diagnosed at a central location with the help of AI. The same principle applies here: The more images that are fed into Wlycloud, the better the deep-learning algorithms become at analyzing them. Wlycloud also works with more than 1,600 hospitals who are aiming to benefit from the cost-effective remote diagnostic services provided by the startup.

The company has long since made a name for itself in the digital healthcare world. In 2016, Ali Health, the healthcare arm of internet giant Alibaba, bought a 25% stake in Wlycloud for 35 million USD. Wlycloud has big plans: It intends to extend its reach beyond China, setting up a regional hub in Singapore from which it can expand into other Southeast Asian countries [14].

Many of the major health platforms, especially those in China, rely heavily and extensively on digital physician assistants that are based on AI. This is the only way to provide the 3.4 billion people who earn less than 5.50 USD per day with access to high-quality health care [15].

### *MedScape*

An equally effective but somewhat less automated support system for physicians is provided by virtual peer-to-peer networks, which offer an opportunity to obtain a second opinion. The largest such network is the New York-based MedScape. It was founded in 2015, and two years later more than 310,000 physicians had taken advantage of the platform – more than 10% of them as active users. In total these visitors, who were on average 56 years old and came from 171 countries on all continents, posted more than 110,000 messages on the platform. More than 90% of their questions received their first answer within 90 minutes [16].

This digital response pattern is aimed at the prevention of misdiagnoses. The problem of misdiagnosis is not a minor one; according to reports, the error rate for outpatient diagnosis was estimated at 3–5% [13, 16]. The problem thus impacts more than 12 million people. The inpatient error rate is between 6% and 7%.

## Online Pharmacies

A few years ago, whoever would have expected to order medications from an internet site? For years now, online pharmacies have been shooting up like mushrooms at a tremendous rate across the globe. While patients around the world purchased drugs worth 42 billion USD over the internet in 2018, by 2025 this figure will have risen to well over 100 billion [17].

Online pharmacies are not without controversy, however. Swissmedic, the Swiss public health authority, cautions against fraudulent websites that distribute medications which are counterfeit or do not contain the correct quantities of active ingredients, and advises against ordering drugs online [18]. The US FDA maintains an ever-growing list of suspicious online providers [19]. The trade in fake drugs is booming on the internet. Some sources claim that one in five medications sold online are counterfeit. The health consequences of such falsified medicines, from non-effective placebos to life-threatening adulterated drugs, can be devastating.

But despite this, the number of online pharmacies is growing – primarily because they make it easier and more convenient to get our prescriptions. Legitimate, licensed online pharmacies, mail-order pharmacies, or telepharmacies all provide the same service: Patients can order their medication over the internet and a package service delivers it to their doorstep. This applies not just to over-the-counter medications, but to prescription drugs as well.

In particular, people whose chronic illnesses require them to take regular medications are happy not to have to keep going back to the pharmacy and standing in line. Furthermore, compared to traditional pharmacies, online pharmacies can offer competitive prices and a wider range of products. They don't have to operate a brick-and-mortar store and can serve a large area from their warehouses, which are located in more affordable industrial zones.

There is also a growing number of technology-savvy people, who are used to shopping over the internet and who can distinguish between reliable and unreliable providers. And precisely these people are growing older. While in the United States, chronically ill patients aged between 35 and 39 years receive 11 different prescription drugs per year, patients who are 65 and older require 21. Last but not least, online pharmacies benefit from the fact that the entire healthcare ecosystem is moving in this direction, with digital prescriptions, the necessary regulatory environment, and same-day drug delivery gradually becoming the norm.

An international comparison shows that the United States is still ahead in terms of the most medications bought online – more than 25%. Next in the ranking comes Europe, represented by Germany, France, and the UK. China dominates the Asian market, with India making a massive push in this direction. Brazil leads the pack in Latin America. In the Middle East and in Africa, internet pharmacies are still gaining ground slowly.

There is also debate in scientific circles as to whether online pharmacies can help increase patient compliance in some cases, such as the supply of insulin to diabetics or the administration of cholesterol-lowering drugs. As early as 2011, the *Journal of Medical Economics* published a study from the United States looking at the possible impacts of online pharmacies on patients [20]. The study looked at more than 22,000 people who had been prescribed an oral anti-diabetic drug, measuring medication adherence – in this case, the percentage of days on which the subjects had actually taken their medication. It was observed that the average patient compliance of people who obtained their medication online was higher than that of people who had to go to the pharmacy repeatedly.

Another study examined almost 15,000 diabetics, again in the United States, who had switched from a traditional pharmacy to an online pharmacy. Average medication adherence increased significantly. At the same time, costs per person and month sank by approximately 80 USD. Another study involving people with high cholesterol levels showed that 85% of the people who used the mail-order pharmacy achieved a reduction in LDL, commonly known as "bad cholesterol," compared to 74.2% of people who had bought their medication from a nearby pharmacy [21].

However, hard scientific evidence of the medical efficacy of online pharmacies has not yet been provided [22]. In addition, not every NCD can be treated with drugs that are available on the internet. Complex combinations of drugs, some of which are administered intravenously or have to be dosed very accurately, also figure in many chronic diseases and cannot be simply be distributed safely and effectively online.

## Digital One-stop Platforms

Why are shopping malls so popular? Because they bring together everything that people need, neatly sorted and in a single location, and do everything possible to provide a pleasant shopping experience. Services and opening hours are coordinated. You only have to drive to one place, look for one parking spot, and not worry about anything else. Of course, shopping malls are not charitable organizations. With their maximum attention to customer needs, they are aiming to retain increasingly pampered customers and ensure that they buy the largest possible number of items within the confines of the building.

Primary medical care still works differently in a lot of places. It is fragmented, not coordinated. The many players barely work together in a systematic fashion. In some regions, you could almost say that it's the lack of cooperation that is systematic. The information that is generated in collaboration between physician and patient disappears into the filing cabinet or computer of the doctor's office. Measurements, X-rays, diagnoses, treatments, medications, and successful treatments remain a secret between doctor and patient. If the patient switches to a different physician, none of this information is available to the new collaborators. This is not only inconvenient for the patient, but is one of the greatest sources of inefficiencies and quality losses in the entire healthcare system.

World Health Organization (WHO) has recognized this, and for this reason is advocating for the creation of integrated health systems, which it defines as follows:

> Integrated health systems are the organization and management
> of health services so that people get the care they need, when they
> need it, in ways that are user-friendly, achieve the desired results,
> and provide value for money. [23, p. 1]

The focus of integrated health systems is providing seamless and coordinated care to patients and their families. The theory is that ensuring patients can move effectively through the healthcare system will lead to higher quality of care and better health outcomes.

And this theory is not contradicted by practice – especially where NCDs are concerned – at least if we lend credibility to the various scientific metastudies on this subject. Integrated health systems have a positive effect on the quality of patient care, result in a higher level of patient satisfaction, and improve access to care.

This is exactly where companies such as Oscar Health, Ottonova, Ping An, and Collective Health come in. They offer customer-centric access to a well-orchestrated ecosystem of healthcare service providers. We can picture these providers of integrated health systems as an all-encompassing health (shopping) center that is available to its customers around the clock through an app; as a quality-tested one-stop shop with a concierge service for both healthy people and those suffering from illnesses. They are evolving into digital platform companies that bring customers together with healthcare service providers. They are relieving both parties of tedious administrative tasks and slowly but surely taking on the role of conductor in the health orchestra. The more customers that sign up, the more attractive they become to service providers. The more service providers that become part of their ecosystem, the better they are for the customers. What's at play here are network effects. In addition to the urgently needed boost in efficiency, however, they also represent a move toward an oligopoly in the healthcare system, which certainly needs to be scrutinized with a critical eye.

At the heart of these companies is the digital patient journey – the record of all of a customer's health-relevant data along a timeline. This forms the starting point and informational backbone of every interaction between the customer, platform operator, and healthcare provider. The most common interactions on such platforms include: finding a doctor and booking an appointment, looking at laboratory results and prescriptions, performing self-diagnosis, using the concierge service, initiating a teleconsultation with the doctor, handling and tracking medical bills, obtaining qualified information about an illness and tips for prevention, organizing preventive screenings, monitoring health data, and tracking fitness data.

So from a patient perspective, platform companies consolidate multiple digital healthcare response patterns and make them easily accessible to a wide range of people. Insurance companies and large healthcare providers are in the best position to lay claim to this pattern. However, the state, society, and citizens must play a defining and protective role.

## Unstaffed Mini-clinics

Ms Liu, a resident of the Chinese city of Wuzhen near Shanghai, reports:

> The weather has been cold recently and my child got sick, so I tried the One-minute Clinic. The online doctors are very thorough, and they save a lot of registration and queuing time. Besides, the One-minute Clinics are open 24 hours and it is convenient to buy medicine at night. If such services can be popularized, it will make life more convenient. [24]

The "One-minute Clinic" referred to by Ms Liu is the most recent and radical innovation from Chinese health insurance provider Ping An Insurance and its subsidiary Ping An Good Doctor, which was founded in 2015. In essence, the company consists of an app that lets users make an appointment with a doctor. In the case of minor illnesses, a video or phone consultation is also offered. Ping An Good Doctor not only covers the doctor's fee, but also the costs of prescription drugs and treatments. Subscribers also have the option of sharing information with other patients in forums. One particularly lucrative market for Ping An Good Doctor is Chinese citizens who are looking for medical treatment abroad. The company establishes contacts with physicians outside of China and organizes the necessary travel.

Ping An Good Doctor is currently working to set up One-minute Clinics across the country. Inside these structures, diagnoses are made and medications and treatments recommended by means of AI. From the outside they look like cheerful, well-appointed transport containers or a cross between a photo booth and a vending machine. In reality, they are small, unstaffed heath centers that make it easy to access all kinds of health services from the Ping An Group.

The One-minute Clinics are designed in the ACG style – "animation, comic and game." After the patient enters the clinic, which measures about three square meters, they can chat with the virtual physician assistant about their symptoms. In addition, it is possible to submit blood, urine, or other samples and take photos. The AI doctor collects the patient's medical history and makes in initial diagnosis. It then transmits the information to one of the 1,000 in-house specialists for a video consultation between doctor and patient, which starts immediately. This allows the flesh-and-blood specialist to verify the accuracy of the diagnosis and the proposed treatment. So that patients can receive their medication immediately after their diagnosis, the mini-clinic also houses a pharmaceutical vending machine containing the 100 most important drugs. The mini-clinics offer state-of-the-art online consultations for more than 2,000 common illnesses and can answer tens of thousands of medical questions immediately.

Initial trials near Shanghai showed that there is considerable interest in this type of treatment involving AI. In the first year following the pilot phase, more than a thousand of these unstaffed mini-clinics will be rolled out across eight provinces in locations where people congregate – schools, universities, pharmacies, shopping malls, airports, train stations, highway rest stops, and factories. In a very short time, they will provide easily accessible health services for more than three million patients. Partnerships already exist with more than 3,000 hospitals and 60,000 healthcare centers. So in critical cases, a physician can intervene and immediately arrange for admission to the nearest hospital.

With increasing volumes of data from which the algorithms can learn, further diseases can be covered and more precise diagnoses made. In addition, the treatment recommendations can be refined over the course of time – it all depends on the amount of data available. In recent years, more than 200 AI experts have been working to develop the technology upon which Ping An Good Doctor is based. Approximately 300 million data sets containing the diagnoses and treatment recommendations of physicians were collected. All of this knowledge, all of this experience, is available to the algorithms for assessing patients' complaints and prescribing the right drugs. The average amount of time a patient spends in a One-minute Clinic is less than five minutes, and the satisfaction rate has grown to 98%.

One such clinic is located in Shanghai at the home office of BiliBili, a company for video-sharing websites. It has already provided thousands of medical and health services to the firm's employees. This not only saves time, but also the customary sickroom and medical staff at the company headquarters – usually two doctors and two nurses. In a country such as China in particular, where there is a shortage of medical personnel, the unstaffed clinics can help alleviate the effects of having too few physicians. Year for year, they also reduce healthcare costs and the amount of sick leave employees take.

Why are innovations like this advancing so quickly in China? According to the World Health Organization, China has an average of only 1.8 physicians per 1,000 inhabitants, a severe shortage. By way of comparison, the United States averages 2.5 doctors per 1,000 inhabitants; Australia, 3.4. Data from the Frost & Sullivan research institute show that in 2016 [25], patients in China had to spend about three hours, including travel and waiting times, when they visited a doctor. The time that the patient then actually spent with the doctor averaged only eight minutes, or about 4.4% of the total time.

In addition, people in China do not place much trust in local and regional hospitals and medical facilities. This is one reason why the Chinese government initiated the Healthy China 2030 program in 2016, the country's first strategic health plan since 1949. This mandate places a priority on health policy. In many areas, people are turning to digital health and AI as a means to close the supply gap without having to spend years training more physicians. This explains why there are now numerous initiatives and companies that are aiming to give patients access to good medical care – usually through apps.

The Chinese model of the unstaffed mini-clinic is, from a Western perspective, definitely an extreme example of this phenomenon. However, it is quite conceivable that the first such clinics will also be tested in Europe or the United States in the foreseeable future – initially on the grounds and in the lobbies of hospitals, which can serve as a safety net, later in the plants of manufacturing companies, and finally in public spaces.

# Chapter 6

# Digital Therapeutics

*The main theses of this chapter:*

- Digital therapeutics and treatments that are supported by digital technologies, coordinate interactions between patient, doctor, medical devices, medications, and interventions. They focus on the patient to the maximum degree, and, in the case of non-communicable diseases (NCDs), become the most important instrument for patient and doctor participation.
- Digital therapeutics are gaining ground in hybrid form –one that combines physicians and computers. They do not replace doctors; rather, they enlarge their sphere of action.
- Wherever and whenever they are employed, digital therapeutics can apply the gold standard of treatment. This means they continuously raise the quality of treatment and self-treatment and reduce the risk of treatments that do not reflect the current state of knowledge.
- Digital therapeutics are a new, different way of managing disease. They significantly improve the quality of treatment, especially outside of the hospital setting. They enable continuous care and a high frequency of feedback on crucial measured values, and include the option of actively calling a doctor.
- Digital therapeutics are significantly more affordable than conventional treatments. So they help democratize access to top-caliber healthcare across the globe.
- The number of digital treatments which can be prescribed will grow exponentially in the coming decades. In the future, it will be just as routine to prescribe digital therapeutics as it is to prescribe drugs.
- Without the corresponding digital therapies, medications often do not reach their optimal beneficial effect. A healthcare provider that does not offer any options supported by digital technologies will be considered a second-class healthcare provider.
- In digital settings, about 99.5% of patient communications are with the chatbot and only 0.5% with the physician.
- Virtual and augmented reality are developing into important technologies upon which interventions for mental disorders and diseases of the musculoskeletal system are based.

The Digital Pill: What Everyone Should Know about the Future of
Our Healthcare System, 81–98
Copyright © 2021 by Emerald Publishing Limited
All rights of reproduction in any form reserved
doi:10.1108/978-1-78756-675-020211006

- Authorities are creating channels for the quality control and continuous approval of "digital medicine," which continues to improve with every update.
- Digital coaches will at some point become as integral to leading a healthy life-style as GPS is to navigating an unfamiliar city.

Can a digital friend become a surrogate family for chronically ill children? It sounds absurd, but it might not be so crazy after all. That was our experience when we were working on a clinical study with obese children at the Center for Digital Health Interventions at the Universities of Zurich and St Gallen. We collaborated with doctors at the children's hospital and the young patients to develop Anna and Lukas, two digital companions. They greeted the children every day with a "Good morning!" After a few days, we switched off this morning greeting as planned. We thought everyone would get tired of it. Some of the children reacted immediately. They sent us, the real-life coaches, a message: "Why doesn't my coach Lukas say hello to me anymore? I miss it, because there is no one else who says good morning to me every day."

Not all children grow up in perfect families. Often the second-best, but available, solution is better for all concerned than the best solution, which is only granted to a few – an intact family. In this context, a digital friend can at least partially assume the role of a nanny that anyone can afford.

The routine contact of chronically ill patients with their doctors mostly looks like this: They have to struggle to get an appointment for treatment, at times even have to skip work or school for it, sometimes sit in the waiting room for a long time, then get to see the doctor for an average of seven minutes, leave again with some advice and a prescription, and are then released back into the wilderness of their illness, where they have to navigate all by themselves. And all the good intentions that the patient has when they leave the doctor's office? They are forgotten within a few days. In order to make a lasting lifestyle change, which is urgently required in the case of NCDs, a personal trainer is needed. In the world of exercise, only the fortunate few can afford one. And this applies doubly in medical matters.

The brave new world of digital medicine looks like this: At the first visit, the doctor not only prescribes the patient a conventional medication, but also access to digital therapeutics in the form of a digital personal coach, who assists the patient around the clock, seven days a week, for weeks and months. The ideal digital personal coach is a sensitive, humorous, unobtrusive companion who can sense when to intervene and when it is better to remain silent. It is not just another annoying, flashing smartphone app, but a digital aid that engages individually with the patient, learns with them, adapts to them. Having someone who is always there is good for body, mind, and spirit.

Artificial intelligence can actually help put a more human face on medicine. In a way, it is putting the "care" back into health care. This sentiment can be traced back to Eric Topol, one of the early pioneers of digital medicine. Digital treatments apply classic behavior-modification methods with the aid of electronic media. They take well-known, long-established, and quality-tested medical interventions and convert them into a digital format – as web-based training, smartphone apps, and augmented reality applications.

To understand the differences, let's look at the most basic form of digital therapeutics: web-based training. Patients sit down in front of their laptop or desktop computer, go to a certain website, log in, and complete that day's unit. The first simple web-based training almost exactly replicated conventional treatment methods. It barely made any use of the new possibilities unlocked by digital devices.

To better understand the doors opened by digital therapeutics, we should look at the development of digital advertising. Before the days of Google, Facebook, and Amazon, advertisements were limited to print media, posters, radio, and television. These forms of advertising still exist despite the ascendency of Google and the like, but the digital alternatives are gaining ground at double-digit growth rates. In 2019, more than half of the advertising budgets in the United States went to digital ads – and two-thirds of this amount went to the mobile segment. In China, the pattern was even more pronounced. In 2019, more than two out of every three renminbi from advertising budgets were invested in the digital world, primarily channeled through Baidu, Alibaba, and Tencent [1].

Why is there this move from analog advertising to digital? First, digital advertising lends itself much better to personalization, that is to say it can be better aimed toward a potential customer group. Fact is, it is simply easier to determine who is using an app than who is walking past a poster. Second, the effect of the advertisements can be more easily measured. The decisive question – who made a purchase because of the advertisement? – can be answered quite accurately in digital channels. And third, payment is increasingly made based on the now quantifiable results of the advertising. In other words, the advertiser only pays if the advertisement is successful – that is to say, for every potential customer who has come to them because of the advertisement.

The same applies more and more to digital therapeutics, which are tailored to specific patients and adapt to them even more over the course of time. For example, by learning what relaxation exercise is most effective at what time, in what place (at home or in the office), and in what situation (e.g., at the computer when fatigue sets in). This knowledge is then shared with all other healthcare entities in anonymized form in the cloud, enabling the entire system to improve itself. To a certain degree, it is self-learning. It continuously monitors the patient's current state of health, for example, through brief questions from their digital personal coach or by recording and interpreting vital signs.

Digital therapeutics consist of three building blocks derived from the monitoring approach, the talk-and-tools paradigm, and the health-psychology concept of just-in-time interventions, as we will explain below.

The first component, based on the monitoring approach, is concerned with the ongoing measurement and evaluation of the patient's state of health, behavior, and lifestyle. If the measurements or estimates deviate from the targets, a so-called "state of vulnerability" is reached and intervention is necessary.

The second component, talk-and-tools, is best explained as an intervention that is agreed upon through a chat. Communication should be as close to natural language as possible, like in a consultation with a doctor. The patients don't use an app with menus, but a digital coach or assistant with whom they can speak ("talk"). The "tools" are then the specific measures suggested by the digital coach or assistant, for example, a smartphone-based breathing exercise or a hike with the family. The system checks whether the patient is able to accept the necessary intervention and implement it as soon as possible, or whether they are currently sitting in a meeting or driving their car, for example.

If the moment appears unsuitable, the just-in-time intervention calculates a suitable time slot. This is important, because currently, some 60% of all smartphone notifications are sent at the "wrong" time, and as a result are potentially not even read, let alone acted upon. The determination of the correct window of time is user-specific and will depend, among other things, on the time of the measurement, the location, the battery charge level, the environment, and the activity. So under this concept, health interventions are only initiated if they are medically necessary and the patient is able to participate. This might seem simple, but is actually very complex to implement and requires a lot of data and machine learning.

The third component is the intervention itself, and in particular concerns the way in which health interventions are communicated.

While conventional medications trigger biochemical reactions and consequently have an effect on the human body, digital therapeutics assist with treatment management and support behavioral changes. Physical pills and digital treatments complement each other to the benefit of all concerned. Our Center for Digital Health Interventions at ETH Zurich and the University of St Gallen describes the characteristics of digital therapeutics as follows:

*Digital therapeutics*:

- Improve self-management in dealing with NCDs, for example, through active, just-in-time management of conventional medical interventions or by increasing health literacy through the use of simplified language.
- Involve the family and friends of patients in collaborative health management, for example, by assisting in certain changes in health behavior and lifestyle in the family.
- Inform patients, healthcare providers, and relatives about critical health conditions in order to ensure support for necessary emergency procedures, including, for example, sending automated emergency calls.
- Recognize whether and when it might be necessary to admit the patient to the hospital by predicting critical health conditions, for example, exacerbations (acute worsening of an illness) in lung patients or health-threatening hypoglycemia (low blood sugar) in diabetes patients.
- Provide physicians with data from the patients' daily lives so that they can optimize treatment, for example, by providing an overview of whether an asthma patient has taken bronchodilators, at what time, and whether the medication was taken correctly.
- Make office hours more efficient, because the digital assistance results in doctors having more time for people who cannot cope with their condition on their own in their daily lives, for example, with strongly fluctuating blood sugar levels or poor asthma control.
- Support research into new digital health interventions with the aid of the data collected on a daily basis.

Do digital therapeutics make doctors superfluous? No, they do not. There has been no evidence that physical practitioners are being edged out by digital ones. As is often the case, this transformation is not an either/or question. Rather, it is more about the collaboration between the digital and physical worlds – about the combination of doctors, medical devices, digital therapeutics, and drugs. Medicine will always retain its physical side.

Under the umbrella of digital therapeutics, we will now consider three digital response patterns that represent different stages of development: the digital personal coach, digital therapeutics by prescription, and the digital coach who monitors patient compliance. We will now explain these three patterns in detail.

## Digital Personal Coach

If I want my body to be in shape and healthily fed, but don't have the necessary time, knowledge, and willpower, I can hire a personal trainer – if I have enough money. Someone who is there just for me two or three times a week, who focuses 100% on my needs, who puts together a tailored exercise routine, who shows me the exercises, corrects me, cheers me on and motivates me, and keeps pushing me to reach new, more challenging goals. A personal trainer can get the most out of me. But there is one disadvantage – this kind of support is very, very expensive. This puts it beyond the reach of most people.

A digital personal coach, on the other hand, is a personal trainer for everyone. That said, digital coaches do have obvious disadvantages. They are not actual, trusted human beings, they cannot return our empathic looks and gestures, and they cannot touch or hug us. They cannot (yet) immediately interpret our gait, look, and posture to know how we are doing and what we might need. They don't wear a white coat or inspire our respect, awe, or fear. They will never be like human personal trainers or physicians. And they should not try to be, because these drawbacks are offset by their advantages.

First, a digital coach is always there – any time, any place. There are no gaps in the care they provide. Second, they cost next to nothing – everyone can afford them, which means digital personal coaches will lead to a further democratization of health care. Third, in certain areas, digital coaches are at least as efficacious as the coaching provided by doctors or therapists, which is invariably subject to gaps in care. Fourth, the ideal digital therapeutics are not subject to quality fluctuations. They are always up-to-date on the latest in medical knowledge, which they deliver regardless of place, time, patient group, and their ability to pay. The best human practitioners will always be better than digital practitioners. But digital practitioners can certainly be better than the average human practitioner. Fifth, digital therapeutics generate an infinite amount of valuable data that can be processed by computers and used to continuously improve and refine the treatment itself. They are part of a self-learning system.

For all of these reasons, digital personal coaches are conquering the world. They already assist millions of people who are living with a NCD and help at least as many more to avoid a developing a NCD. This applies to all the most common diseases.

Companies such as mySugr, Omada Health, Virta Health, Livongo, and Lark help diabetics keep a diabetes journal, encourage them with witty remarks, collect and synchronize data from blood glucose testing devices, remind them to perform the tests, offer assistance with nutrition, and provide important data for the next consultation with a flesh-and-blood doctor.

### *mySugr*

The idea for the Austrian startup mySugr came in 2010 during a stop at a Romanian gas station. Frank Westermann, who at the time was a corporate consultant, was on his way to see a client in Bucharest. As a diabetic, he had to regularly record his blood sugar levels in a paper notebook – and that day was no exception. Couldn't something like this be done electronically? Although more and more apps were coming out at this time, Frank couldn't find one that took care of this tedious form of bookkeeping to his satisfaction. When it comes down to it, a lot of the day-to-day treatment of diabetes consists of recording and managing data: determining amounts of carbohydrates, measuring blood sugar levels, calculating insulin quantities – again and again, every day.

After returning from Romania, Frank decided that an app could help with all that. Finding co-founders, attracting investors – the process of founding a company began. He had to endure setbacks and overcome obstacles, but his desire for better digital assistance and connection always carried him through. Two of the five original founders – the two developers, of all people – left the company after only one month, because they no longer believed in the idea. But because the investors stayed on board, the development of the app was able to continue.

Once the app was on the market, many doctors were baffled – what were you supposed to do with it? To the founders, it felt like an eternity until collaboration with the industry became possible. Health insurance providers also failed to understand the technology at first; it was like nothing they'd seen before. But

Frank's persistence finally paid off. Today the app has grown into an established platform that offers a range of functions that help users better manage their diabetes. Thanks to the documentation of the relevant data, patients, doctors, and diabetes advisors gain insights into the diabetic's daily life, allowing targeted decisions to be made about their treatment.

After the startup was founded, it took several years before the initial financial hurdles were overcome. All of the founders repeatedly invested their private capital and a great deal of their time; in some cases they even had to change residences. The turning point came in 2017, when mySugr was acquired by the Swiss pharmaceutical and diagnostics company Roche. Now mySugr is firmly established in the digital healthcare industry and, with more than 2 million registered users, is one of the most popular diabetes management apps. The mySugr headquarters are located in Vienna, with an additional head office in San Diego, California.

As of March 2020, the mySugr app is available for free in 79 countries and 14 languages. Once they connect a compatible device, users can also access the Pro version of the app for free, which offers additional features such as meal photos. In addition, patients in Germany and the United States can take advantage of the mySugr package, which gives them access to trained diabetes advisors through the app as well as free, usage-based test strip delivery and other benefits.

mySugr was developed by diabetics for the use of other diabetics – of its over 160 employees, more than 20 are living with the disease. This means the corporation understands the concerns and needs of the patients very well indeed.

### *Meru Health*

Meru Health, a company located in Helsinki and Palo Alto, California, has dedicated itself to fighting depression and anxiety. At its heart is a digital chatbot, in other words a digital communicator that combines familiar treatment modules made up of mindfulness exercises and behavioral therapy to create a new integrated concept.

The digital coach, which sets new tasks and exercises and offers new insights every day, is backed up by a human coach who communicates with the patient by telephone. In addition, the patient can engage in anonymous exchanges with other patients. That the therapy is useful is suggested by the data continuously collected by Meru Health: 75% of all patients who complete the program reduce their PHQ-9 score by at least 20% after 12 weeks. The PHQ-9 patient questionnaire is the industry standard for measuring the severity of depression. The patient stories send an even clearer message.

Mary is one of these patients. She had too much stress at work and eventually suffered from burnout. At first she was not sure if an app could help her. After trying Meru Health, today she recommends the app to others:

> I had doubts that a mobile treatment program could do anything about the burnout, anxiety, and depression that I'd been experiencing for the past 10 years, and, since I'd been meditating on and

off for 10 years, I thought I had nothing new to learn. I was wrong. Mixing mindfulness and behavioral therapy was revelatory, and having online access to a personal therapist was an essential part of my success with the treatment program. With the aid of the app I learned to cut back on my extreme work hours and to practice self-compassion and kindness when I'm gripped with anxiety. Getting more rest and minimizing the anxiety has been the key to significantly reducing the depression. [2]

Similar approaches are being pursued by numerous companies, some of which are growing rapidly, such as Ginger.io, Happify, Lyra Health, Pathmate Technologies, and 2Morrow, all of which aim to combat anxiety, depression, obesity, smoking, stress, and chronic pain. They all translate the existing store of knowledge about behavioral change approaches into affordable, scalable, digital healthcare services that are accessible and affordable for everyone.

In the fight against mental disorders, it is especially important to make treatment easily available. The symptoms worsen gradually, the patient can successfully ignore them for a long time – and often does so because conditions like depression are still not socially accepted. This applies just as much to new mothers in Singapore, who are showing signs of postnatal depression as to stock traders in London, who are struggling with symptoms of burnout. The expectations they place on themselves, which often reflect the demands and requirements of society, at first do not allow them to ask around for the name of a good therapist and take time for the initial and follow-up visits. They would have to talk to their family or their supervisor about their problem – a disease that is frequently viewed as a personal weakness. So they prefer to simply suffer in silence. Until they break down.

In the world of digital coaches, all this could change. The barriers to entry for this type of therapy are very low. The patients do not have to give their names; they receive advice at the time and in the place that suits them best. The treatment costs are much lower than for classical therapy, not to mention the overall costs.

### Propeller Health

Asthma and other chronic lung diseases are the focus of Propeller Health. It aims to help patients better understand and manage their condition. The patients receive a sensor by regular mail, which they then attach to their inhaler and connect to the Propeller app. Propeller then measures all inhalations, regularly checks on the patient's state of health, learns to understand the individual disease pattern, and provides the patient with reminders, information on air quality, and the like.

If desired, parents can be sent a text message when their child uses the inhaler, helping them stay involved in the treatment. In the asthma coach function, the parents are even asked to take a video of their child using the inhaler and share it with the digital coach. With the knowledge of the child and its parents, the responsible physician uses a predefined list of criteria to check whether the inhalation was performed correctly. If the doctor discovers an error, they contact the patient using the chatbot and give them some pointers. Like all other apps in this field, the Max app focuses on the patient's ability to understand and deal with their illness. This is also very important for children. The digital coach explains the basics of asthma to them in small, easily digestible, and child-appropriate steps over a number of days.

Digital coaches are now also available for people with cardiovascular conditions – Hello Heart, for example, and the Sanitas Coach App. The Sanitas Coach App, offered by Swiss health insurance company Sanitas, offers daily assistance for patients. The bots in this app are named Tim and Anna. In an interactive chat, they encourage users to regularly measure their blood pressure and pulse, record the readings, and improve them over the course of the coaching program – through more exercise and relaxation and better nutrition. The patients receive push notifications to remind them to take their medications regularly.

### Kaia Health

The startup Kaia Health, located in Munich and New York, is very much like the traditional personal trainer. Kaia produces a digital physical therapist that is modeled on the gold standard for back pain treatment and follows national care guidelines. The company also employs a multimodal approach: the app not only assists patients with back exercises, but provides information about the causes of the pain as well. And, based on the latest findings from mindfulness and pain research, it helps them cope with chronic pain using gentle methods. Like other digital coaches, when necessary the Kaia coach can quickly set up contact with human coaches, who can answer complicated questions directly and offer the patient additional encouragement.

The Kaia Motion Coach even goes a step further: It not only shows patients which exercises to perform, like hundreds of other fitness apps, but also counts reps and offers corrections. For this function to work, users have to position their smartphone so it can film them doing the exercises. The software interprets this data in real time, assesses the exercise, and gives feedback. This is technically very challenging, because the smartphone has to be able to tell which exercise has been selected and whether it is being performed correctly.

These apps have the advantage of being able to access dozens of smartphone sensors, from the motion sensor to the tracking function to the camera, as well as offering cost-effective chat functions. A mature application can be recognized by its focus on communication. So it is not surprising that digital coaches are increasingly taking on the form of a chatbot, and now incorporate elements of gaming and artificial reality techniques.

### Magic Leap

Magic Leap is a case in point. After sitting in a room for a few minutes wearing the Magic Leap glasses, you will no longer be surprised to see dozens of pink jellyfish swimming across the room in swarms, changing direction when they come to the walls, and disappearing behind chairs before reappearing. You can watch little toy knights fighting on the ground and admire the grass slowly growing under the buzz of nearby bees. If you touch one of the virtual plants – which are hard to tell apart from the real thing – a blossom may open up and start to glow. And because the human brain associates light with warmth, you will feel warmth in your hand, triggered by a virtual flower that only exists in your head. When a charming virtual woman approaches a man, the scene appears so real that he will naturally return her smile and reciprocate her gestures, just as if all mirror neurons were firing simultaneously.

At this point at the latest, the power of good artificial reality applications becomes clear. And it is no wonder that Magic Leap and other companies in this segment are taking a closer look at the healthcare market and testing their first digital therapists.

### Akili Interactive Labs

Now let's turn our attention to gaming as a means of digital treatment. Akili Interactive Labs is building a platform for developing digital therapeutics in the form of creative action video games. The games are designed to be fun and entice people to keep playing, while at the same time fulfilling a strict medical purpose. Akili's most impressive project is called AKL-T01, and it is used to treat attention deficit disorder (ADD) and hyperactivity. When young people with ADD play the game, they move through a winter wonderland or a lava flow, where they complete certain tasks to receive rewards.

AKL-T01 could soon become a prescriptible digital treatment – all necessary clinical testing has already been completed. It is now undergoing the US Food and Drug Administration (FDA) certification process. If the FDA approves the application, AKL-T01 will have the same status as other approved treatments and any doctor will be able to prescribe it just like a medication. Akili also has other irons in the fire: digital therapeutics for the treatment of autism, depression, and multiple sclerosis.

Confirmed findings about the efficacy of virtual reality as a therapeutic tool are still thin on the ground. Large-scale studies performed in 2017 on the effects of virtual reality in the areas of pain therapy, eating disorders, and anxiety and other mental disorders have at least come to the conclusion that the acceptance of such interventions is very high among patients, and the majority of the studies indicate clinical efficacy. However, the research also shows that the scope and quality of the individual studies are very heterogeneous and that further, large-scale clinical studies are necessary [3, 4].

Brennan Spiegel, Director of Health Services Research at Cedars-Sinai Medical Center in Los Angeles, and his team use a variety of applications to free patients from the confines of their hospital rooms. They let patients experience virtual flights over Iceland, dive underwater with playful dolphins, or enjoy front-row seats at the Cirque du Soleil. By using virtual reality, they have achieved robust results in their pain therapy, with short-term pain reduction of up to 50%, and up to 25% in the long term [5]. They have also been able to help members of ethnic and religious communities, whose members consume too much salt because of their special diets, and as a result many suffer from high blood pressure. With the aid of virtual reality, the patients are shown how much salt is in different foods and, in a simulated flight through the human body, what effect this salt has on them. It certainly seems like the applications of this behavior-modifying technology are far from exhausted [5].

### Mindmaze

Based in Lausanne, Switzerland, the Mindmaze startup uses virtual reality to provide people who have suffered a stroke with much faster assistance than would have been possible using conventional methods. Mindmaze developed Mindmotion, a three-dimensional virtual environment that makes it possible to supplement rehabilitation measures with exercises using an avatar, a digital alter-ego of the patient. Following a stroke, some forms of paralysis are permanent, whereas others can be reversed – but only with enormous effort. Patients often quickly become frustrated when they begin the rehabilitation process. They feel that they are not getting anywhere. But the camera system can capture even the tiniest amount of progress and show it through the avatar. This lifts the spirits of the patients and motivates them to persist, day after day, with the hard work necessary to regain control over their bodies.

The avatar is also employed in a virtual mirror trick. It works like this: A patient whose left arm is paralyzed has to move their right arm, but on the screen they see their avatar making the same movement with their left arm. The patient has the impression that their damaged arm is moving again. This targets precisely those areas of the brain that need to be activated and trained to facilitate healing.

As we can see, the true value of the digital coach lies in its power to motivate. The following patient testimonials speak for themselves [6]:

- "I can feel my brain firing up. I have never used a computer and I love this!"
- "My mum comes alive when she uses the Mindmotion, I can see the sparkle in her eyes."
- "The time spent during these exercises makes me forget that I am in a hospital."

Its immediate availability and comparatively low costs also make this an attractive alternative form of treatment. It might be that, in this field at least, virtual-reality-based digital coaches will become the new standard. As the examples above illustrate, digital coaches can take on many forms. They are still in the early days of development. Noteworthy are their power to modify behaviors and the opportunity to help a lot of people at a low cost.

Most providers of digital coaches start with a one-trick pony – in other words, they create a coach for a single condition, like type 2 diabetes. But since this type of diabetes is often accompanied by high blood pressure, obesity, and depression, many companies are expanding their reach to offer a patient-centric platform that includes the most common associated diseases. So at some point, many digital coaches share the same content modules: behavior-modification interventions related to food, exercise, health knowledge, and mindfulness.

## Digital Therapeutics by Prescription

Digital therapeutics may look good, but are they also effective? Just because a lot of people and organizations believe in something that does not mean that it will actually do anything, let alone have the desired effect. Could the thousands of medical-related apps in the Apple and Google stores in fact be digital snake oil or a modern version of applying leeches? What does the statistical evidence tell us – can a digital chatbot or avatar really compete with a flesh-and-blood coach, delivering a similar level of measurable results?

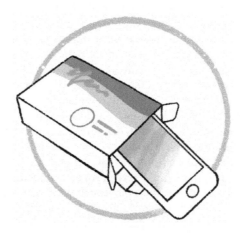

This question is not only of interest to the champions of the supposedly invariably superior treatment provided by human beings or those who are constantly critical of innovation, but also to doctors and hospitals who are looking to scale and reproduce their knowledge and services so they can be made available to everyone. And it is of particular interest to health insurance companies and regulators, whose business models seem to be struggling to bear up under the growing pressure exerted by NCDs. So can digital therapeutics offer comparable or better services at significantly lower costs over the long term? Are they a valuable building block in the democratization of the healthcare system? Will they be sand or granite in the foundation of the future healthcare system?

The subject is still relatively new, so as yet there are only a few conclusive scientific studies. Meta-studies, which examine several original studies and attempt to draw overarching conclusions, provide a good overview. However, none are yet available. Only one finding seems to be consistent: Digital interventions have at least demonstrated no negative medical impact, and they can achieve similar results to physical interventions. And every study that measures adherence as an outcome – in other words, the compliance of the patient with the prescribed treatment – arrives at a clearly positive conclusion [7–13].

When the economic potential of a new technology is recognized as being high, then the scientific community is often quickly overtaken by the industry when it comes to both innovation and the speed at which it occurs. The field of digital therapeutics is no exception. Digital therapeutics by prescription – that future is already here. And the company Pear Therapeutics, headquartered in Boston, provides a striking example.

## Pear Therapeutics

Working in collaboration with researchers at Dartmouth College in the US state of New Hampshire, Pear Therapeutics developed a 90-day digital treatment program called reSET. Its goal is to fight the abuse of alcohol, marijuana, cocaine, and stimulants. Guided by their smartphone, addicts complete behavioral therapy programs. On the one hand, the app is aimed at helping the user get their alcohol and drug abuse under control, and on the other, at continuing a previously started rehabilitation program outside the inpatient setting.

Pear Therapeutics is very different from the other healthtech companies who together upload more than 200 new health apps to the Apple Store and Google Play every day. In September 2018, the US FDA certified reSET, meaning it has formally been recognized by the government as an effective treatment. This represented a seal of approval not only for Pear Therapeutics, but also for the entire market for digital therapeutics. Such certified digital interventions have to meet the same standards as conventional physical medications. Pear's software was tested in more than 20 clinical trials with over 3,000 patients. Now reSET can be prescribed by doctors and covered by health insurance. In other words, it is anything but snake oil.

In December 2018, Pear received approval for a second treatment, this one aimed at the opioid addition that is plaguing the United States with an average of 118 deaths per day. Like reSET, it is being marketed in cooperation with a commercial partner, Sandoz, which is a subsidiary of the Novartis pharmaceutical company. Additional therapeutics for the treatment of insomnia, depression, schizophrenia, epilepsy, pain, and migraines are currently being developed [14].

Numerous providers are rushing to get on the bandwagon, also developing evidence-based digital therapeutics with the intention of seeking FDA approval so these treatments will be prescriptible. This includes, as discussed above, Akili and its therapeutic video game for the treatment of ADD and hyperactivity. Proteus Digital Health has an approved product for monitoring patient compliance; Voluntis, an approval for a diabetes product.

The FDA has laid the groundwork for the future. It has recognized that the traditional logic for the regulation of hardware no longer matches the requirements for software. Software must be constantly updated to keep up with the latest technology and customer expectations – lengthy and complex certification processes for each update would kill innovation and are simply not compatible with the current state of the software world. With this in mind, the FDA founded a quality assurance program called Pre-Cert as part of its Digital Health Innovation Action Plan. As the name suggests, it represents a way for companies to become pre-certified. Once this is done, the software products of these companies go through a non-bureaucratic approval process aimed at ensuring continuous certification [15].

When it comes to digital health regulations, Europe is still lagging behind the United States. Because there is no standard set of rules, startups complain that the European market is fragmented. If they want to expand from one European market to another, they not only have to deal with a new language, but also with new regulations and a healthcare market that is completely different in structure. The European Commission, working in conjunction with leading digital companies and associations, has so far only developed a European Code of Conduct that defines data protection principles for medical apps. However, the Code has not yet been approved [16]. Up to now, the approval of medical apps for digital therapeutics in Europe has been subject to the same regulations as for medical devices, which require a time-consuming process [15]. In the field of digital health care, Germany has preempted a European solution by passing the Digital Healthcare Act (DVG – *Digitale-Versorgung-Gesetz*) in 2019. The law simplifies the approval process for medical apps. In the future, such apps will be able to be covered by the state health insurance providers even before their efficacy is proven. In each case, the developers of the apps have one year to establish clinical efficacy. The German law accelerates the process, fostering digital health innovation. It is no wonder that the startup sector has applauded the move.

### *Evidation Health*

In the last 10 years, an indeterminable number of companies offering digital services in the healthcare sector have emerged across the globe. It is estimated that in this field, more than 100,000 apps have now been developed. For many of the companies, the challenge is proving the efficacy of their digital products. Many of these companies come from the consumer goods sector, so they are not aware in advance of the importance of this clinical proof-of-concept, which is standard in the healthcare industry. In addition, many players in the healthcare sector are cautious and conservative in their approach, which is why considerable empirical evidence must be presented before a new product is accepted.

So when it comes to testing the efficacy of digital apps, there is significant need for assistance. This is where Evidation Health enters into the equation. The company provides support to other companies in the healthcare industry in creating and conducting the necessary tests, which can be very complex. They range from 72-hour intervention studies with a small number of patients to analytical studies lasting a year, for example, to compare the effects of a new app with the traditional use of medications. It is not necessarily the case that the promised benefits are not delivered, says Deborah Kilpatrick. However, most companies have yet to learn that this proof of efficacy must be provided. Many company owners are surprised when they learn about the costs and length of the tests.

This was the case with the California-based health startup Omada Health, which offers companies a 16-week program aimed at changing the eating and nutritional habits of employees with NCDs such as diabetes or high blood pressure. At first, Omada Health had planned to launch its app as soon as it was finished, but then found out it needed a series of data extending over a period of one year to demonstrate the efficacy of the digital product. These series of tests can quickly burn through millions of USD, but are also essential – because people's health is at stake.

## Digital Adherence Coach

In the case of NCDs, patient compliance is the key to the success of the treatment. Unfortunately, many people – consciously or unconsciously – tend to let things slide. They forget to take their meds or skip some exercises. This is no way to manage a chronic illness.

First a brief explanation of the term "adherence": It describes the degree to which patients cooperate in the treatment of their disease. Adherence measures the difference between the treatments prescribed by the doctor or therapist and the actual actions of the patient. So it describes whether the patient is complying with the behaviors agreed upon between them and their doctor. Does the patient accept and apply the treatment? Do they take their medications regularly, at the correct times, and in the correct quantities? Do they use medical devices such as inhalers correctly? Do they stick to the recommended diet? Are they really making the agreed upon changes to their lifestyle?

Good adherence means consistently following the treatment plan agreed with the practitioner. According to the World Health Organization (WHO), an average of only 50% of patients achieve good adherence. In many therapeutic areas related to NCDs, only about half of the patients are still on the agreed track after one year. More than 50% of the prescribed medications are not taken in the manner in which they were prescribed [17]. Or they are not taken at all. The consequences of poor adherence include – in addition to unmanaged health conditions and the resulting suffering – the costs of medications which are not taken and must then be disposed of, as well as unnecessary hospital stays and visits to doctors and emergency rooms.

There are many different reasons for poor adherence. In no particular order, here is a very long list of reasons based on WHO data illustrating how complex the issue is: Illiteracy; low level of education; unemployment; lack of supportive social networks; unstable living conditions; long distance to healthcare facilities; high travel costs; high cost of medication; cultural perception of the disease and its treatment; advanced age; patient–carer relationship; poor distribution and accessibility of medications; lack of knowledge and experience of carers in dealing with NCDs; overworked carers; short office hours; lack of capacity to support self-help groups and self-management; severity of symptoms; extent of disability (physical, psychological, social, or occupational); nature and severity of the course of the disease and the availability of effective treatments; complex drug regime; duration of treatment; lack of rapid progress in treatment; side effects; unsuccessful treatments already experienced; the resources, knowledge, attitude, beliefs, perceptions, and expectations of patients; forgetfulness; emotional stress; fear of side effects, low motivation; poor knowledge and skills in dealing with side effects; pessimism about the treatment; lack of acceptance of the disease; fear of addiction; failure to understand the treatment instructions; bad experiences with people from the healthcare system; and feeling stigmatized by the disease [17].

It really is a long list, and it shows that poor adherence is not just the result of laziness or bad intentions on the part of the patient. Conditions such as depression, Alzheimer's disease, or drug addiction have additional negative impacts on adherence. So it is not surprising that the entire healthcare industry is desperately looking for affordable and scalable assistance to get a handle on the adherence problem, not only during the treatment of chronically ill patients, but also during clinical trials.

A digital coach can help solve this problem. Probably the most spectacular approach is being taken by Proteus Digital Health of Redwood City, California. Patients are literally taking a digital pill.

David, 58 years old, is one patient in the Proteus world. He has suffered from type 2 diabetes for more than 10 years. Because he likes eating and is not so fond of exercise, he is 20 kilos overweight and has cholesterol levels that are considerably too high. And because his blood pressure is also too high, he has to take several different medications at several times of the day. As a result, he often lost track and did not know exactly what drug he had taken and when.

Cases like this represent a serious challenge for the healthcare sector. A study funded by America's National Institutes of Health reveals the financial consequences of non-adherence. In the United States alone, some 500 billion USD per year are spent on follow-on costs because patients like David take their medications in incorrect quantities or at the wrong intervals, or do not take them at all [18]. The goal of Andrew Thompson, one of the founders of Proteus, is to relieve the healthcare system of this burden.

## Proteus Digital Health

With the pill that Proteus Digital Health started developing in 2001, it is possible to precisely reconstruct whether David has taken the medication prescribed by his doctor regularly and in the required dose. How does it work? Proteus has developed an ingestible sensor the size of a grain of sand and already had it certified. The sensor is a microchip made of silicon which is coated in minerals that are common in the human diet. It is added to the tablets, the actual medication. Once it has arrived in the stomach, it sends a signal that is received by a special patch on David's torso, and from there relayed to his smartphone as well as the Proteus cloud, which his doctor and care team can access. The patch not only records all ingested medication that contains the sensor, but also periods of patient activity and rest. In other words, Proteus has developed the most radical form of digital pill yet. Every single tablet is a hybrid of the physical and digital worlds.

There have been applications since 2016, focusing primarily on monitoring the intake of medication by chronically ill patients – in particular, patients like David who suffer from diabetes and high blood pressure. If a patient does not feel like the drugs are working and stops taking them, even though their doctor thinks they are adhering to the regimen, it can lead to extremely expensive follow-on treatments. This is the argument put forth by Clint Purvance, CEO & President of Barton Health, the hospital where the sensor pill was used for the first time.

The sensor pill is especially suitable for the treatment of high-risk patients, such as people who are addicted to drugs or intellectually impaired. It also enables a significant improvement in the accuracy of the drug efficacy analyses. In many studies, it has proved impossible to verify whether and to what extent the patients have actually taken the medication they were administered. The hybrid pills help patients remember their medication and take it at the right time. Because they make it possible to determine whether the medication has actually been taken, they deliver significantly more trustworthy data than basic reminder-apps, of which there are many. The difference can be seen in the adherence rates, which increase from less than 60% to over 90% [19]. The data set that is compiled over time, comprising patient data, medication administered, and actual intake provides an increasingly better understanding of the way drugs work.

In addition, the collected data, which with the patient's permission can be shared in the cloud, assist the physician in providing medical care. It helps verify the success of treatments – an important criterion in the remuneration of doctors and for value-based contracts between pharmaceutical manufacturers and insurance companies. So it comes as no surprise to find that more and more pharmaceutical companies are working with Proteus and incorporating the sensor into their tablets and capsules for the treatment of mental, metabolic, and oncological disorders as well as cardiovascular and infectious diseases.

The digitally enhanced pill from Proteus helped David establish a reasonably sound routine for handling his medication. Andrew Thompson, founder of Proteus, points out that the wonder-sensor does not necessarily have to be used forever. Most patients use the Proteus treatment for three or four months. Later they try to get along without Proteus' assistance [20].

In the digital world, a long-term boost in adherence is not limited to hybrid pills. It is part of all good digital therapeutics and applies a variety of methods. One is notifications in the form of text messages, in-app messages, and phone calls. There is still great potential for optimizing and personalizing the frequency, timing, and communication style of these notifications. A lot of questions have not yet been answered. How should the chatbot talk to the patient? Should it make jokes and act like a buddy or employ a tone of authority? How often should it communicate with the patient each day? Once? Eight times? Or only if there is an important matter to clarify? And should the chatbot adapt to the patient, know their preferences, be tailored to them?

Good digital coaches regularly remind their customers to stick to their treatment plan and document their actions – for example, by taking photos of their daily walk or a lunch that complies with their diet plan. Or shoot a video when their asthmatic child uses their inhaler. Patients are asked to complete exercises, such as a guided breathing exercise with their smartphone. Or to measure vital signs such as blood pressure. Or to take medication – please take the pills from slot 3 of the red pill dispenser every evening. Or to answer questions like: On a scale of 1–10, how severe is your pain this morning?

All of these data are then made available to the patient along a timeline. Not only to the patient, however, but also, provided the patient agrees, to the human practitioner, who can review the data at regular intervals and use it as a basis for interventions. The practitioner is also notified as soon as the patient's engagement levels sink – not just when the vital signs start to get out of hand. This way they can reach out to the patient as early as possible. However, for this form of cooperation between patient, digital coach, and human practitioner to work, they all have to be seamlessly connected. Human practitioners can only utilize the growing flood of data when the medically relevant facts are presented in an easy-to-apply fashion – and are compatible with the computer system they use. Interventions that can coordinate and leverage the combined efforts of human beings and technology have proven particularly effective.

# Chapter 7

# Digital Health Data and Data Security

*The main theses of this chapter:*

- Digital data derived from clinical practice, referred to as "real-world data" (RWD), supplement clinical trial data. In addition, lifestyle data and everyday observational data are becoming increasingly relevant. Together, they are the lifeblood of medical progress.
- Comprehensive, quality-controlled, and machine-readable health data translate into better health for everyone as well as an improved healthcare system. Together with a functioning digital infrastructure, these data are increasingly becoming a competitive advantage for healthcare companies.
- The way we handle health data impacts on both the quality and the cost of the healthcare system.
- The use of health data in research, which is subject to increasingly stringent rules and regulations, is becoming a driver of innovation. Artificial intelligence (AI)-based tools are becoming the stethoscope of the twenty-first century.
- Increasingly, digital literacy is now a prerequisite for health literacy.
- Healthy individuals and patients alike are keenly interested in clean, comprehensive, and high-quality health data. As long as privacy is maintained, they do not mind if their data are collected.
- Patients and healthy individuals are only willing to purchase from companies that are actively committed to protecting their privacy. Patients will only collaborate with trusted brands.
- Encrypting all data is becoming the new standard and a precondition for sharing.

All the organizations and institutions described in this book have one thing in common: They collect and analyze health-relevant data. Whoever has the data can generate medical expertise and knowledge about the healthcare system.

**The Digital Pill: What Everyone Should Know about the Future of Our Healthcare System, 99–120**
Copyright © 2021 by Emerald Publishing Limited
All rights of reproduction in any form reserved
doi:10.1108/978-1-78756-675-020211007

Randomized double-blind studies (where patients are randomly allocated to a group) have been viewed as the gold standard for gaining medical knowledge and the approval of new drugs and treatments. Even if these clinical studies have enabled medicine to make great strides and there is currently no viable alternative, they are not without challenges: Studies often do not run for very long, which makes it difficult to track long-term effects and side effects. Study participants have frequently been highly pre-selected and do not correspond to the average patient in subsequent clinical practice. Clinical trials are impractical when it comes to rare diseases, since it is difficult to find a sufficient number of patients with the disease, and they impair the ability to detect effects that only occur after the study is completed. Preparing and conducting them is very time-consuming, and they are generally extremely expensive [1]. Clinical studies cannot always keep up with the rapid development of active ingredients or infectious diseases or with the explosion of scientific expertise. And they often present an ethical dilemma: Clinical studies require a control arm, where patients receive a treatment that might be inferior – or even a placebo that has no effect.

This contrasts with observational data, which, as the name suggests, is based purely on the observation of clinical practice. Such data are constantly being generated but – and therein lies the problem – not always systematically collected. In the late 1980s, for instance, these data helped reduce the risk of sudden infant death syndrome in New Zealand, a situation where ethical reasons do not allow for a controlled comparative study. Doctors often rely on their previous practice and conventional treatments. This leads to the repeated reaching of clinical decisions that are based on incomplete and error-ridden "data sets." Waiting for better data is not an option for many patients, as this would simply mean not taking any action at all. Therefore, we need to strive to gain useful RWD that is robust enough to justify interventions [1]. It makes sense to digitally collect the RWD continually being generated in the healthcare sector, and to do it systematically and at a quality that allows us to objectively and rapidly analyze a large volume of this data using scientific best practices – in addition to data from clinical trials, which will continue to be needed in the future.

## Health Data as a Strategic Asset

Health data are generated in many places: during doctor's appointments and hospital stays, interactions with health insurance companies and at the pharmacy, through continual self-monitoring with apps, blood testing or genome/microbiome sequencing at a lab, and when patients participate in clinical studies or move around their smart home or nursing home. The data sources are as varied as their use and the actors in the healthcare sector. So how has the collection and analysis of health data developed historically?

## *A Brief History of Health Data*

The history of medical progress and the development of medical records run parallel to each other, since information about patients has always been just as important as medication and treatments. The earliest forms of medical records can be traced back to ancient Egypt. At the time, medical information was stored on papyrus scrolls that today bear witness to the various medical practices that were routine nearly 4,000 years ago – from surgery to dentistry, and always touching upon magic, astrology, and astronomy as well [2, 3].

Medical records have always been a valuable source of medical progress. Just like his predecessors, Hippocrates, the "father of modern medicine," born around 460 BCE, gained his rudimentary knowledge based on documents he likely studied in an Asclepeion (a temple dedicated to Asclepius, the god of medicine) with an attached *sanatorium* on the Greek island of Kos. These records were simple in form, but served the same purpose they serve today: to improve the treatment of patients, to advance medicine, to pass on and preserve knowledge for future generations, as well as to manage billing [2, 3].

However, many centuries would pass before patient data would be collected in a standardized manner that would allow it to be shared. In the Western world, Grace Whiting Myers at Massachusetts General Hospital is considered to have been the first official medical records librarian. Sometime around 1900, after being asked to put together some medical and surgical statistics, Myers began collecting the many administrative and medical records that had been kept all over the hospital in closets, attics, and vaults. In the end, she had assembled all the records, extending back to when the hospital opened in 1821, in a central location. She studied Latin and Greek so she could decipher and understand the contents of the cards and later categorize the information working alongside her colleagues from neighboring hospitals. Thus, the American Association of Medical Record Librarians was born. This marked the beginning of the data-based healthcare sector, at the time exclusively on paper [4].

It was not until 1960 that the first digital information systems began to be used in the healthcare sector. At the time, computers were still large and expensive, and a system's applications were very limited. They were primarily used for book-keeping and billing. In the 1970s, computers gradually shrank in size and became more affordable. The first information systems around hospital pharmacies and laboratories as well as for patient administration were developed. This resulted in ever-growing data silos, since no provision was made for the exchange of data across departments [3].

Because health insurance companies pressed for a diagnosis-based reimburse-ment scheme, a selective networking of systems across some departments occurred in the 1980s. The silos remained, however. In the 1990s, internal computer net-works began to gain popularity. At the same time, the first hospital-wide patient lists – known as "master patient indices" – were introduced. It was now possible to interlink the systems of the departments to create more comprehensive systems that at least covered every department in a single hospital and was therefore also suited for ensuring seamless patient care within the organization [3].

With the advent of the internet, we gained the technical ability to extend this exchange of information to parties outside the hospital. Since the begin-ning of the millennium, every doctor, pharmacist, lab, naturopath, psychologist, and physical therapist as well as the majority of patients have had access to the internet, both in the developed and, increasingly, in the developing world. New cloud-based information systems are capable of interlinking the entire patient ecosystem and sharing the resulting data and insights to benefit the patient and society as a whole. At least this is the idea.

History shows – which is why we mention it here – that the biggest drivers for the digitization of patient data have been administration, billing, and reim-bursement. While the effort also required clinically relevant data, it was noth-ing more than a byproduct. This is unfortunately also reflected in the quality of the patient data we have available today. Even though the internet provides every opportunity for networking and although more and more medical meas-urement methods have ben digitalized over the past decades, especially imaging data (ultrasound, X-ray, and MRI), in many countries, the majority of medically relevant data continues to be tucked away in isolated data stores just as they were nearly a century ago. What this data lacks is consistent quality, compatibility, and machine-readability. This is also true for many of our modern data sources and for the millions of measurements that patients generate on their own today or order from omics labs. The term "omics," which we will return to later, desig-nates fields of biology such as genomics, epigenomics, microbiomics, proteomics, and transcriptomics.

Individual countries and companies recognized the tremendous importance of health data years ago and began to structure, standardize, and collect it. The millions of data points that occur per patient can be roughly divided into three categories: data from traditional medical records, omics data, and self-monitor-ing data.

Frequently, the image of an onion is used for the totality of data. Onions con-sist of a core surrounded by multiple layers that can be used to visualize different types of health data. We would like to continue with this image by examining three of these layers.

### Electronic Medical Records (EMR) as the Core of Health Data

The data stored in a traditional medical record are at the core of the data "onion." It contains all the information that describes any contact between patients and healthcare providers such as physicians, hospitals, pharmacists, and insurance companies. The data reservoir starts with the identification of the patient and the physician with information such as age, sex, language(s), profession, and place of residence. It also lists risk factors such as allergies, contains information about health-related lifestyle factors such as smoking and alcohol consumption, and provides data from doctor and hospital visits arranged by time and health episode. This also extends to records of visits, meeting notes, the results of blood, urine, stool, and tissue tests, images (e.g., X-rays), examination results, diagnoses, vaccination data, treatment plans, surgeries, doctors' recommendations, and prescriptions. It ends with achieved medical outcomes, costs, and other billing-related data. Living wills and informed consent data such as for organ donation are also stored in this pool of data.

This list shows the challenges associated even with just the digitization of conventional medical records, which constitute a tremendous volume of extremely diverse data. Many of these records are only available on paper or tucked away in isolated electronic systems. They are created by different parties, most of whom are not very interested in sharing data, let alone in sharing it in a format that can be read and understood by machines.

**Practice Fusion.** One currently unsolved problem in medical care is that almost nowhere in the world is there an electronic patient file that is easy to manage and fully compatible. This means that a doctor never has all the information about a patient. Generally, doctors are only aware of conditions they have personally diagnosed. This information deficit is what Alan Wong, Matthew Douglass, and Ryan Howard hoped to combat when they founded Practice Fusion in 2005. The company provides physicians with software that lets them enter and update all medically relevant data about a patient, evaluate data in various ways, and create graphic depictions of the results.

The data collected here serves two purposes: to research new medicines and innovative treatments and to simplify and accelerate the treatment process. For instance, if a patient is required to have several examinations at a hospital, doctors can access the data at any time and any place in the hospital. There are no information gaps, and nobody has to carry medical records from one department to another. Patients also have access to their own EMR and can thus track their process through doctors' offices and hospitals.

**Apple.** In 2017, Apple added Sumbul Desai to its team, a renowned professor of medicine and digital health expert from Stanford University who has headed up its health business ever since. The latest health innovation by Apple is Health Records, a comprehensive EMR that Apple launched on the US market in 2018 in collaboration with more than 120 hospitals. The clinics enter comprehensive information about vaccinations, X-rays, blood test results, surgery reports, and other data directly into the app. Patients benefit from this transparency and access to their health data, and follow-up exams can be made more efficient since tests do not have to be repeated unnecessarily. Many renowned hospitals are already using Health Records, among them Mount Sinai, Duke, and the US military hospitals.

As early as 2016, Apple CEO Tim Cook stated that the healthcare market makes even the smartphone market look small in comparison. In a time where the iPhone market is increasingly weakening, we can expect many other health innovations. What might that look like? Since 2018, Apple has operated its own healthcare centers for its employees. These practices have implemented a holistic, preventive approach to medicine. In industry circles, there is speculation that these employee practices could constitute a test run for US-wide expansion.

### Omics Data

Staying with the image of the onion: A second layer of health data is the omics data, as mentioned above. The omics data most frequently used in medicine is derived from *genomics*, in other words, working with the human genome, our DNA. The numbers hint at the volume of data we are looking at when it comes to describing the genome, which consists of DNA molecules with more than 3 billion base pairs. Pulled apart, a DNA strand would be 2 meters long. Nonetheless, it resides at the nucleus of every human cell, which is only 5–16 μm in size – about a seventh of the diameter of a human hair. Humans themselves consist of $10^{13}$ of these cells, 50 million of which die every second while about the same number is newly formed.

The DNA strand organizes itself into 46 chromosomes in every cell nucleus, 23 of them from the mother's egg cell and 23 from the father's sperm cell. Specific sections of the DNA strand that provide the blueprint for specific characteristics are referred to as genes. About 20,000 of these sections, or genes, are known today. They are between 100 and one million base pairs long, and their sum makes up less than 2% of the entire DNA strand.

During fertilization, the two initial cells fuse and immediately begin to divide. Up to the third cell division, all cells are identical and have the potential to fulfill any purpose. Afterwards, the cells – which continue to hold the same blueprint in their nucleus in the form of the DNA strand – begin to develop differently. Thus, cell differentiation, which is referred to as epigenetic fixation, begins: The descendants of the first cells increasingly develop according to their desired function in the body. They then specialize and become one of the 200 cell types in the human body. They become muscle, nerve, skin, bone, intestinal, or liver cells, because only part of the blueprint is executed and therefore not every gene is actually used. While the genome describes the blueprint, the field of epigenomics – the study of the meta-aspects of the genome – is dedicated to the exact implementation of the blueprint for every cell.

Human bodies are not only made up of human cells, however, but are generally host to up to 10 times as many bacterial cells or cell structures such as fungi.

The sum of these mostly *beneficial* and even vital residents are referred to as the microbiome, and the associated field of study, microbiomics (see Chapter 4). The microbiome not only represents 90% of the cells in our bodies, but the DNA strands of the microbiome also contain 100,000 genes, five times as many as in human cells. The genome, epigenome, and microbiome doubtlessly impact our health and our wellbeing. This is also true for other discussed "omics" such as transcriptomes, metabolomes, proteomes, dieseasomes, and environmentomes.

Omics data, for instance those generated through genetic sequencing, are becoming increasingly crucial in the fight against severe chronic diseases, whether for the development of targeted medicines that dock to specific proteins, determining the risk of disease, or predicting whether a specific drug will or will not work for a patient.

## Self-monitoring Data

A third layer of data is derived from self-monitoring. Fitness trackers as well as smart watches, rings, scales, and even toilets help collect this information. Self-monitoring allows us to gather information about blood pressure, blood sugar, cholesterol, uric acid, ketones, gait pattern, pollen count, outside temperature, environmental noise, fine particulate matter, and more. Together, over time, these data form a giant, nearly gap-free tapestry of data. The individual data sets, such as the pulse that can be measured every minute instead of just once at the doctor's office like before, may seem trivial at first glance. However, they form the threads of a data tapestry of potentially life-saving value, both for the person collecting the data and for society.

Those who self-monitor collect what is referred to as longitudinal data, which provides more than an isolated snapshot of their health status, but instead an entire movie that shows changes and allows us to draw conclusions about cause and effect. Among the frequently collected data are body temperature, body weight, heart rate, steps taken, distance covered, food consumed, blood sugar, calories, sleep (duration and sleep phases), respiratory rate, medication, and stress levels [5].

## Exponential Growth in Data Volume

According to Siemens, every medical image requires about 0.5 MB storage, and the average processing of this type of image generates an additional 30 MB. In contrast, an average picture taken with a digital camera requires 4 MB, every X-ray 30 MB, every mammogram 120 MB, every MRI more than 150 MB, and every CT generates 1 GB of data [6]. It is no wonder medical image archives grow by about a third every year. IBM estimates that the clinical data at the core of the data onion make up about 400 GB per patient and lifetime. The second layer of the onion, the omics data, uses at least 15 times that amount, in other words a minimum of 6 TB. (1 terabyte stands for 1,024 GB.) The lion's share is made up of the data from the third layer of the onion model: The continuous self-monitoring data over the lifetime of a patient amount to a surprising 1,100 TB. This almost unimaginably large volume corresponds to approximately the storage needed for an HD video that lasts 63 years(!) or for more than 7 billion pages of documents. If these pages were printed out and stacked, you would have a tower that was 715 kilometers high [7–9].

The yearly data volume doubles every 12–24 months, depending on the source, more than in any other area of life. Soon, the health data in countries with very large populations such as China, India, or the United States will reach a data volume measured in zetta- and yottabytes. In addition, about 80% of all data are unstructured and stored in hundreds of different formats, for example, as lab test results, images, or medical transcripts. These huge amounts of data represent both a tremendous opportunity to drive treatment and prevention as well as a massive challenge for everyone in the healthcare sector, from scientists to health-care policy-makers and companies [10].

## Collecting, Processing, and Analyzing Data

Faced with data volumes this large, differentiation is crucial: "Big is better" only conditionally applies to the healthcare sector. Instead, it is important that useful information and insights can be derived from large data volumes. This is more challenging in the healthcare sector than in online retailing, for instance.

Almost all the actors in the healthcare marketplace, from patients to pharmaceutical companies, use information technology both to gain easy access to health data that can be processed and to transform this data into medical knowledge.

## Data Collection

In order to make collecting data as user-friendly as possible, consumer-facing and internet-savvy companies are getting very creative. They are looking for data sources that are as clean as possible and will over time be able to provide insights on the health status of data subjects. There are many ways to do this. For instance, smartphones and wearables may be paired with sensors to elicit clues to neurological conditions. Simple, game-based user interfaces can be created and use "nudges" – incentives based on behavioral economics – to encourage users to enter even more data. Multiple companies from Apple to PatientsLikeMe offer a particularly strong incentive, however: Many services are free for users. They pay through other channels – and with their health data.

At the same time, large databases are being built, for instance in the field of clinical genome sequences: data sets about different tumor profiles, their genetic expression, and even information about the outcomes of certain treatments. And finally, in many countries, EMRs are being created to allow individuals to be able to trace their entire medical and health history.

The tremendous benefit of digital health data is undisputed and has already led to many regulatory initiatives. In the United States, 96% of all hospitals and 86% of all doctors in private practice already had access to EMRs in 2017. Patients, too, are convinced of the benefit. In 2019, 45% of US citizens stated that these medical records had improved their treatment. Only 6% said the opposite [11].

However, in 2018, nearly 60% of physicians believed that the systems for maintaining medical records needed to be completely overhauled. A year prior, eleven CEOs of US medical centers wrote an open letter to their peers, warning them that current systems had a negative impact on patient care. A study among 142 general practitioners in Wisconsin demonstrated the unreasonable working conditions computers are forcing upon physicians: During an average 11.4-hour workday, a doctor spends nearly six hours at a computer to maintain the EMRs. Nearly 2.5 hours of that time are spent simply entering text and another two hours processing incoming messages [11, 12]. In the eyes of many physicians, the herculean effort required to input all this information simply does not correlate to the gains in output.

One solution to this problem could be dictation software. Companies such as Google, Microsoft, Nuance, NoteSwift, and Saykara are already marketing such solutions. Olive and Apixio are developing digital office assistants that take the majority of the administrative workload off the doctor's hands.

Another problem is the blind faith that many doctors and healthcare professionals have in computer-based data. While they will look critically at the hard-to-decipher hand-written content of index cards, characters on a screen appear to be associated with a high degree of authority, something that has caused life-threatening mistakes to occur. In general, experts agree, EMRs have improved patient safety. Whenever the system detects an unusual pattern, it sounds the alarm to point out potential errors as early as possible. However, if the data quality is insufficient, a certain amount of alarm fatigue can set in. We have all experienced this in the real world; after five false alarms at a hotel, the local fire department might not respond to the sixth alarm – with potentially lethal consequences.

### The Problem with Distributed Incompatible Data

In many countries, patient data are still stored on paper, for example, in the form of hand-written notes or lab printouts. Of course this data could easily be scanned and digitized, but entering it digitally at the source would address the problem at its roots. The diverse data formats different manufacturers use to store structured (readings) and unstructured (written reports and images) health data present a tremendous challenge. These make it impossible for hospitals and sometimes even departments in a single hospital using different software to exchange patient data or process the data outputs of medical devices. Binding standards prescribing the syntax and semantic structure of key data elements would be helpful. Another approach could be the use of software modules that automatically "translate" data from one system to another. Frequently data are stored in different places, which present an additional challenge. The internet suggests a multitude of potential solutions, such as the services provided by Practicefusion, Health Gorilla, Redox, and LiveHealth.

**Redox.** Doctors, healthcare policy-makers, therapists of all kinds, health insurance providers, and patient groups have repeatedly called for EMRs. Altogether too much information about patients gets lost or is not communicated where physicians in private practice or hospital-based specialists work with medical records created manually. In addition, the information is not up to date and generally is not available at the location where it is needed.

An EMR can solve this problem in theory; however, numerous versions have been developed and often they are not compatible with each other. This prevents data from being shared or results in an incomplete or error-riddled exchange. This is why James Lloyd, Luke Bonney, and Niko Skievaski founded the Redox platform in Madison, Wisconsin, in 2014. All people and organizations involved in the treatment of patients can enter their data on this platform and access the data entered by others.

The interfaces are designed in such a way as to allow different systems to communicate with each other. In addition, Redox invites companies to develop software to analyze patient data. Redox intends to use its system to create a platform that provides up-to-date, complete, non-redundant data that is made available to all parties concerned. This data can be accessed in real time to improve the assessment of symptoms and decisions about treatments, medication, or medical interventions.

**LiveHealth.** LiveHealth, an Indian company, takes a somewhat different approach. The Indian healthcare system is spinning out of control; as in other countries, healthcare spending is growing at an alarming rate. More than two thirds of all healthcare costs in India are paid out of pocket, which makes the rising costs particularly painful for the population. One important reason for this is the insufficient exchange of data, especially between hospitals, but also between hospital departments. If a patient visits a hospital in India and is released, they will generally not be recognized as the same person if they go to a branch of this hospital for another examination a few days later.

In the light of these and other cases, LiveHealth aims to simplify processes in the healthcare sector and especially to overcome data fragmentation. It has developed an app to guide patients through different interactions with physicians, hospitals, and health insurance providers. The app helps not only the user, but also health insurance providers, because all medical exams as well as the resulting diagnoses and treatments are collected here. This helps prevent repeated examinations of identical symptoms and redundant consultations, significantly reducing costs for health insurance companies.

Once a physician decides that a patient needs to have blood or urine tests or X-rays done, the app takes over. First, it registers the patient and assigns a barcode to the sample (X-ray, blood test, etc.). This allows it to track the location of any given sample and determine who is currently working on it. The test results are then used to generate a report, which in turn is sent to the doctors selected by LiveHealth. They make the diagnosis and suggest a treatment and/or the next stage of testing. Abhimanyu Bhosale and Mukund Malani, the two founders of LiveHealth, continue to stress that their app is intended to improve processes in the healthcare system, not to replace the doctor.

The most difficult problem to solve is that of the divergent, deficient data quality and completeness that often occurs when data were originally collected for a specific purpose but then used for another. A lack of quality especially constitutes a problem when it is necessary to merge data from different sources. As a rule, ensuring a consistent level of minimum quality in medical RWD requires a tremendous amount of expensive manual effort by specialists. Ensuring this level of quality is a core competency of companies such as Flatiron Health in oncology (see Chapter 9).

## Transforming Data into Medical Knowledge

Almost all medical tasks described in this book are supported by AI. This ranges from medical consultations using triage tools to chatbot-based coaching, screening, diagnosis, clinical decision-making assistance, documentation, and resource planning all the way to support in making behavioral changes, identifying active ingredients, and carrying out clinical testing.

All these apps derive their knowledge from data. Therefore, the data must of the best possible quality, that is to say correct, complete, readable by humans and machines, easy to comprehend, and verifiable. And in many cases, it needs to contain a so-called fundamental truth. It is not enough to feed thousands of melanoma images into an algorithm for the classification of malignant and benign cases. While the algorithm is learning, programmers must also provide the fundamental truth of whether each melanoma is actually benign or malignant. This is the only way the algorithm gradually learns to differentiate between good and bad, between true and false. The fundamental truth comes from people passing on their knowledge to the machine.

In these applications, the data play a unique role. The use of AI requires high-quality mass data. Without data, the best algorithms are as useless as a piano without a pianist – even if it were the most beautiful grand piano in the best concert hall in the world. Today, the algorithms used in such applications are taught at any self-respecting university and can all be accessed online. Any organization can acquire the necessary knowledge about algorithms the way you would buy a piano. High-quality data are a different matter. They are truly a scarce resource.

In addition, many applications follow the laws of the network economy. They exhibit the following network effect: The more data these algorithms are exposed to, the more informative value they have. The more informative value a digital tool has, the more frequently it is used. The more frequently a tool is used, the more data are entered into it. The more data these algorithms are exposed to ... which brings us full circle [7].

Services based on AI become better and better over time. At some point, they become so good that the competition cannot keep up – at least as long as the data are not accessible to these competitors. The same network effect is responsible for Amazon's tremendous success, to take just one example. This is why almost all players in the digital healthcare market strive to use this effect for their own benefit, from patient-oriented platforms to insurance providers and pharmaceutical companies.

When physicians enter some of their knowledge into AI systems, their knowledge is not just passed on from one person to another – which, it should be noted, would require a lot of time, energy, intelligence, and labor. Instead, this knowledge enters into an artificial neural network or system of rules that never takes a day off, never has a skiing accident, and never retires. In addition, the artificial digital system can pass its knowledge onto many other systems at the click of a button, works 24 hours a day, never forgets anything, and is always available where an internet connection and the right password are provided.

There is one caveat, however: For the foreseeable future, such systems will continue to have a "one-track mind." As opposed to humans, they are only capable of executing narrowly defined, limited activities and serve as tools to support patients, physicians, therapists, nurses, employers, and many others. Step by step, they are becoming indispensable, however, and are on their way to being the stethoscope of the twenty-first century.

The proliferation of digital health data has also attracted the attention of the large online companies specializing in data processing, such as Amazon, Facebook, and Google.

**Google.**   Google is also working on collecting and analyzing health data. Over the past 20 years, Google has become specialized in big data and AI in advertising, something the company intends to use creating lasting change in the healthcare market. Google CEO Sundar Pichai is convinced that over the next five to 10 years, the biggest advantage of big data and AI will be within the healthcare sector.

Today, the company is already active on several fronts in the healthcare industry. In 2014, it launched Google Fit as a counterpart to Apple's Activity Tracker. The app measures users' activity levels using Android smartphones and motivates them to become more active. In the United States, since 2015 the company has been displaying "health panels" above the Google search results if a user searches for information about a disease. The content of these health panels was developed in collaboration with the US-based Mayo Clinic. They are intended to provide verified information about the symptoms and treatments of various conditions and prevent the spread of false information.

Another health service Google offers is Google Genomics. DNA sequencing is progressing ever more rapidly, and the flood of data is growing. Instead of testing a small group of patients, it is now possible to analyze the genome of thousands of people – although this requires tremendous computing power. This is where Google's big data expertise comes in. Google Genomics is an IaaS (Infrastructure as a Service) model that allows hospitals, universities, and other institutions to store their large data volumes in the Google cloud for a fee and use Google servers to process those overwhelmingly large data volumes. "The processing time for highly complex searches in [Google] BigQuery is at four seconds, whereas a search used to take significantly more than 10 seconds or even several minutes," says the CEO of DNAstack, whose company uses Google Genomics.

Alphabet, Google's parent company, is approaching the health sector from various angles. It bundles the majority of health-related activities in its subsidiary Verily, previously Google Health Systems. So far, the results are mixed: While Verily has achieved promising results in working with its partners, the attempt to use Google Health to establish an EMR failed. Experts believe that this is because Google's offering does not adequately take the true needs of patients and physicians into account. In addition, there were data privacy concerns [13]. Even Google Flu Trends, which provided predictions about the danger of flu infections, has now been taken off the market.

At the same time, large pharmaceutical companies have not been idle. They are hiring scores of programmers and sometimes self-administering a radical change in corporate culture in order to become more flexible and responsive in the use of digital technology. For instance, pharmaceutical company Novartis has declared digitalization to be one of the key pillars of its new strategy. Partnerships are very popular at the moment. The German company Merck created a joint venture with data company Palantir, while the pharmaceutical and diagnostic company Roche added two leading startups for the analysis of oncology data to the group by acquiring Flatiron Health and Foundation Medicine and is now increasingly developing software solutions meant to assist doctors in making decisions.

At the moment, it appears that the large online companies are unable to gain a foothold in the highly regulated healthcare sector when going it alone. The healthcare sector is highly regulated and requires a great deal of experience as well as scientific expertise. The actual research continues to be dominated by large and small pharmaceutical and biotech companies. They frequently continue to view digitalization in the healthcare sector as more of a means to an end than a completely new business area – and are therefore not forging ahead to the same degree. Nonetheless, the large, established corporations need data analysis and AI expertise in drug research. What looks like a race between new and traditional actors at first glance may therefore well lead to many different models of collaboration.

### Primary and Secondary Use of Health Data

In terms of the use of health data, we need to distinguish between two forms of use. Consultations with primary care providers are an example of primary use. Data are collected during or for the patient's visit with the goal of providing that patient with the best possible health care. This data only applies to the patient, for example, their blood pressure, cholesterol, or blood sugar levels. It follows that patients have a personal interest in their data being collected and assessed.

This primary use, however, is only the tip of the iceberg. It is the only use that the patient sees and is aware of. The much greater share of potential data use is beneath the surface, however. This secondary use of data is not visible, and its benefit is not immediately apparent to patients. However, in the medium and long term, it is highly relevant to society.

While primary use refers to the use of data in direct patient care, secondary use designates the use of health data to enhance treatment. This data-driven improvement takes place everywhere empirical data, statistics, and machine learning are required – in other words, in evidence-based medicine. From your personal digital health coach to personalized medication: All these innovations depend on the availability of health data from millions of people and benefit from secondary use on a massive scale [14].

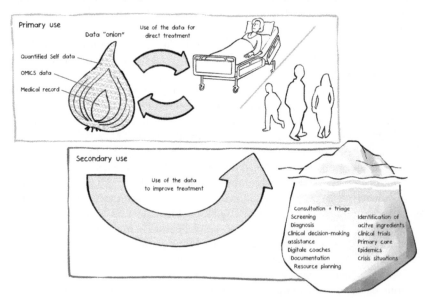

The goal is not merely to stabilize and increase the quality of healthcare services. Efficiency gains made through transparency and automation simultaneously lower costs and allow for the impending switch to results-based billing. In addition, the general availability of internet access increases the accessibility of high-quality medical care for all regions and populations. The secondary use of health data allows states to place their basic medical care and the healthcare sector on stronger footing, and it allows research and industry to compete at a higher level and be better prepared for epidemics and other crisis situations.

We may be at another turning point in the healthcare sector, just as we have been several times over the last 150 years as medicine developed from a trade to a science. This is likely also the reason why the entire world is discussing or has regulated the use of health data as a public good. Some countries are using their authority or their digital vision to make these data available for use as early as possible, while others are engaging in a broad-based process of forging public consensus that specifically delves into the risks and dangers of the collection and secondary use of health data [14].

### *Digital Biomarkers*

Digital biomarkers play a key role with respect to primary and secondary health data. Raw sensor output such as the acceleration data measured by a medical ring or fitness tracker is useful neither to the patient nor to the doctor. This is because they are unable to interpret it. In order to provide a benefit, this raw data must be transformed into medically relevant parameters, that is digital biomarkers. Data generate knowledge that can be used to further medicine. The term biomarker was originally used to designate detectable parameters that provide an indication of a potential treatment or therapy – for example, the hyperexpression of a protein on a tumor cell as an indicator for the use of a specific medication or the presence of a specific hormone to predict cardiovascular risks. *Digital* biomarkers are physiological and behavioral measurements collected through digital technology that explain, influence, or predict health-related results. A simple and widespread example related to the accelerometers mentioned above is the sum of daily steps taken.

The number of available digital biomarkers and those in development is vast. Here is a long – but still incomplete – list of topics: Sleep quality, calories burned, rest, respiratory rate, sleep efficiency, duration of sleep phases, calories consumed, fats, carbohydrates, floors climbed and descended, running distance, nightly coughing fits to assess control of asthma, inhalation and exhalation, breath volume, breath duration, number of daily social contacts, mood, falls, loss of cognitive performance, changes in posture, early detection of Alzheimer's and Parkinson's disease, diagnosis of attention deficit syndromes in children by measuring eye vergence, diagnosing depression by means of voice analysis, and nighttime scratching.

Digital biomarkers are used both by established pharmaceutical and diagnostic companies as well as by startups like Altoida and Freenome to assess disease risk, make diagnoses, and determine whether someone is at particular risk for an impending threat or reacts particularly well or poorly to medication. Research regarding the identification and validation of clinically useful and usable biomarkers is still in its early stages. In order to develop digital biomarkers, sensor technology experts, programers, data scientists, and researchers in hospitals and companies need to work together across disciplines. They must develop a detailed understanding of the nature of the clinical phenomenon they are trying to measure, find the appropriate sensors and adapt them for clinical use, collect data, use machine learning to discover biomarker candidates, and conduct clinical studies to validate digital biomarkers. Just like other fields where AI is used, they can and should continue to learn in order to evolve.

**Roche.** Pharmaceutical company Roche uses digital biomarkers in the field of clinical neuroscience. Smartphones and wearables contain numerous built-in sensors that make them useful for the measurement of health data, for example, accelerometers and motion sensors. This allows us to track the progression of neurodegenerative diseases such as Parkinson's and MS. In the analog practice of medicine, disease progression is generally tracked through doctor's visits. Standardized testing is conducted, and patients are asked how they have been doing. The challenge here is that these diagnoses are only a snapshot. Conditions like Parkinson's and Multiple Sclerosis (MS) develop in stages with flares and times of remission. Patients can have good and bad days. However, the way patients perceive their condition often becomes very vague if remembered over several days. As a consequence, if patients see a doctor every couple of months, the diagnosis can sometimes be very imprecise. The progression of the disease is only partially documented. This is where the Floodlight app comes in. It uses smartphone sensors to measure and recognize the subtle changes in the motor function of MS patients. In addition, standard testing such as shape drawing can be done daily. Overall, this makes for a much more precise picture of the disease progression, which is documented accurately every day.

## Managing Privacy, Security, and Ethical Concerns

Digital health data, as we have seen, are one of the keys to a quality, high-performing, efficient, and fair healthcare system. Not collecting health data and not analyzing it for research, patient care, and the efficient use of resources would be an unparalleled waste and would serve neither patients nor society. Does this mean we all should collect data enthusiastically and carefully and make it available for secondary use out of pure self-interest?

Even if data will be an integral part of the healthcare sector of the future, we need clear rules for how to handle it, just as we have rules regarding information on consumer behavior and location data.

## Data Security

Especially because health data are so crucial and highly personal, data security and privacy are crucial. This is reflected in the occasional data security breaches in the healthcare sector that already occur today.

Because even if these breaches occur much more rarely than with other data (e.g., email passwords), we have nonetheless heard sobering reports from many countries such as England, Australia, Singapore, Germany, and South Africa. The most notable numbers are from the United States: Between 2009 and 2017, 1,863 breaches were reported. They affected more than 173 million people [15], 100 million in the context of health insurance data breaches, with the remaining ones mostly occurring with service providers in the healthcare sector as well as device manufacturers and suppliers.

The good news is that the secondary use of data is less about the identity of the individual than about databases that contain the aggregate data of many patients that can be searched for biological or medical insights. This gives the majority of affected actors – as well as the healthcare industry – a strong incentive to protect the identity of the individual and ensure that data is properly encrypted, anonymized, and aggregated. In the pharmaceutical industry and in clinical research, this procedure has been practiced for decades in handling patient data for clinical studies.

Nonetheless, in more than half of all successful attacks in the United States, healthcare companies are the victim. Why? The reason is unfortunately both simple and shocking. The going rate for stolen credit card information on the black market is currently 1 or 2 USD per card. Stolen medical records fetch about 10 times that amount. This is because medical records contain a person's social security number, health insurance number, and address as well as the credit card information. And this information allows people to sign up for multiple new credit cards, gain access to loans, buy narcotic drugs, and much more [16].

With the increased networking of medical devices, security becomes an even bigger issue. Today, about one in four clinical devices is on a wireless network. During an average hospital stay, a patient comes into contact with 10 devices. The frequently discussed fears about the manipulation of insulin pumps are not the real issue here, however – to do this, hackers would have to physically near to their victim. Criminal hackers will always focus on attacks they can launch from their secure basements while targeting hundreds of thousands of potential victims.

The problem of data security will probably never be solved completely. It is comparable to a race where the good guys always need to be a few steps ahead of the bad guys. How can patients, healthcare providers, medical device manufacturers, and insurance providers fend off the constant threat posed by hackers, software bugs, and inadequate risk management?

There are two primary approaches to this. The first is training, training, and more training! After all, users continue to be the biggest security gap. Everyone using information systems in the healthcare sector, from patients to insurance employees, needs to be aware of the potential dangers and correct behaviors. Many of the breaches occur simply because of unintentional mistakes made by employees, for instance by leaving their unencrypted laptop in the car or forgetting a folder with medical records on a commuter train. Others dispose of entire file cabinets and computer hard drives improperly or fall prey to increasingly cunning emails that trick them into disclosing passwords.

The second approach is a technical one. Not even 10 years ago, data security was a fringe topic in the manufacturing of medical devices. Once the development of a device or a software program was completed, it would then be made safe. Security was more of an afterthought, a patch to be applied later on. In the meantime, authorities have reacted with clearer regulations – the National Institute of Standards and Technology of the US Department of Commerce passed its regulatory framework in 2014, and the EU regulation on in vitro diagnostics now also contains data security rules. Data security must be a major focus from the very beginning. It needs to play a role in design, architecture, choice of technology, concept of use, and hardware and software development. Security experts need to be given a major, active role in every step of the development process [16].

### Privacy or the Right to Informational Self-determination

Security, privacy, and the right to informational self-determination are related, but not identical. Data security refers to the technical and organizational protection of data. Data stored on a computer need to be kept confidential and safe from theft. Health data must not be taken from the cloud by unauthorized users.

The right to informational self-determination, on the other hand, means that personal rights and freedoms are not infringed upon when a person's data are processed – and that this processing only occurs where it is lawful, legitimate, and ethically justifiable to do so. Data security is indispensable to implementing these controls. There can be no privacy without security.

The debate about privacy as a right originated in the Western world outside the healthcare sector. In their ground-breaking article "The Right to Privacy," which Samuel Warren and Louis Brandeis published in 1890 in the *Harvard Law Review*, the authors defined the right to privacy as "the right to be let alone." They were motivated by the rise of gossip columns in newspapers at the time that printed intimate details from the lives of celebrities, enriched with images from the then-new technology of photography. In it, they traced the development of the right to body, life, and property. Initially, legal remedies existed only for physical damage, bodily injury, or theft. Only later did threats and attacks on immaterial property become punishable offenses. Warren and Brandeis argued that information needed to be handled in the same manner to prevent both reputation damage as well as slander and libel.

We should not forget that the notion of universal individual privacy is a modern idea of the Western world. In other parts of the globe, the culture of privacy is not nearly as pronounced. However, we must acknowledge that even in the Western world, we lost control over our private data a long time ago, at least in part. Many of this personal information is already public. Those concerned just do not know who has it and what they are planning to do with it. At least that is what Michael Chertoff, the former US Secretary of Homeland Security, says. And he is right, of course, for instance regarding all the unencrypted data we send through the internet. In terms of privacy, the internet resembles a giant copy machine and eavesdropping device that anyone who has access to the right resources and knowledge can use. Once we have disclosed personal information without encryption by email, Facebook, or Twitter, we have lost control of that information [17].

Everybody needs privacy. This is why we have front doors, bathroom doors, bedroom doors, and curtains. As soon as people feel they are being observed, they are no longer free. Jeremy Bentham used this concept as early as 1790 when he devised a prison with a tower in the middle. The guards on the tower could observe everyone and everything. However, the tower was constructed in a manner that prevented prisoners from seeing whether they were being watched. This allowed a single guard to keep hundreds of prisoners in check. Bentham called his concept a "panopticon." George Orwell would later include it in his novel *1984*. The internet with its cookies and all its connected cameras and speakers also has the potential to become a panopticon of sorts.

But let's get back to the context of health. In addition to the data "onion" we have described, there is another data set that needs to be controlled: All the data trace users generate when, for instance, searching for information about depression on online forums, watching a video about HIV/AIDS, ordering certain types of medications, or simply doing a Google search on abortion.

Even if medical data are made available anonymously, the potential for re-identification lingers. This may be a fairly easy process, as was the case with former Massachusetts governor William Weld. Governor Weld had made the medical records of 135,000 state employees available for use by third parties in 1997. The data contained neither names nor social security numbers. Latanya Sweene at Harvard University was able to correlate this data set with a voter list for the town of Cambridge, Massachusetts, she had purchased for 20 USD. She was very quickly able to locate the governor's personal medical record, since he was also an employee of the state. Only six data sets in the patient files shared his birthday, only three were of male patients, and only one lived in Weld's neighborhood. She proceeded to mail that medical record to Governor Weld. The effects of this letter on the privacy regulations in the Health Insurance Portability and Accountability Act (HIPAA), which was passed in 2003, are described as significant [18, 19].

It is therefore crucial that we do not allow personal data to be accessed or used by third parties without a legal basis and without the consent of the data subject. Personal data refers to all information that can be used to identify the patient.

So how can we strengthen data security and privacy? First, we need to heighten awareness of potential misuse. Next, companies and organizations need to be held to clear rules. At the same time, we all need to assume personal responsibility and ignore questionable e-health offers. New digital technologies and the operation of health databases should be regulated appropriately, just as we already regulate the approval of drugs and the banking sector. The data subject's right to transparency and disclosure must be respected, including the right to deletion and the right to be forgotten, wherever and to the extent that privacy laws provide this option. And we should never again send anything without encryption, never have another unencrypted exchange of information. The privacy and security we are used to in online banking needs to become the standard in the healthcare sector as well.

### Ethical Challenges

The topic of privacy in the digital world raises many issues that come with hard-to-solve dilemmas and are therefore difficult to answer conclusively. This is why, in this section, it is our aim to approach the challenges of the digital healthcare sector with some ethical considerations. The principles of correct action in a medical context are the focus of the field of medical ethics.

English physician Thomas Percivals coined the term "medical ethics" around 1800, and today, ethical considerations in medicine are more relevant than ever [20], especially when it comes to topics such as abortion, end-of-life care, reproductive medicine, organ transplants, and gene therapies. At least in the Western world, the debate around medical ethics is mostly taking place within the framework of four established ethical and moral principles, which we would like to touch on briefly.

The first principle calls for patient autonomy on medical issues. Every patient must be allowed to make their own decisions about the goal, purpose, and administration of medical treatments. Prior to every intervention, the patient must be informed and capable of consenting. This principle endows patients not only with the prerogative to make decisions, but also with personal responsibility. In the world of digital health, this means that patients should be able to gather information and educate themselves. They should be provided with easy access to their health data and be given the opportunity for self-monitoring. At the same time, patients should be able to push back against unwanted surveillance. And finally, they should be able to determine who may view their personal data and who may not.

The second principle is "do no harm." It requires that medical treatments not harm the patient or others involved. Although this seems obvious, many exams, treatments, and procedures are associated with risks that can lead to damage. It is no coincidence that in many legal systems, medical interventions without consent are viewed as "medical battery." The benefits and risks must be weighed continually. In the world of digital health, the risk of harm can also be present when patients digitally self-diagnose. This can occur in the form of cyberchondria, as described earlier, or during self-monitoring, for instance if perfectionists start to track their sleep patterns and then fall prey to orthosomnia based on the constant fear of getting the wrong kind of or not enough sleep.

The welfare principle centers around a patient's life, health, and quality of life. It obliges caregivers to always act with the best of intentions and to apply the current standard of knowledge. If we follow this notion into the digital age, not only do healthcare providers have a duty to pursue continuing education, but also to obtain second opinions digitally. They should make decisions based on the entirety of available health data and, if warranted by the clinical picture, support their patients around the clock with the assistance of digital coaches and ensure their compliance with the prescribed treatment.

At this point at the latest, it becomes clear that this principle might conflict with a patient's autonomy. Is a doctor allowed, or perhaps even obliged, to verify a patient's compliance using the latest digital methods if a patient only has a realistic chance of survival with a high level of compliance? Can patients simply opt out of this monitoring? Who will cover the unnecessary cost of low patient compliance?

The fourth principle relates to equity. It demands the fair distribution of notoriously scarce health services. Identical cases should always receive identical treatment. This principle also states that the burden and the benefit of new or experimental treatments must be equally distributed among all societal groups

Digital technologies improve access to medical care and therefore bear out this principle. However, this is only true for regions and populations that are connected to the internet. Low-income populations, senior citizens, and the disabled, as well as people living in rural areas, are often at a disadvantage. At least that is what a study published in the renowned *New England Journal of Medicine* concludes [21]. In addition, dividing populations into Apple and Android users could contribute to a further division: Android users, who make up more than half the users in the United States, have a lower average income than those who use Apple products. And it is conceivable that the digital ecosystem provided by Apple systematically produces better medical solutions, especially due to the very advanced access that Apple has to the innermost layers of the data "onion," the EMR. That fact that doctors can now bill for the time they spend organizing and interpreting data from medical devices such as blood pressure monitors, electrocardiographs, and glucose monitors has accelerated this development.

On the other hand, there is the question of whether it is fair and in keeping with this principle if only a small part of the population provides clinical data for the purpose of gaining knowledge that everyone benefits from. Would it not be more just if all members of society contributed to the generation of this data? If the data of all citizens were automatically available in a secure, aggregated, and non-traceable way for purposes such as research and the quest for effective treatments? Just as with organ donation today, where citizens are automatically listed as donors in some countries and have to fill out an organ donor card in others, we will need to debate the question of opting in and opting out of the sharing of health data.

### Do We Need a "New Deal on Data"?

Different cultures take different views of these issues, especially when it comes to ethics and privacy. Western cultures are pursuing different regulatory, entrepreneurial, and personal paths than Eastern cultures. They not only look back on a different history, but also have different individual and collective expectations, values, goals, and norms. But from Asia to Australia to Africa, from Europe to North and South America, they all have one thing in common: They have recognized the value of health data and everyone is trying to do justice to this value in the context of their specific worldview.

In 2008, MIT professor Sandy Pentland presented his – admittedly very Western-centric – view of the handling of RWD at the World Economic Forum in Switzerland [22]. His "New Deal on Data" can be directly applied to secondary health data and may be seen as an imperative to answer key questions surrounding privacy. Pentland assumes that the benefit of data drawn from the real world must be weighed against the danger of its misuse. Therefore, the New Deal on Data would need to strike a balance between those providing the data and those benefiting and deriving value from these data.

But what exactly would such a "New Deal" look like? Pentland rightfully wants citizens to own their data – like a vault you can open and close, as well as the option of removing personal data from databases. Technically and legally, this is almost not doable given the current circumstances – often, data *have* to be stored without a right to request its deletion, such as the data stored by tax authorities. However, one thing is clear: This will require rules that clarify access and usage, protect the privacy of the individual, and generate trust. It will require guidelines that allow for and/or promote the use of anonymized aggregate data for the common good.

Such pillars and guidelines are being created by countries from Estonia to New Zealand. They are being implemented by companies that range from small spin-offs and health co-ops such as Midata.coop and Healthbank.coop (both based in Switzerland) to large health and technology companies such as Novartis, Apple, and Google. Doctors' offices, pharmacies, and integrated health care and insurance companies, such as Ping An, are playing a role as well.

In the end, the deciding factor will be whether and whom patients trust. They are in the driver's seat and will decide whether data donation will become the new blood drive. It is important to be aware that the medical treatment we receive today has benefited from the insights gained from the data "donated" by previous generations of patients. And this trust is something the industry players listed above need to earn by ensuring the lawful, appropriate, transparent, and ethically impeccable processing of personal data in all cases.

Chapter 8

# Value-based Medicine

*The main theses of this chapter:*

- Digitalization permits well-organized collaboration between patient and selected healthcare providers. It fosters integrated healthcare systems. The glue that bonds the healthcare providers together in such a system takes the shape of the electronic medical records that are managed by the orchestrator, for example, a health insurer, the state, or even the patient.
- Digitalization leads to greater transparency concerning who does what within the healthcare system. It sheds light on costs, quality, and core competencies and reduces misuse and waste.
- Digitalization permits the objective measurement of lifestyle. As a result, programs that reward a healthy lifestyle will become an established standard. In this respect, healthy people, the chronically ill, employers, insurers, and legislators are all pulling in the same direction.
- Digitalization makes it easier to measure the success of treatment, advancing the cause of value-based remuneration.

At a healthcare conference in New York, Jeff Immelt, the former CEO of General Electric, forecast that healthcare costs in the United States would soon reach 25% of gross domestic product. The United States already has the world's most costly healthcare system, with 18% of the nation's value added being spent on health care – almost 1 USD in five. Nevertheless, as we have already seen in the case of David Maldonado, even many middle-class families are barely able to afford health insurance. According to the United States Census Bureau, in 2018 almost 28 million people had no health insurance in what is one of the richest countries on earth.

So how can we contain the escalating costs? For Jeff Immelt, incentive systems provide one of the key levers. As things stand, he said, failure and unnecessary treatment get rewarded. We need a new compensation model in our healthcare system, Immelt argued. The healthcare providers – doctors, hospitals, and pharmaceutical companies – need to be called to account more effectively. And they

**The Digital Pill: What Everyone Should Know about the Future of Our Healthcare System, 121–133**
**doi:10.1108/978-1-78756-675-020211008**

should only be paid for their services if these services also lead to an improvement in the patient's health [1].

In the Swiss healthcare system, doctors use the billing codes defined in the TARMED tariff system to charge for their services: M2, TP, TPW AL, 001, 00.0141. How transparent is that? These codes appear on Swiss doctors' bills, and they are incomprehensible. Two out of three people in Switzerland say they do not really understand their doctors' bills [2]. Each code stands for a service provided at the doctor's office. As in most other countries, doctors are paid in line with the services they provide. These can include diagnoses, consultations, various examinations, prescribing medication, and much more besides. Whether or not these services actually improve the patient's health does not necessarily affect the remuneration. When there are several options, a complicated course of treatment can prove more profitable than a simple one that would nevertheless have the desired effect.

### GoodRx

But back to the United States: Doug Hirsch is a tall guy with a beard. It is hard to say how old he is. He is casually dressed in jeans and sneakers. You cannot tell by looking at him that he co-founded the most popular medical app in the United States and continues to manage it successfully. Back in the day, Doug was one of the first employees at Facebook; today he is co-CEO of the GoodRx startup that operates an app which helps patients to obtain prescription drugs at the lowest possible price.

Here's how the story of Doug Hirsch and *GoodRx* began a few years back: Doug went to the pharmacy to pick up a drug the doctor had prescribed for him and he was in for a shock: The drug was priced at 500 USD. Doug did not know what to do: Should he really go ahead and buy the drug? He almost walked away without it. Let's assume for a moment that he had not bought it: Then his visit to the doctor would have cost money but without the prescribed drug it would, of course, bring no benefit. Doug Hirsch turned this typical dilemma into his personal business model. Fifty percent of all drugs prescribed in the United States are not picked up from the pharmacy by patients. The most common reason is cost – the high costs that patients still have to pay themselves, despite their health insurance.

As things stand today in terms of remuneration, doctors have little or no incentive to prescribe less expensive drugs that are equally effective. And in many cases, they do not even learn whether or not patients pick up their prescriptions. If doctors' remuneration were tied to whether or not the patient's health improves after a visit to the doctor, then doctor and patient would work together to find an effective and financially viable solution. Even after organ transplants, only 55% of all patients in the United States actually collect their medication from the pharmacy. By failing to do so of course, they increase the risk of their body rejecting the new organ. Imagine the awful state of affairs if a successful organ transplant that cost thousands of dollars and was designed to save a life were really to fail due to the patient's inability to afford the necessary drugs. It soon becomes clear that, even setting aside the human tragedy, existing performance-based incentives are often not cost-effective. In the new digital world of health care, there is already a name for the incentive system of the future: "Value-based medicine" and "outcome-based medicine" are common terms in the vocabulary of many digital healthcare startups.

So how can technology help create the right incentives for doctors, hospitals, and pharmaceutical companies, as well as for patients, in the interests of the best possible medical outcome? In what follows, we present three patterns that we have repeatedly encountered: data-driven healthcare networks, Lifestyle reward programs, and Pay for performance.

## Data-driven Healthcare Networks

The new digital world of health care creates transparency, and this transparency can form the foundations of a healthcare network, in which efficient providers are rewarded and inefficient providers penalized. This topic is particularly relevant in the United States, where the fees for medical services are largely unregulated and can be set by the respective providers of these services. This explains why the cost of identical medical treatment can vary dramatically from one provider to the next. Why, for example, does a cesarean section (C-section) cost more than 20,000 USD in San Francisco but only just over 4,000 USD in Texas [3]? Even within the same region, there can be substantial differences in price for the same medical services. Let's stay with the C-section: In Knoxville, Tennessee, a city in the Bible Belt with a population of 200,000, it costs between 3,000 and 5,000 USD. That equates to a 66% difference in cost for an identical service within the same city. This would not be so bad if providers published their prices. But they do not. Comparing prices is a complex and time-consuming process.

## Oscar Health

"In the United States, patients are not normally aware of how much they will pay for a course of treatment. They feel out of their depth and insecure," confirms Thorsten Wirkes. For the last five years and more Wirkes has been working for Oscar Health, where he is responsible for Medicare Advantage, which concerns itself with state-regulated insurance policies for retirees. Oscar Health was founded in 2012 and insures patients in the United States. The company aims to take out-of-their-depth, insecure patients by the hand and guide them through the healthcare system. What primarily sets Oscar Health apart from conventional insurers is the way, in which the insured can interact with the insurer. Instead of being kept waiting in long call center queues, Oscar members can speak with a customer advisor at a single click on the Oscar app, while five clicks or so will connect them to a doctor around the clock via telemedicine or let them call the insurer's concierge team who will help find the right doctor.

A concierge team is made up of customer advisors and medical specialists, each team being responsible for a specific number of members. "For instance, we have one team that only looks after patients on the Upper West Side of Manhattan. For our members that's great because this team is intimately familiar with the doctors, pharmacies, and hospitals in that area and can provide genuinely personalized advice," says Thorsten Wirkes, speaking in one of the bright and modern conference rooms at the Oscar office in Soho, New York.

To stay cost-effective, Oscar has established a network of doctors and hospitals with whom the company collaborates. "In the United States, the incentive systems for doctors, insurers, and patients are often counterproductive. This leads to high costs. Instead of collaborating with as many doctors and hospitals as possible, at Oscar we aim to work only with the best and to network with them. We treat hospitals fairly and pay them well. But by collaborating very closely with a limited number of partners and defining efficient processes together, we are able to work cost-effectively," says Wirkes.

In addition, Oscar prioritizes providing cost transparency for its members. If a member reports in the app that they are feeling dizzy, they find that with these symptoms they can either consult a general practitioner or a neurologist and the Oscar app indicates the approximate cost in each case. The Oscar algorithm bases its cost estimates on the thousands of doctors' bills that the insurer receives every day. The insured can also compare the projected costs and the patient ratings of two different general practitioners and then select the cheaper of the two or the one with the better ratings. When the patient has reached a decision, they can use the app to make an appointment.

As Oscar's smart insurance policies show, good medical care does not have to be expensive. These policies encourage the patient to first consult a general practitioner before calling in an expensive specialist. Oscar members can go to a general practitioner free of charge. On the medication front, Oscar also provides incentives to avoid using expensive branded products and buy cheaper generic medication instead. Oscar also wants members to consult a doctor without delay if they present serious symptoms. Delays in seeking treatment can often lead to drastic increases in healthcare costs in the long term. Which is why Oscar tries to keep the barriers to a visit to the doctor low.

Through smart solutions like these, Oscar manages to offer its members the best health care at a good price. So it's not surprising that 40% of Oscar members first consult the app or the concierge team before they see a doctor. "Our members trust us because we offer solutions that add value for them. Instead of asking their friends or colleagues, they turn to us," says Wirkes. "And that's something we're proud of."

Consulting the app or the concierge service can also prevent incurring costs for an unnecessary trip to the emergency room. In the United States, the average visit to the emergency room costs around 2,000 USD. Estimates indicate that 38 billion USD in unnecessary costs are incurred annually in this area [4, 5]. An analysis conducted by Oscar reveals that around one half of all emergency room visits are unnecessary. As Thorsten Wirkes says: "Through the app we have been able to persuade 21 percent of all patients who wanted to head for an emergency room to choose a less expensive alternative." Patients often find telemedicine or outpatient clinics a source of help.

In the case of chronic illness, Oscar also uses technology to provide good, less expensive health care. "All calls to the concierge team and all bills are analyzed systematically with the aid of artificial intelligence," says Wirkes. If, for example, a patient picks up insulin at the pharmacy but does not have a primary care physician that they regularly visit, they get a call from the Oscar team, who explain how important it is to have blood sugar levels regularly checked by a general practitioner and help the member find a suitable doctor nearby. "We network closely with our members but also with the doctors. The doctors ensure that patients with chronic illnesses are well looked after. This helps to prevent follow-on costs."

Ultimately, all data that Oscar generates through the many touchpoints with the insured, the doctors, and the pharmacists, go into the electronic medical records. As Wirkes says: "We don't want to create data silos." Data generate the most value when it provides a holistic picture of an individual. If a patient has spoken with an Oscar doctor on the weekend through the telemedicine service, the physician responsible for them when they next visit the Cleveland Clinic can see at a glance what the Oscar doctor advised them to do. The patient's medical record also contains all lab results and details of the prescribed medication.

What does the future hold for Oscar Health? Thorsten Wirkes is convinced that Oscar has so far attained just 10% of its potential. At present, 250,000 US citizens are insured with Oscar and clearly very happy with the service provided. The aim of company founders Mario Schlosser, Joshua Kushner, and Kevin Nazemi is to introduce Oscar to everyone in the United States. So far, however, the startup still has to show a profit – although one reason for this is that it has prioritized strong growth.

### Collective Health

Collective Health is another startup that is using a data-driven healthcare network to boost efficiency. In the United States, companies with more than

50 employees are required to offer health insurance to their full-time employees and their families. Companies have been complaining about a substantial rise in healthcare costs for years now. This has led increasing numbers of employers to look for alternatives, which generally means terminating their agreements with conventional health insurance companies. Many companies develop their own plans for the health insurance of their workforce. This is where firms like Collective Health come in; they put together insurance packages that are tailored to the respective companies.

Collective Health was founded in 2013 with the purpose of offering companies with their own health insurance plans a platform on which to manage all aspects of the insurance process. The platform also provides employees with lots of information to help ensure they get fast and easy access to treatment in the event of illness. And indeed, a comparative study covering several years shows that companies can save substantial amounts by offering their workforce their own company insurance plans.

Collective Health helps its customers set incentives in such a way that their employees utilize the most economical but effective medical services. In much the same way as at Oscar Health, the app tells the user in advance what a visit to the doctor will cost. This leads to savings not only for the employees, who reduce their deductible, but also for the company.

Evangeline Mendiola is a manager at Zendesk, a Collective Health customer. She knows from personal experience that the changeover from a health insurance company to a proprietary corporate insurance plan represents a huge challenge for many companies. You need companies like Collective Health, she says, to provide the IT platform that lets you handle all kinds of insurance transactions. Zendesk's employees love the new system, she adds, because there are no high hurdles to clear to access it and in the event of illness the associated app guarantees the best possible health care.

### Amino

Another startup that specializes in the smart analysis of medical data is Amino. As with many healthcare startups, this one too originated with a very personal experience: A good and caring doctor saved the life of 19-year-old David Vivero, who had just begun his studies at Harvard. A blood test showed that David was suffering from a rare hereditary disease called hemochromatosis or iron overload. The disease leads to an accelerated rate of intestinal iron absorption, which can cause serious liver and heart disease as well as infertility. Thanks to his attentive doctor, in David's case the disease was caught at an early stage and he suffered no lasting consequences. However, he soon discovered to his cost that, because of this pre-existing condition, many health insurance providers now refused to cover him. This was what led David Vivero to join with three friends and found Amino in 2015.

David was not the only one facing the problem of finding affordable health insurance. In recent years, deductibles for those insured have risen six times faster than incomes. So Amino is working to bring transparency to what is an opaque and expensive US healthcare world and thereby save money for those insured. To this end, the Amino team, who previously acquired experience in one of the leading online real estate portals, spent two years aggregating more than 9 billion health insurance claims. Amino's strongpoint is big data analysis, and this enables its database to accurately predict what a patient's co-payment will be for a specific treatment, or which local doctor treats a certain disease most frequently.

"The special advantage of the Amino database is that it is hyper-specific. We can break down the data into the tiniest details, so that each user gets truly personalized recommendations," says David Vivero. So far, Amino has listed more than 800 illnesses in its database, so that even patients with rare diseases can locate a specialist in their vicinity.

But what sets Amino apart from conventional aggregation portals? The team has undertaken not to accept any advertising or paid services going forward. The choice of recommended doctor is entirely objective and based exclusively on the symptoms and wishes of the patient. After initially offering this service directly to the user free of charge, the startup now offers a fee-based service to companies who in turn can provide the Amino app to their employees. In the comprehensive Amino database, the employees can search for the best doctor for a specific illness and identify the clinic that will offer them the best price for their treatment. When they have found the doctor they want, they can book an appointment using the app. But it is not only the company's employees who benefit. Amino also promises that employers' healthcare spend will fall dramatically. In its advertising, Amino claims that a company with 1,000 employees can save more than half a million dollars per year by using its services.

The latest innovation from the Amino team is a proprietary health savings card, launched in 2018. In the United States, employees who have health insurance plans with a high deductible can make tax-free provision for their private healthcare costs. To make this option easy to use for its customers, Amino now offers a debit card with which they can pay their deductible and benefit from the tax break.

In Europe too, new players who use data to build efficient healthcare networks are entering the market. In Switzerland, for example, health insurer Sanitas has been collaborating with Medbase since 2019, while in Germany, digital health insurance provider Ottonova was founded in 2017.

## Lifestyle Reward Programs

Health care is not the exclusive preserve of the medical profession or pharmaceutical companies. Every individual can make their own impact. The risk of suffering from a chronic illness can be approximately halved by adopting a healthy lifestyle. This is where the second mechanism within value-based medicine comes into play: Lifestyle reward programs. These programs are normally created by health insurance companies to motivate their customers to adopt a healthy lifestyle.

For example, CSS, the biggest health insurer in Switzerland, offers those it insures around 150 Swiss francs a year in discounts on their premium if they reach the target of 10,000 steps a day. To qualify for this discount, customers must download the CSS app and connect it to their fitness tracker. For every day on which they reach their target, they get a 40-Rappen credit from CSS (1 Swiss franc = 100 Rappen). If they reach at least 7,500 steps, they get 20 Rappen.

Oscar Health also offers a lifestyle reward program through which those it insures can earn up to 100 USD. In this case, they are not motivated to hit a fixed step count, but are assigned dynamic goals. If an insured person is more of a couch potato, their initial target will be a relatively low number of steps that is then gradually increased. Because consumer research shows that goals are at their most motivating when they are challenging but seem attainable.

Why are health insurance companies so keen to get their customers up off the comfy couch? Studies conducted in the United States show that just 30 minutes' exercise three times a week cuts the costs per patient by an average of 30% [6]. So both the insurers and the insured stand to benefit from lifestyle reward programs.

### Walgreens

The US drugstore and pharmacy chain Walgreens also offer this type of program. For Walgreens, it is important to be perceived as the go-to provider in healthcare matters. In a Walgreens store in the United States, people can buy not only medications but also vitamins and supplements, personal care products, and a basic assortment of grocery products. Walgreens aims to set itself apart from the competition by offering a "Healthy Choices" program that encourages people to adopt a healthy lifestyle. Customers can take part in health challenges that last four weeks. They are then challenged, for example, to walk a certain number of steps or exercise several times a week. Their participation is tracked either by means of manual input or by linking the Walgreens app to a fitness tracker or a smartphone. Customers can also earn points by healthy eating or getting enough sleep.

People with chronic illnesses are encouraged to check their blood pressure or blood sugar level at regular intervals and awarded points for doing so. This is made possible by smart gauges that are connected to the Walgreens app by means of Wi-Fi or Bluetooth. The Walgreens program is also linked to the company's customer loyalty card, so that additional points can be scored by shopping at Walgreens. Points can be exchanged for coupons. Walgreens aims to be perceived by customers as a partner who supports them in their healthy behavior, as was reflected in the company's longtime advertising slogan: "Walgreens, at the corner of happy and healthy."

At the University of St Gallen's Institute for Customer Insight, we too are working on designing lifestyle reward programs in such a way that people remain motivated in the long term. Because all the current programs have the same drawback: They rely heavily on monetary incentives, and these incentives have an extrinsic effect – an impact that comes from the outside. Psychology teaches us, however, that extrinsic incentives undermine people's intrinsic – natural – motivation. Or to put it simply: over time the prospect of a reward will displace our self-motivation.

This is readily visible in children. Take, for example, 14-year-old Ricky, who lives near London. In his spare time, he likes to play football. He's a good student; his favorite subjects are biology and math. When Ricky comes home from a long day at school, he flings down his backpack and sports bag in the hall. His room is decorated with heaps of clothes, books, and magazines. Cleaning up is not one of Ricky's strongpoints. As his parents are out at work all day and have had enough of the mess to which they come home, they decide to pay Ricky two pounds a week for keeping the house tidy. Ricky signs on to the deal and for a few weeks the house looks much tidier. His parents are relieved. But then comes the summer break and Ricky has nothing to do all day except play football with his friends. His mother, Lydia, sees no reason to go on paying him two pounds a week for tidying up when he now has plenty of time at his disposal. The outcome? A house that looks even messier than ever. Ricky refuses to tidy up without the two pounds. Why should he? He has learned that tidying up is such an unpleasant task that you have to be paid for doing it. Any intrinsic motivation that he may have had has vanished.

When we transpose these findings to the incentives paid by insurers for exercise, it soon becomes clear that they need to proceed with caution. A study by an American researcher shows that when extrinsic incentives are applied, exercise is perceived as something negative and feels like work [7]. So any incentive programs should ideally trigger intrinsic motivation.

Today there are many different players on the lifestyle reward market, with even governments getting involved. In Canada, the Ministry of Health of the Province of British Columbia launched the Carrot Rewards app as part of a public–private partnership. Citizens could earn consumer reward points by playing sports or exercising more than they would otherwise do and then exchange these points for discounts at movie theaters or grocery stores, for example. The app proved very popular and was used by more than 1 million people. However, government funding expired in 2019 and the app is no longer available. In South Africa, the Discovery insurance group offers a Vitality Reward app. Users can not only qualify for discounts on healthy purchases, but also earn bonus points when they undergo medical screening. *Dacadoo* in Switzerland, *Yodo Run* in China, and *Nandoo* in India are further startups aiming to corner a share of this growing market.

## Pay for Performance

The third approach in value-based medicine is Pay for performance, or in other words, only paying for services that demonstrably have the desired effect.

This calls for a new mindset in the healthcare sector. Because right now, we reward the treatment provided and not its efficacy. Treatment is paid for by the health insurer regardless of whether or not it has the desired therapeutic effect for the individual patient. There is a dilemma here: On the one hand, this remuneration model appears fair because the person providing the service expends their time and resources and should be compensated accordingly. But on the other hand, this form of remuneration also encourages the performance of as many services as possible, even if the medical benefits are limited.

In this context, a major debate has been in progress for some time now over how to assess the value of medical treatment and medication. Because in almost every healthcare system on earth, prices for medical services are not set arbitrarily, but negotiated and agreed centrally – at national or regional level. Even in the United States, where competition between insurers is at its fiercest, major insurers have a major say in setting prices. The fact is, though, that the actual value of what is provided is hard to quantify. One prominent institution in the healthcare community is the UK-based National Institute for Health and Care Excellence, which bases its calculations on what it calls "quality-adjusted life years." Basically, this means that a medical intervention is not considered cost-effective if it costs more than 30,000 pounds sterling per quality-adjusted life year gained. Setting a price on life in this way is, at least in some societies, highly controversial. And yet there are many different factors that can certainly be taken into account in assessing the value of medicine: Are we talking about a major innovation that represents a quantum leap in the treatment of a disease? Does it allow someone to return to or remain at work or care for family members? Does the intervention take place early or late in the progression of the disease? And finally – and ultimately unanswerable as a rule in the context of severe illnesses – what is the value to the individual of prolonging their life, gaining time to attend grandchildren's high school graduations or undertake one more journey of a lifetime?

New forms of treatment for cancer mean that the debate over pay for performance models is highly topical. For the last few years, conventional chemotherapy and radiation therapy have been joined as standard approaches in the field of oncology by targeted treatment, in which drug molecules dock directly with tumor receptors. With personalized treatment of this kind, it must first be determined whether or not the specific receptor is actually present in the patient. Another new arrival on the cancer treatment scene is immunotherapy. Instead of attacking the cancer cells directly, immunotherapy stimulates the body's immune system to fight cancer. Oncologists are pinning great hopes on these new forms of treatment. They can be used to successfully treat patients who would otherwise have little chance of survival. These innovations also underline the fact that individual factors specific to each patient are becoming more and more important for the successful application of medication and forms of treatment – factors such as the mutated genome of the tumor, the presence of certain proteins, or the patient's DNA.

Medical jargon refers here to ALK and EGFR mutations, HER2 overexpression, or BRAF pathways. The abbreviations stand for parameters that indicate the likelihood of a medication being effective or not. They are referred to as biomarkers.

Often, however, there are no direct indications of whether or not a form of treatment has been or will be effective. As a rule, recovery, improvement, or additional life expectancy are gradual processes. Digitized health data enable us to evaluate the efficacy of treatments even after the event with no major investment in terms of human resources or capital.

In the case of immunotherapy, for example, we know that depending on the type of cancer, the approach is effective for between 20% and 80% of patients and very expensive. Treatment can cost approximately 150,000 euros per annum [8]. In many cases, remuneration systems based on pay for performance could represent a value-based form of compensation.

The digital healthcare revolution is spurring on the debate over pay for performance models by facilitating better assessment of the efficacy of a particular treatment. Today there are already growing numbers of pricing models, in which drugs are only paid for in full if the treatment has the desired effect. The pharmaceutical company Roche, for example, has been testing such models for years, not least in Italy where, thanks to the existence of a cancer database, it is also possible to determine whether or not a particular treatment is really proving effective for the patient.

### Omada Health

Startup Omada Health has also adopted the pay for performance principle, although in this case in the battle with obesity. Some 85 million people in the United States suffer from obesity, linked with a substantial risk of developing type 2 diabetes. There is no secret about the remedy: Be careful what you eat and drink, and get much more exercise. However, many people find it very difficult to change their established behaviors. Omada Health has developed a digital preventive health program to help obese patients.

The program comprises an app, a preconfigured scale, support from a health coach, a peer group, and lessons in health literacy. Through the ongoing interaction, the system learns which tips and insights work best for the patient. At the same time, the Omada system can tell where and when someone is more open for advice.

The company's business model is particularly interesting: Omada Health offers its preventive health package to companies that want to encourage their employees to adopt a healthy lifestyle. Omada agrees on a basic fee with the customer, which is then multiplied by the weight loss of the users. So if the basic fee is, say, 10 USD and an employee loses 5% of their weight within a predefined period, Omada receives 50 USD. This model also makes financial sense for the employer: A person with type 2 diabetes will generate healthcare costs of around 10,000 USD a year. As even a 5% reduction in weight cuts the risk of developing this disease during your lifetime by 70%, the deal is well worthwhile for all concerned.

### Spark Therapeutics

Another field in which pay for performance models will play a central role is gene therapy, where scientists try to combat genetic diseases by inserting healthy genes into a patient's DNA. One company that is focused on gene therapy is Spark Therapeutics. Its purpose is illustrated by the story of Caroline Carper. When Caroline was 10 years old, for the first time ever she saw rain falling.

> I was at school and suddenly it started to pour. I was thrilled and asked my friend what it was. She couldn't believe that I'd never seen the rain before. Back then a whole new world opened up for me.

Like her younger brother, Caroline Carper suffered from an extremely rare genetic disease, in which the retina becomes more and more dysfunctional. It is called Leber's Congenital Amaurosis. There are only some 6,000 cases in the United States and Europe, and most of those affected are children, who become almost completely blind at an early age. For many years, the disease was considered incurable. In 2017, Spark Therapeutics launched its Luxturna gene therapy on the US market.

Luxturna is the first gene therapy to be approved by the US Food and Drug Administration – a revolutionary new category of medication. Instead of merely alleviating the symptoms of a disease, gene therapy endeavors to eliminate its underlying genetic origin by replacing the defective or missing gene with a healthy one. It is hoped that it will prove possible to cure certain genetic diseases with a single dose of medication.

This turns the existing pricing model for medication on its head: Instead of pricing a drug based on several months or even a lifetime of treatment, in the case of gene therapy for rare diseases, the single dose required must be priced very high indeed in order to repay the investment in the necessary research. So at first glance, gene therapies like Luxturna look like the world's most expensive medication. In the United States, the dose required to heal both eyes costs 850,000 USD. Compared to the cost of lifelong treatment of a person who has lost their sight, including care and loss of productivity, however, such prices appear in a different light and are reimbursed accordingly. Spark also negotiates compensation models, in which insurers receive discounts or refunds if the success of treatment decreases again over time.

Chapter 9

# Digital Drug Development

*The main theses of this chapter:*

- Digital health data in the form of "real-world data" (RWD) collected from everyday clinical practice are a multiplier and of immeasurable value for drug development. In a well-designed healthcare system, all digital health data are made available to researchers in the form of anonymous RWD.
- Access to health data is more important than ownership, and data quality trumps quantity.
- Digitalization simplifies and accelerates patient recruitment while enhancing the accessibility of clinical studies. It also drastically reduces the duration of the drug development process.
- Any kind of robust data can become part of a virtual clinical study. RWD is starting to replace control groups in clinical studies and complement data derived from clinical studies.
- The time of "one size fits all" drugs is drawing to an end. Data-based drug personalization improves efficacy and minimizes side effects.
- Digital expertise is a new core competency pharmaceutical companies can no longer do without.

The development of new drugs still plays a major role in medical progress and will continue to do so despite the impact of preventive care and the more effective use of resources. We already elaborated on the revolutionary cervical cancer vaccine as an example of preventive medicine in Chapter 3 of this book. This vaccine, developed by German physician Harald zur Hausen, prevents infections with the human papillomavirus (HPV), which causes cervical cancer. Thanks to this vaccine, a reduction in new cases is already measurable. The cancer immunotherapies presented earlier in this book have also wrought ground-breaking change by providing ways to treat late-stage melanoma and lung tumors. Both Harald zur Hausen and immune therapy pioneers James P. Allison and Tasuko Honjo were awarded the Nobel Prize in Medicine. But what is even more important is that these innovations in medicine are changing the fate of millions [1].

**The Digital Pill: What Everyone Should Know about the Future of
Our Healthcare System, 135–152**
Copyright © 2021 by Emerald Publishing Limited
All rights of reproduction in any form reserved
doi:10.1108/978-1-78756-675-020211009

Nevertheless, in many areas, medical research is still only scratching the surface. Here, digitalization can help us achieve long-anticipated advances in knowledge and discover new therapies. Every year, 10 million people develop Alzheimer's disease, and the number of cases rises sharply as the population ages. To date, there are no drugs that might prevent or slow the development of the neuro-degenerative disease. When writer Kate Neuman opened up about her mother's Alzheimer's disease in a stunning article in the *New York Times*, it raised public awareness about the tragic nature of the disease. Initially, Kate's mom Nancy just became increasingly forgetful. And then the day came when Kate found her mother confused in her New York City apartment: both the oven and a burner were on, even though Nancy did not cook. Kate was shocked and brought her mother to live with her and her family in Massachusetts. One day, Kate's mom told her she couldn't remember how they'd met. That was the point where it became clear that she had lost her mother to the disease [2]. How digitalization can contribute to diagnosing and treating of Alzheimer's patients is something we will cover later in this chapter.

In the field of oncology, on the other hand, digitalization promises to facilitate rapid acceleration along the current path – one of ever-increasing personalization of cancer treatment. Whereas a good 20 years ago, cancer was considered a uniform disease, experts today view it as an assortment of more than 250 different types of entities that have significant differences on a molecular level. Accordingly, pharmaceutical and biotech companies have developed treatments that, for instance, dock to specific proteins frequently found in various types of cancer or that target tumors with a highly specific gene mutation. But this personalization comes at a price – drug research and development are becoming incredibly complex.

Today, technology companies are tackling this challenge alongside traditional pharmaceutical firms. Thus, Apple has stated that one of its business goals is to simplify the process of drug development, which is protracted and can last 10–15 years.

The process of drug development is divided into three stages [3]. In the first stage of early, preclinical research and development, potential active ingredients are identified and tested in test tubes ("in vitro") (Fig. 9.1). This can take up to six years. The first step is to identify a need, for instance, a disease for which there are currently no satisfactory medicines or where the drugs available are associated with severe adverse effects. Next, researchers attempt to understand the cause of the disease on a molecular level and identify a mechanism of action and/or a target for the active ingredient to be developed, such as a receptor on the surface

**Fig. 9.1.**   *Stages of Drug Development.* **Source:** *Hoffmann – La Roche (2019)*

of a tumor cell. Once molecules that meet these requirements have been discovered, their efficacy and tolerability are tested in vitro as well as in animals ("in vivo"). On average, only 1 of 5,000 active ingredients tested in this early stage of development is later approved [4].

Once an active ingredient is identified as a potential candidate, it enters the second stage of development, which involves clinical testing in humans. This stage takes approximately seven years and is extremely costly. Clinical studies are strictly regulated. The competent regulatory body as well as an external ethics committee must give permission before this stage can even begin. In a three-phase process, the active ingredient is now first tested in a small group of healthy volunteers to find a suitable dose (phase 1) and then (phase 2) tested for efficacy, drug interactions, and tolerability. Later, in randomized clinical trials (phase 3), the active ingredient is tested against the current standard of care or a placebo in larger groups of several thousand patients, who are allocated randomly in a lottery-type system. Neither the patients nor the administering physicians know who will receive the new active ingredient and who will receive the placebo or the currently approved standard of care.

If a candidate drug passes clinical testing, the third stage – drug approval – begins. In this stage, the results of the clinical studies are submitted to the regulatory authorities who will evaluate the risk–benefit ratio. They will focus both on therapeutic efficacy as well as on the side effects documented in the study. If a drug is approved, its efficacy and safety will often be monitored in an additional observational study after approval. In this type of study, the drug is generally reviewed in a diverse group of participants. These studies also evaluate combination therapies, where the drug is administered in combination with other drugs.

How can digital technology help accelerate this protracted development process without embracing higher risks? This chapter presents four examples – exciting companies and startups – that are all stepping up to meet this challenge.

## Computer-aided Drug Discovery

Computer-assisted methods can support every aspect of the drug discovery process, especially the identification of genes or proteins that are the root cause of diseases. This section focuses on examples of how new active ingredients can be identified using automation and artificial intelligence (AI).

Before clinical studies in humans can begin, you first need a promising candidate. But how do you identify molecules that could potentially have a highly specific pharmaceutical effect? This has traditionally been – and still is – the job of hundreds of chemists and biologists who would sometimes spend years doing research in the laboratories of biotech and pharmaceutical companies. But now, the digital revolution has also reached this sector.

Lab robots were widespread well before so much of society became digitalized. Pharmaceutical companies have been using robots for many years, primarily to automate laboratory processes. Robots are extremely well suited to perform repetitive tasks that require the utmost precision. Sometimes, these machine-based assistants work alongside human chemists in a collaboration referred to as "collaborative robots" or "cobots" [5].

Whereas the first generation of robots still consisted of analog and mostly mechanical devices, they have now become increasingly intelligent. Today, robots not only replace humans in carrying out mechanical processes, but also perform cognitive and research tasks. In fact, the University of Cambridge developed the lab bots Adam & Eve specifically for this purpose. These two robots are capable of developing hypotheses, testing them, interpreting the results of their experiments, and adapting the hypotheses accordingly. Adam & Eve perform hypothesis-driven drug research significantly faster and with much greater precision than humans. In early 2015, the team at the University of Cambridge published a study describing how Eve had discovered drug candidates for the treatment of malaria as well as the less well-known tropical disease chagas and African sleeping sickness. Year after year, these tropical diseases afflict millions. However, since they only occur in less economically developed countries, developing drugs to combat them is not very lucrative for companies – despite the fact that, according to Steve Oliver at the University of Cambridge, the cause of the disease is known. Lab bot Eve has now helped accelerate drug development and make it less costly.

First, Eve tested a list of potential chemical molecules and conducted a series of experiments to determine how the respective molecules reacted to the proteins of the disease-causing parasite. In addition, the robot tested the reaction of the molecules to human proteins. Whenever Eve found a molecule that attacked the parasite but was safe for humans, it would then search for similar molecules that might also have a beneficial effect. Thus, the robot learned more with every test and finally found what it was looking for: TNP-470 is a molecule that was already being studied in several oncology studies. Eve found that it also works against the parasite that causes malaria. The results that Eve produced are so far based only on in vitro studies. But if the effect is confirmed in clinical studies, Eve may well have improved the lives of millions of people [6]. Digitalization in drug discovery therefore means that algorithms increasingly enhance and sometimes partially take over the work of chemists. This saves both time and money.

Over the past years, large pharmaceutical companies have launched many innovative work processes and projects that use digital tools or algorithms for drug discovery. In addition, many startups have developed innovative business models in which they research active ingredients using algorithms. Often, they have close ties to universities, because unlike a medical lifestyle app, computer-aided drug discovery is a field that requires a high degree of expertise and is very high-tech. These startups describe themselves as "next-gen biotech," among them Insilico in Hong Kong, Benevolent.ai in London, Exscientia in Oxford, Deep-Genomics in Canada, as well as Atomwise and TwoXAR in Silicon Valley.

### *Atomwise*

While the startup Atomwise has not developed an intelligent robot to identify new active ingredients, it promises to dramatically speed up drug discovery using its AI-based platform. First, a pharmaceutical company has to identify a protein that plays a key role during disease progression that can be targeted by the new drug. Atomwise aims to help pharmaceutical companies identify potential "hits" – a molecule that interacts with a specific protein. Atomwise then uses AI to optimize these "hits" into "leads" – molecules that interact with the protein in the desired manner. Its algorithm digitally examines the active ingredients and predicts the likelihood of success in research before it even starts. This allows Atomwise to focus exclusively on testing only the most promising molecules [7].

### *Novartis*

Swiss pharmaceutical corporation Novartis began using virtual reality (VR) headsets in 2017 to allow development teams to experience potential active ingredients in 3D. While chemists are able to visualize molecules on two-dimensional computer screens and predict what the potential active ingredient might bind to, it takes a 3D image of the molecule for them to truly experience all the structures of the potential active ingredient. Viktor Hornak is a member of the computer-based active ingredient development team and is convinced that VR is transforming communication between chemists in development teams [8]. This is because spatial visualization is extremely helpful for chemists in explaining how they hope to optimize a candidate drug. It allows researchers to "walk around" the protein together, rotate it, and view it from all angles. At Novartis, researchers use regular VR headsets and controllers like the ones used for computer gaming. The only thing they had to develop in-house was the software. Novartis hopes to use this innovative approach to reduce the time required to develop drugs. In the past, the search for candidate drugs could take between three and six years.

### *TwoXAR*

TwoXAR is another startup hoping to optimize the active-ingredient development process with the help of AI. The two founders of TwoXAR are researchers who met at MIT; both are named Andrew Radin. This also explains the name of their startup, which is an acronym of "2 times Andrew Radin." The first Andrew is a biomedical IT specialist who developed the technology TwoXAR is based on. He describes the company's approach by using an analogy to self-driving cars:

For many years, automotive development was driven by engineers. Frequently, a change in perspective helps advance a field of research by leaps and bounds, and in the automotive industry, the change came by viewing things through the lens of programmers. Their response to the problem of fatal car accidents was not to develop seat belts or airbags, but instead taking the driver – the main source of risk – out of the equation. This perspective is currently driving the automotive industry.

Similarly, programmers are bringing smart answers to the field of drug development. TwoXAR launched more than 10 projects last year to search for new active ingredients. Sometimes they work alone, and in other projects they collaborate with biotech or pharma companies such as Santen Pharmaceutical in Japan and Adynxx in the United States.

Like Atomwise, TwoXAR does its testing digitally. The molecules they find are 30 times more likely to be successful in animal studies than molecules identified through biological tests. In initial studies, the startup achieved promising results in the treatment of rheumatoid arthritis. Early successes were observed in animal studies, and this was achieved much more rapidly than would have been traditionally possible in the pharmaceutical industry. TwoXAR is a startup we are likely to hear more about in the future [9].

However, examples such as the startup Theranos presented in the chapter on DIY testing show again and again that not every promise made by an up-and-coming entrepreneur should be taken at face value. Startups in the field of AI for drug development are extremely ambitious. They hope to dramatically accelerate processes with a significant reduction in cost. Austin Huang, who works in biomedical IT at Pfizer, remains skeptical, however: "Just because artificial intelligence can drive a car, it is not automatically capable of solving complex medical problems" [10]. This is why the majority of applications for discovering active ingredients are developed by traditional pharmaceutical companies using their unique combination of biological and IT-related expertise. They tend to view these tools as a closely guarded secret that can give them a competitive edge. Be that as it may, humanity can only benefit from less expensive drugs that get to the market more quickly than they have in the past.

## Digital Patient Recruitment for Clinical Studies

Clinical studies often fail due to simple issues. The biggest challenge is recruiting a sufficient number of qualified patients. In the area of cancer immunotherapy alone, more than 2,000 clinical studies were conducted in 2017, which would have required 600,000 participants. Alas, only 50,000 patients were recruited [11]. A study by the National Institutes of Health (NIH) shows that 85% of patients were not aware that they could have participated in a clinical study. In addition, 75% stated they would have been open to the possibility of participating [12]. Clearly, the issue is not so much the unwillingness of patients to participate, but rather a lack of information. However, keeping track of all the clinical studies which are recruiting participants at any given time presents a challenge for both patients and physicians.

## *Antidote*

The startup Antidote was created with the goal of accelerating clinical studies by optimizing the recruitment process. "While medicine has become more complex in the past 30 years and progressed immensely, it's shocking to me that patient recruitment for clinical trials has not evolved at the same pace. Three decades later, it remains one of the major bottlenecks to accelerating medical research. Solving this puzzle is very compelling to me," says Antidote CEO Laurent Schockmel [13].

Antidote is an aggregator and a global search platform for clinical studies. Today, their machine-readable database lists about 15,000 clinical studies for more than 700 conditions. This allows specific studies to be found quickly, and patients can more easily determine whether they are interested in participating. To create the database, Antidote had to define standards in describing clinical studies, since every pharmaceutical company and every investigator had a different process.

The Antidote platform – which is free for patients - currently reaches up to 15 million people per month. Antidote achieves its reach by collaborating with many partner organizations such as the American Kidney Foundation and subsequently using their networks to make patients aware of Antidote.

Patients interested in participating in a study are asked to enter their condition, their location, their age, and their sex. For instance, a 50-year-old woman living in St Louis, Missouri, who has lung cancer would be presented with more than 600 studies she could participate in. However, if she were not willing to drive more than 20 miles, this number would go down to fewer than 70. The selection process can be further refined if the patient knows which mutation triggered her lung cancer.

The service Antidote provides can be immensely valuable to pharmaceutical companies. As a rule, they apply for patent protection on new active-ingredient candidates when they enter the development stage. From that moment on, the clock starts ticking: Depending on the country, companies will have 20–25 years from that date to exclusively market the active ingredient. After this time, patent protection expires, substantially reduces the price for the drug. With an average development time of 10–15 years, companies only have around 10 years to exclusively market the drug and earn back the cost of development, which averages more than 2 billion USD. If Antidote manages to accelerate the speed of development, this will increase the time a company has to exclusively market the drug. Recruiting clinical study participants often takes months, if not years. On its website, Antidote promises to save pharmaceutical companies up to six months of recruitment time [14]. Time is money – and this old adage is particularly true in this industry. Antidote has clearly understood this.

### IBM Watson

With Antidote, the patient or the physician still needs to fill out a search form to find relevant clinical studies, whereas IBM Watson takes a fully automated route based on AI. IBM Watson's algorithm searches a patient's electronic medical record and compares it with the clinical studies registered on the platform www.clinicaltrials.gov. If a doctor has a patient with a rare disease, all they need to do is open the Watson Clinical Trial program to instantly view a list of suitable trials. This service is extremely helpful for physicians, who frequently lack the necessary time to search for clinical studies for specific patients in their day-to-day clinical practice.

In addition, the tool simplifies patient enrollment in clinical studies. Traditionally, clinical trials have been carried out in university research hospitals. With IBM Watson, non-university hospitals can now more easily enroll their patients in clinical studies. Steven Alberts, the chair of the division of medical oncology at the renowned Mayo Clinic, is enthusiastic about IBM Watson. The Mayo Clinic collaborated with IBM to train and test the algorithm. Using IBM Watson, the team was able to recruit 84% more patients per month for their breast cancer studies. In addition, doctors in Steven Alberts' team reported that Watson had made the recruiting process simpler and less time-consuming [15].

### Science 37

Digital health startup Science 37 has devoted itself to another challenge of clinical study recruitment: More than 70% of potential participants in the United States live more than a two-hour drive away from where the study is being conducted. Since some studies involve regular on-site testing, patients have to make a significant effort and sometimes travel long distances several times a week in order to participate. This prompted Science 37 to develop a platform that allows participants to take part in studies from home. According to Science 37 CEO Noah Craft, this helps solve the widespread problem of participants dropping out of clinical studies prematurely due to travel requirements. The technological basis consists of a cloud-based application with terminals that allow for video calls and the exchange of images. Participants receive detailed information and are walked through the study step by step. Where needed, an investigator can always be called in. The advantage of this approach is that even patients living in the country can participate in clinical studies without the burden of commuting. This should also reduce the cost and duration of testing.

## *Apple*

Technology giant Apple also offers a solution to simplify recruiting and performing clinical studies. Health technology has become one of the mainstays of the corporation: "I believe [in] the future, if you look back and you ask the question, 'What was Apple's greatest contribution to mankind,' it will be about health," Apple CEO Tim Cook confidently stated in an interview with broadcaster CNBC in January 2019 [16]. Apple launched its ResearchKit platform, which allows pharmaceutical companies and research institutes to conduct clinical studies through the Apple platform, in 2015. ResearchKit is an open-source framework that researchers can use to simply and securely program their own apps and make them available on the App Store. Apple's ResearchKit has three major benefits for researchers when compared to traditional studies: easier recruiting, reduced expense and effort in conducting clinical studies, as well as more accurate observational data, since participants can continuously enter their symptoms on their smartphones in a very user-friendly manner.

These advantages become very clear when you look at the example of the ResearchKit-based app mPower programmed by the University of Rochester in New York in partnership with the non-profit organization SageBionetworks. The team at SageBionetworks is currently using mPower to research the progression of Parkinson's disease.

Melinda Penkava has Parkinson's and is participating in the trial. She was recruited directly through her iPhone. More than 720 million people use an iPhone, making them potential participants in clinical studies. Over 16,000 people enrolled in the Parkinson's study, nearly 15,000 of whom qualified to participate. These excellent figures are explained by the fact that ResearchKit makes enrolling a breeze. Patients can enroll from home using the device that Melinda Penkava and others already have on them as they move about their everyday lives – their smartphone [17].

Several times a day, Melinda enters information about her symptoms in the mPower app. In Parkinson's patients, these can vary a great deal throughout the day. In a traditional clinical study, Melinda would have to visit a study site every time she needed to make an entry. This would not only be time-consuming, but her data could also never be collected with the same precision or frequency as with mPower [17]. In addition to answering questionnaires, the participants are given different cognitive and motor tasks in mPower that they have to perform before and after taking their medication. In one task, Melinda is asked to tap on her iPhone as quickly as possible. In another, she has to take 20 steps and walk in as straight a line as possible, while sensors in her iPhone measure her gait. Researchers hope to use this data to gain key insights into the long-term progression of Parkinson's disease.

In addition to the companies listed here, many additional startups are active in the field of clinical testing. The previously mentioned patient network Patientslikeme is now also recruiting study participants. In addition, the association Clinical Trial Transformation Initiative, a public private partnership comprising more than 80 government and business organizations, is leading the way in improving clinical study processes.

## Evidence Gained from Digital Real-World Data

Statistical evidence from RWD is a second pattern that is having a major impact in drug research. The term "RWD" is used to refer to data that is not derived from strictly controlled clinical studies. These can include diagnoses, lab test results, X-rays, and ultrasound images added to a patient's electronic health record during routine clinical practice. The billing information maintained by health insurance companies also constitutes RWD. In addition, wearables such as Fitbits and Apple Watches record vital parameters like blood pressure and heart rate. This, too, is RWD from a patient's everyday life.

To date, RWD have rarely been used for drug research, since it was generally stored on paper in the filing cabinets of doctors' offices, hospitals, and health insurance companies. This RWD was unavailable and had also never been systematically collected. The second challenge in terms of RWD is the sheer volume of these data sets. Unlike data from clinical studies, this data does not have a defined beginning or end, nor does it follow a specific narrative. Looking at the totality of all medical data, it is safe to assume that only about 4% of it was collected through clinical studies, whereas 96% is RWD [18]. This is important because clinical practice often differs from clinical studies – patients might forget to take their medications regularly, occasionally miss a treatment, or switch drugs.

It was previously not possible to detect or research exceptional phenomena such as rare cases, where a patient responds unusually well to a treatment.

The digitalization of RWD in electronic health records as well as the use of AI now allows us to systematically evaluate data that was mostly disregarded in the past. In research circles, the availability and use of RWD is considered to be one of the most impactful transformations in drug development. These data have multiple advantages over data from clinical studies, which is why increasing attention is being paid to them in drug development:

### *RWD Allow for Time Travel*

RWD allow us to go back in time, making it indispensable for researching conditions where preventive care has the greatest effect. According to what we know today, Alzheimer's disease is one such condition. In the story about Kate Newman's mother Nancy, we detailed the fate of an Alzheimer's patient. We do not know whether Kate's mom was offered the opportunity to participate in a clinical study. If that had been the case, the only symptoms that could have been studied would have been those after her official diagnosis. The data from Nancy's medical record before she became ill, however, could also provide insights when compared to those of other Alzheimer's patients: Are there mutations in Nancy's genome and that of other Alzheimer patients that could have predicted the disease before its onset? Are there symptoms common to all Alzheimer's patients prior to diagnosis? Are there sociodemographic similarities between patients? RWD allow us to systematically search for clues that help us better understand diseases and their development and diagnose them at an earlier stage.

### *RWD can Replace Control Groups*

RWD can even play a role within clinical studies. For the most part, clinical studies are conducted in the form of randomized controlled testing. This means that participants are randomly allocated to an intervention or a control group, where neither the participants nor the physicians know which group a patient is in. The new drug or treatment is administered to the patients in the interventional group, while those in the control group receive a placebo or the current standard of care. Ethical concerns arise if the new treatment is promising and the illness is life-threatening. After all, half of the study participants are receiving a treatment according to the current standard of care and not the new, potentially life-saving drug.

This is where RWD can come in. Instead of analyzing a control group within a clinical study, RWD from the past could be used to evaluate the current standard of care. This process has already been implemented in US oncology trials and has been accepted by the Food and Drug Administration (FDA) under certain conditions [19]. The key question is whether the data are "regulatory grade," in other words of the necessary quality to be used in the context of strictly regulated drug approval processes. Cathy Critchlow, a VP at biotechnology giant Amgen, led this process.

In order to put the data from the active arm into context, we felt it was important to characterize treatment response rates and safety issues in a highly similar real-world population of patients who had not received our investigational therapy. [20]

If control groups can be created from RWD, this not only makes the clinical study less expensive, but simultaneously accelerates patient recruitment, potentially also accelerating the path to approval of the new drug.

## RWD can Help Discover New Uses for Existing Drugs

With the development of sildenafil, an active ingredient better known under the brand name Viagra, the public became aware that unforeseen indications can be discovered for medications. The pharmaceutical corporation Pfizer initially carried out a clinical study to determine the benefits of sildenafil for patients with chest pain due to coronary heart disease. Pfizer assumed that sildenafil would relax the blood vessels in the heart, alleviating chest pain. However, the clinical study did not confirm the anticipated effect. The study participants could not confirm that their chest pain disappeared; instead, they reported that sildenafil caused increased erections. By the time unknown perpetrators broke into the clinical laboratory to steal the sildenafil stocked there, Pfizer realized that they had inadvertently struck gold. In 1998, they began to market sildenafil under the trade name Viagra as a drug to treat erectile dysfunction. It was to become one of the world's best-selling drugs [21].

Drug approval is always tied to the specific application, referred to as the "indication," being evaluated in the clinical study. Frequently, however, medicines are known for other uses besides their original indication. Since clinical studies are very expensive (an average of 30–40 million USD; [22] and take a long time to carry out, rare indications can often not be researched. In such cases, despite the lack of clinical validation, physicians are permitted to prescribe drugs for uses that go beyond the evaluated benefit. This is referred to as "off-label use." This is by no means a rare phenomenon: It is estimated that approximately 20% of drugs are used "off-label." One example is prazosin, a medication approved for the treatment of high blood pressure which is also used to treat posttraumatic stress disorder (PTSD)-related nightmares.

RWD allow for inexpensive testing of off-label uses without the need for a costly clinical study. The advantage is that the benefit of the medication is clearly documented and side effects can be systematically studied. In addition, it creates a safe legal framework for prescribing and reimbursing these medications for new indications. The US FDA is already encouraging pharmaceutical companies to assess existing drugs for broader use based on RWD.

## RWD can Improve a Study Design's Probability of Success

It is difficult to comprehend how apparent minutiae can impact the duration, expense, and success of a clinical study. Should the age of the participants range from 45 to 65 or from 45 to 75? This issue could determine the success of the trial.

RWD can accelerate the approval of new drugs by helping to make clinical trials as efficient as possible. Robust RWD can also help optimize the recruitment criteria for clinical studies. For instance, they may show the breakdown of a specific group of patients in terms of age, sex, and other sociodemographic criteria. In addition, RWD can show in which patients the current standard of care may be less effective or cause an unusually high number of side effects. Clinical studies can then focus on these patient groups, which can increase their probability of success.

### RWD Add to the Knowledge Gained in Clinical Studies

How does a drug work in real-life situations, such as when patients do not always take it at the prescribed time? What side effects occur if a patient simultaneously takes other medications? How does a drug work on overweight versus underweight patients?

While a clinical study only allows researchers to study side effects in a few thousand patients at best, RWD can document them in millions of people. So RWD add to knowledge gained in clinical studies. This is particularly relevant when it comes to rare but dangerous side effects. One example is the thalidomide scandal of the 1960s in Germany.

To her students, Bärbel Drohmann is just a regular math teacher. Her co-workers describe Ms Drohmann as "approachable yet strict." In 2006, the German broadcaster *Westdeutscher Rundfunk* reported on the courageous teacher, who teaches a full course load at a secondary school in Selm, a town in central Germany, in spite of missing arms and not having fully developed hands [23]. Bärbel Drohmann was one of more than 5,000 children born with deformities from 1958 to 1962. These were caused by the sedative thalidomide that led to fetal deformities if taken in the early stages of pregnancy. These side effects had not been recognized at the time in the studies conducted by Grünenthal, the drug's manufacturer, and for good reason: Pregnant women are generally excluded from participating in clinical studies in order to prevent any side effects from impacting the unborn child. This was also the case in thalidomide studies.

When, in 1958, an increased number of children were born with deformities, German scientists were in the dark about the cause. The German parliament debated whether they might be linked to nuclear weapon testing conducted at the time during the Cold War. They were also lacking reliable statistical data to confirm a definitive increase in the number of children born with deformities. It took three years until thalidomide was identified as the cause. Only in 1961 was the sedative taken off the market.

How would this situation have evolved in an era where we have access to RWD? It is safe to assume that RWD and smart algorithms would have established a connection between thalidomide use during pregnancy and birth defects in children much more quickly and with greater precision. Databases of RWD clearly can improve safety in the medical field.

But in spite of all the advantages that RWD provide for drug development and the medical field in general, we need to proceed with caution. Because as always, when data are in the mix, the question is: Who does this data belong to? Is treatment data owned by the physicians treating the patient and the hospitals that document it? Does the data belong to the patient? Or is a country's health data a national resource because, taken together, it provides added value to society? These issues are subject to different regulations on a national level and require societal consensus. First and foremost, medical data naturally belong to the patient whose personal rights must be respected. However, most countries allow anonymized data to be used in medical studies. It is also important for high-quality data to be collected and assembled in databases that can be analyzed. After all, data are only useful if it can be evaluated.

In Finland and the UK, the processing of data on a national level is managed by the state. In the United States, clinics can sell their data to private businesses for processing and aggregation. This is where the potential of RWD is currently most evident. In 2016, Congress passed the 21st Century Cures Act, which allows the FDA to accept RWD to help support new uses for existing drugs, as well as to simplify the approval of new drugs through hybrid test designs. In Germany, too, the Federal Ministry of Health is driving the digitalization of the healthcare system. The Digital Healthcare Act (DVG – *Digitale-Versorgung-Gesetz*) lays the groundwork for creating a RWD of all 73 million patients who have statutory health insurance in Germany. No matter what the result of discussions about RWD is in various countries, RWD are likely to play a key role in the research departments of universities and pharmaceutical and biotech companies. It is no coincidence that almost all of these companies are focusing strongly on the use of medical RWD in their research and development or that many startups are actively working in the field of RWD. Among them are Flatiron Health, Hello Heart, Healthbank, Data4Life, Redox, Aetion Health, and China-based iCarbonX. Let's take a look at two of them.

**Flatiron Health.**   Flatiron Health maintains one of the leading databases of RWD in the field of oncology. In addition to software solutions for the more targeted treatment of cancer patients, this database is also used by third-party companies for research and development purposes. In the United States, only about 4% of cancer patients participate in clinical studies, which mean that all insights about the remaining 96% of patients are lost. Taking every patient into account would be very valuable, especially for the advancement of drugs and therapies. Flatiron is a very personal affair for founders Nat Turner and Zach Weinberg: Nat's cousin Brennan was diagnosed with a rare form of leukemia at age seven. From one day to the next, the family found itself living a nightmare. They were completely overwhelmed by the situation. What was the best treatment? How could they best help Brennan? Nat was shocked by how fragmented the healthcare system was and the siloed thinking that prevailed. Since Nat and Zach had previously founded and successfully sold a startup to Google, they decided to collaborate once again in 2012, building a company that would provide the maximum amount of data for cancer research.

They developed a cloud-based platform to store the electronic health records of cancer patients. These contain all diagnostic testing results as well as the medicines administered and the therapies prescribed. In addition, multiple analysis functions are integrated that allow physicians and researchers to perform any necessary assessments.

At this writing, the platform contains the data of more than three million people. Nearly 300 hospitals are part of the network and provide data that are analyzed by more than 2,500 researchers. Not only the founders of Flatiron, but multiple health organizations also view this approach as an opportunity to learn significantly more about the efficacy of drugs and therapies and – crucially – to do so much faster than ever before. In the meantime, Flatiron has expanded its services beyond its RWD database and now also provides software solutions for oncology practices and departments. The Swiss pharma company Roche saw enough potential in Flatiron to purchase the company in 2018. Nonetheless, Flatiron Health continues to operate as a separate company in collaboration with other third-party companies. By acquiring its analytical capacity and database, Roche made one of the industry's largest investments into RWD – betting on a future where robust health data will become increasingly important.

**Aetion Health.** Founded by Jeremy Rassen and Sebastian Schneeweiss in 2013, the startup Aetion Health is another significant player in the industry. At a conference in New York City, Jeremy explained the history behind the name Aetion Health:

> Aetion is based on the Greek word for causation. At Aetion Health,
> it is our mission to discover causal relationships in RWD using IT to
> influence critical medical decision-making processes. [24]

Unlike Flatiron Health, Aetion Health is not focused on building a database of RWD. Instead, its aim is to develop the best possible platform to analyze RWD. To do so, it has partnered with the FDA. In the context of the Repeat project, Aetion is replicating the results of 40 clinical studies based on RWD in conjunction with the FDA. In addition, it is attempting to forecast the results of seven current clinical studies based on RWD. If this is successful, it could have a lasting impact on regulations that determine drug approval in the United States.

## Precision Medicine

From a historical perspective, the pharmaceutical industry has always been driven by the search for blockbuster drugs – medicines that are highly relevant for a maximum number of patients and therefore particularly lucrative. This has all changed completely, however, with the decoding of the human genome and the extremely rapid progress of knowledge about diseases on a molecular level. The term "personalized medicine," also referred to as "precision medicine," describes the opposite development: Finding the right therapy for clearly delineated patient groups. Instead of manufacturing medicines for millions of people, personalized medicine sometimes leads to the development of drugs that allow us to know in advance whether they are likely to work for any given patient based on specific molecular or genetic criteria.

US President Barack Obama launched the "Precision Medicine Initiative" in 2015, which promotes basic research in the field of personalized medicine. He described personalized medicine as "one of the most pioneering medical developments" [25]. Naturally, physicians have known for a long time that every patient should be viewed as an individual with unique characteristics. Austrian hematologist Karl Landsteiner discovered the blood type system in the early twentieth century and received a Nobel prize for his discovery [1]. In effect, adapting blood transfusions to each blood type is already a form of personalized medicine. But what would medicine look like if tailoring a cancer drug to a patient's genome were equally simple and routine? President Obama saw the potential of personalized medicine in "administering the right treatment to the right patient at the right time." Certain scientific and technological developments are helping us fulfill this promise. They are laying the groundwork for state-of-the-art personalized medicine.

Digitalization will only increase the trend toward personalization. This will extend to methods such as customized tumor vaccines and CAR-T-cell therapies developed specifically for a single patient. Certainly, patient cohorts are being more precisely defined on an ongoing basis. This is done by linking data and the genetic profile with machine-learned correlations derived from real-world databases. This is then turned into patient-specific treatment suggestions.

### Decoding the Human Genome

In 2003, the human genome was fully sequenced for the first time by the Human Genome Project. The process took many years and cost around 3 billion USD. Today, genetic screening takes very little time and is available for a few hundred USD [26]. Access to genetic information provides greater clarity about the differences between patients and their conditions. It is now possible to sequence the DNA of a tumor to determine which therapy might be most effective. Tumors can have different surface structures, which explains why certain therapies are efficacious for some patients but not for others. In 2018, the US Federal Health

Insurance Program Medicare began covering the cost of genetic screening for cancer patients [27]. The same is true in Germany and Switzerland. The era of one-size-fits-all cancer therapy (surgery, chemotherapy, and radiation) is now over.

### Continuous Improvements in Computer Processing Speed and Smart Algorithms

In the past, RWD were largely disregarded, because its sheer volume was not manageable. Only clinical study data were evaluated. But advances in computer processing speed and continually improving algorithms have now made it possible for computers to determine patterns and associations zettabyte-sized data sets.

Numerous startups are now working on the next generation of personalized medicine in addition to large corporations in the pharmaceutical and technology sector that continue to strongly impact these developments. Among them are the Chinese company iCarbonX (personalization through collecting a maximum amount of data and AI analysis), Biovotion and Encellin (continuous measurement of patients through innovative sensor technology), InsightRX and Celcuity (determining the best-suited medication based on patient demographics, genetics, and biomarkers), Freenome (innovative blood tests for cancer diagnostics), Nostos Genomics, and many others. Let's take a closer look at two exciting startups in this field.

**Celcuity.** Celcuity was founded by an experienced executive team in 2012: Lance Laing is a biophysicist with more than 20 years of experience in drug development, some of which he spent working for Novartis. Brian Sullivan brings a business perspective to the founding team. Prior to founding Celcuity, he successfully managed and sold several medical companies and hopes to make Celcuity yet another success story, which is already well under way – Celcuity was listed on the Nasdaq in 2017.

The company works in oncology and develops tests to help improve the more targeted use of cancer drugs. Celcuity analyzes a patient's live cancer cells to identify the most promising treatment option for that patient. To date, the company has focused on breast cancer, developing a test to identify the HER1, HER2, and HER3 sequences and evaluate whether the corresponding signaling pathways have been abnormally activated. The team is convinced that these sequences, much like the BRCA1 and BRCA2 genes, can be key indicators for the treatment of breast cancer patients.

**iCarbonX.** iCarbonX is a startup that is well on its way to becoming a sort of Amazon for healthcare services. How? By combining insights in biotechnology and genetics with other indicators such as metabolites, bacteria, and lifestyle to digitally quantify every individual. Their aspiration is to know every participant inside and out, complete with their DNA, pheromones, enzymes, and proteins. The tremendous volume of data is managed by AI algorithms.

All of these data are collected on the Meum platform and used to develop services for the company's clients. However, not all of the recommendations on Meum are based on robust medical insights. For instance, urinalysis may indicate that a patient should take probiotics to improve their skin. A DNA analysis might suggest that the patient should aim for 40 minutes of cardio every day due to a genetic predisposition to diabetes. Even the reaction of the body to a cup of coffee or exercise can be quantified. This creates a digital image of the individual to assess his/her various actions in terms of their effects.

iCarbonX was founded in 2015 by Jun Wang, the former head of the Beijing Genomic Institute. He wanted to create something completely new, focusing not merely on genetics, but on bringing together all kinds of data about the individual. This was his vision in founding the Digital Life Alliance, a collaboration between companies that aggregate data. More than one million people in China, North America, and Israel are already participating in the project.

You might wonder whether Jun Wang subjects himself to the same testing. Indeed, he has blood drawn every three weeks and provides urine samples on a daily basis. But does he adhere to all the suggestions he receives based on the assessments? "I'd love to, but I have too much to do," he sighs. "Also, every human being has free will." iCarbonX is like a GPS: If you absolutely want to take a different route than what it suggests, nobody can prevent you from doing so.

What is the company doing with all those personal data? Generally, Chinese patients are more prepared to share data than Westerners, Wang confirms. Nevertheless, customers can choose whether or not their data may be anonymized and shared with third parties. iCarbonX promises to adhere to all international privacy laws. The company's founder firmly believes in one thing: More data and more specific therapies make for a better life for every individual.

# Part III

# The Five Pillars of the Healthcare System of Tomorrow

*Chapters*

In this section, we set out to provide orientation for the healthcare systems of the twenty-first century. We have developed guidelines for the healthcare systems of the digital era. The idea is for these guidelines to be clear and practical – for ordinary citizens, physicians, patients, and all other actors within the healthcare sector. In Part II of this book, we described the most important developments in a digital healthcare system using 25 response patterns, supported by theses and examples. In this short, final Part III, based on these patterns and theses we outline a concise framework for the healthcare system of tomorrow.

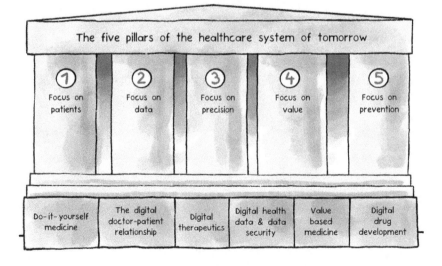

The question is: In the digital age, what will be the guiding principles of "ideal" healthcare systems? What will be the main pillars that provide lasting orientation and stability to everyone involved, from patients to policy-makers? Based on the patterns and theses of Part II, we believe that five pillars have emerged which will guide tomorrow's health systems. We present these pillars on the following pages.

Chapter 10

# Re-allocation of Roles: Patients Gain Power – and Responsibility

*Our key message:*

In the digital age, healthcare systems are adapting to the new role of patients. The do-it-yourself (DIY) response pattern, new channels of patient–doctor communication, and digital therapeutics all necessarily mean that the way patients view themselves is changing and a new balance of power between patients and the healthcare system is emerging. The patient will sit in the driver's seat; the doctor will become a valued partner in a relationship of equals. In addition to more power, the patient is gaining personal responsibility. And the term "patient" is becoming increasingly inaccurate. The patient of tomorrow will often be a person who wants to remain as healthy as possible, and who produces health data in the process of doing so. Patients are turning into a more and more autonomous hybrid of consumer, producer, and patient.

The Digital Pill: What Everyone Should Know about the Future of
Our Healthcare System, 155–157
Copyright © 2021 by Emerald Publishing Limited
All rights of reproduction in any form reserved
doi:10.1108/978-1-78756-675-020211010

Digitalization means self-service and self-determination wherever possible – including the healthcare sector. In the course of this transformation, the role of the patient will fundamentally change as well.

The word "patient" has its roots in the Latin word for "suffering." And of course in modern English, the adjective "patient" describes someone who calmly accepts difficulties or delays. So the very word "patient" attributes a passive role to the person experiencing the illness. In addition, it expresses a hierarchical relationship between the patient (the one who endures) and the physician (the one who acts and makes decisions).

This role is now changing in two ways. First, the patient is taking on an active, more expectant role through the move toward DIY. Depending on the country and region, some 50–80% of all patients already do some internet research before they go to the doctor. The internet is changing the institutions of the healthcare sector just as the printing press changed the Christian church. It is becoming a source of advice for patients on a similar footing as a doctor. As a result, patients are assuming greater responsibility and demanding a say in the choice of treatments. In addition, they can obtain diagnoses independently by carrying out tests at home and treat their non-communicable diseases (NCD) with the help of a digital coach, as is already the case today with the mySugr app. At the same time, this shift from therapeutic to preventive medicine is also changing the picture of what a patient is.

New technologies make it possible for patients to access medical information more easily and quickly than in the past. And with electronic health records, people will also have all the information pertaining to their own health at their fingertips.

What role will doctors play when individuals, not to mention algorithms, take on more responsibility in the future? Will we still need them? The answer is a definite yes. But the packed waiting rooms might still soon be empty. Because doctors will be freed of their administrative work. They will be transformed from "gods in white coats" into coaches. And they will have to adopt a new mindset. The individuals sitting across from them in their offices will have increasingly done some online research before their visit. They have been empowered, and wish to be involved in the decision-making process. Eric Topol, a pioneer in the world of digital healthcare, refers to the traditional doctor–patient relationship as one of "eminence-based versus evidence-based medicine" – in other words, medicine that is more based on the physician's prestige than on medically proven facts [1]. The actions of doctors will become more transparent in the future. They are no longer the omniscient, almost god-like healers of Hippocrates' day. Modern doctors appreciate it when patients gather information about their illness and assist them by recommending trustworthy internet sites.

Patients are increasingly likely to write online reviews about treatments they receive from their physicians. In this respect, they are becoming more like customers, and the doctors more like service providers. So in addition to correct and good treatment, it is becoming increasingly important that doctors take the time to explain the therapies they have prescribed to their patients. This goes hand-in-hand with a shift in language. Why do we need Latin medical terms for a conversation between doctor and patient?

This sort of linguistic demarcation is already a thing of the past in many places – instead, doctors and patients engage as equals. And using language that is easier to understand automatically makes patients more responsible for their health. Never before has it been so clearly and unambiguously shown that certain behaviors have a negative or positive impact on health. A person's lifestyle is responsible for around half of all NCD. Society therefore needs to discuss the extent to which people should be held accountable for taking care of their own health. We need to weigh individual liberty against civic duty. When does the community of the insured or the taxpayer step in, and when is the individual held to account?

And physicians, just like many other professional groups, are increasingly called upon to recognize and accept the limits of their own knowledge. Numerous technological applications now make it possible to draw on the world's accumulated knowledge and thus arrive at better diagnoses and select more appropriate treatments. Just think of a scanner for skin cancer capable of machine learning and with access to a network of millions of images and correct and incorrect diagnoses. In real time, it can draw on a knowledge base that the best dermatologist could never acquire in an entire lifetime. In order for such technologies to be put to effective use for the patient, a coordinated effort between physician and machine is called for. At the end of the day, it is the human being who must accept and bear the responsibility, not the machine. Part of doctors' new identity is applying the power of digital medicine in support of day-to-day treatment.

In the healthcare system of tomorrow, patients and physicians will assume new roles. The transformation will not happen overnight; the process has long since begun.

Chapter 11

# Digital Health Data and Infrastructure: Data Donation is the New Blood Drive

*Our key message:*
   In the digital age, healthcare systems will very much be guided by the opportunities offered by digital health data and a digital infrastructure. For the sake of everyone involved, they must be structured in such a way that the collection of data as well as the exchange of information between the different actors is easy, secure, clearly regulated, and trustworthy. People's privacy must be safeguarded. Data and infrastructure will be the lifeblood of the healthcare system of the twenty-first century – essential for its survival.

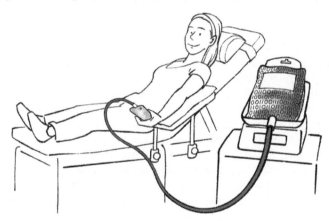

   In the healthcare system of tomorrow, data about patients, their illnesses, and the treatments they undergo will play a key role. This data will no longer be a mere by-product of the therapy, but just as important an element of effective treatment as diagnosis and medication. Many aspects of medical research will also revolve around patient data, which have the potential to accelerate and reduce the costs of medical progress. In short, data represent the cornerstone of every modern healthcare system.

The Digital Pill: What Everyone Should Know about the Future of
Our Healthcare System, 159–162
Copyright © 2021 by Emerald Publishing Limited
All rights of reproduction in any form reserved
doi:10.1108/978-1-78756-675-020211011

160 The Digital Pill

For the data to be useful, we must rethink how it is collected and aggregated. We need to change from accounting-driven data collection to patient-oriented data collection. Up until now, diagnoses and treatments have largely been recorded digitally so they can be reported to the health insurance companies for billing purposes. Here, diagnoses are reduced to billing codes that cannot be read or interpreted by the patient. In addition, the information collected in this manner can seldom be used, aggregated, or consolidated for purposes of analysis. This despite the fact that such data are urgently needed in the healthcare sector for research and efficiency-boosting measures. Nor is the focus on documenting the state of health of the patient. IT systems are optimized for accounting, not for machine-readable patient health records. So new IT solutions and data collection standards are called for here as well. The question remains as to what role the physician should play in patient-oriented data collection.

Today doctors already spend too much time on administrative work. In the United States, such tasks take up about one-sixth of their working hours [1]. And in Switzerland, the situation is even more pronounced: doctors here spend more than 50% of their working hours on administrative tasks, in particular on patient record-keeping and entering codes for billing [2, 3]. Data collection must be made easier and faster in the future. This is the key to ensuring that doctors support the transition.

The first digital solutions have emerged here as well, like the Suki digital assistant that uses speech recognition to assist medical staff. In addition, in the future medical devices such as computed tomography and ultrasound machines will be networked directly with the patient's electronic health records. This will allow data to be sent directly and immediately from where it is generated to the electronic health record. Advances in sensor technology are also making the continuous collection of data possible. Today motion and blood pressure sensors are already built into watches, fitness trackers, and clothing. In the future, we will be able to inject sensors directly into the bloodstream [4]. The quantity and, above all, the quality of the data are set to continue to improve. The availability of high-quality and high-resolution data is an absolutely essential prerequisite for medical progress.

Besides the collection of data for medical purposes at the patient level, the aggregation of data sets will play an important role. "Aggregation" means pooling the data sets of as many patients as possible into one vast, possibly national – or even international – database. Because the larger the database, the better and more accurately the algorithms can identify patterns in the data sets. Machine-readable, quality-assured health databases that are as comprehensive as possible will represent a competitive advantage for national economies and lead to health innovations. The secondary utilization of health data looks set to emerge as a driver of innovation in the healthcare sector. This trend can already be observed today, when we look at the pioneering role played by China and the United States in the field of data-driven startups such as iCarbonX, Flatiron, Aetion, and TwoXAR.

When it comes to the analysis of data, digitalization is opening up untold new possibilities for the medical sector. The use of AI-based IT tools will therefore prove essential, because without them it will no longer be possible to be evaluate the growing volumes of data. Smart data analysis systems will become the stethoscope of the twenty-first century. They can lighten the load on a healthcare system that is threatening to buckle under the almost epidemic-like spread of non-communicable diseases. We can find countless examples of this in everyday medical practice: (1) the diabetes app monitors fluctuations in the patient's blood sugar levels, making a regular visit to the primary care physician unnecessary; (2) the smartwatch automatically detects atrial fibrillation in an at-risk patient; (3) algorithms provide assistance in the interpretation of X-ray images; and (4) artificial intelligence searches a genome database for rare forms of cancer.

A key factor here is the facilitation of the transfer of data between the individual actors in the healthcare system and the patient. In the future, it should be standard practice to forward the information from a diabetes app or a heartrate monitor to the general practitioner – just as lab results are sent today. Of course this system will only spring into action when any of the measured values gives cause for alarm. In such cases, the right analysis tool will automatically notify doctors so they can contact their patients, thereby improving the quality of care for the chronically ill.

Data from everyday medical practice (known as "real-world data") are of vital importance to medical research. Such data could make the use of control groups in clinical studies unnecessary (see Chapter 9). This could make it possible, for example, to ensure that patients with serious diseases do not merely receive a placebo when participating in a study. At the same time, research will become faster, more precise, and safer, because thanks to real-world data, researchers can obtain a better understanding of the efficacy of medications in a large population under everyday conditions – outside of a clinical study and not just in a relatively small test group.

The topic of data protection plays a key role on the road to digital data-based medicine. This particularly applies in Europe, where data privacy is much more deeply rooted in society than in the United States or in China. We can already observe the paradox surrounding data privacy in many areas of life, which has the following implication for the field of medicine: People do not want to share their data if they do not know what it will be used for. Data privacy is extremely important to them. But if they understand the purpose behind it – helping themselves or sick people – then they are also willing to share. And if they are personally affected, people often voluntarily begin to discuss the full details of their medical history online, with the aim of seeking advice from others with the same illness or even just receiving emotional support. In his book, the German Health Minister Jens Spahn sums up this paradox as follows: "Data privacy is for healthy people" [4, p. 39].

It is indisputable that health data are among the most personal information. So as a matter of principle, the individual must be the owner of their personal health data. To the greatest extent possible, they should determine who can access it, when it can be accessed, and what aspects are accessible. Security standards must be developed to regulate the exchange of data and how it is secured – and thereby also enable it to be used in research and analysis. The general encryption of medical data should be the new standard. In the future, patient data should only be stored and transmitted in encrypted form.

Anyone who voluntarily makes data available is also making a contribution to medical progress. And those who do not share their data risk raising healthcare costs and lessening the prospects of effective treatments. Evidence-based medicine relies on corroboration, on statistical findings from scientific studies that make it possible to classify treatments as either effective or ineffective. To achieve this, data are essential, as reflected in the famous quotation from American physicist and statistician William Edwards Denning: "In God we trust. All others must bring data." And American economist Peter Drucker is quoted as saying, "You can't manage what you can't measure." A similar principle applies in medicine. Digitized data are making it possible to detect diseases earlier and to understand and heal them better. More precise, detailed, and up-to-date – or in a word, better – health data mean better health for patients. Which is why patients should have the greatest interest in high-quality, comprehensive health data.

The most important question we have to answer is: How can medical data be stored by all the various actors involved in the healthcare system in such a way that each can access it? What should a future-proof data infrastructure look like? Medical technology must also be configured in such a way that X-ray images and ultrasound scans can be transferred to the electronic medical record if required. Doctors, hospitals, pharmacies, and other medical service providers need assistance to meet the challenges of digital transformation. They will only cooperate if they are not left to struggle on their own – and if they understand the benefits.

What we need are standards for the safekeeping of medical data, not only by all those involved in the healthcare system, but also using cloud solutions. Lawmakers have to decide if health data are communal property and should be stored by the state, or if it can also be managed by private companies. Important questions remain to be answered, such as how to protect health data from hacker attacks. Completely encrypted patient data could help make data theft more difficult.

Concerns about electronic medical records remain significant in many countries, among both patients and physicians. So instead of stoking public fears, health policymakers should highlight the benefits of digital records. Because at the end of the day, it is the patient who will benefit the most from a data-driven healthcare system. First, through better quality of care, and second, from decreasing costs that will lead to lower health insurance premiums. In the United States, unnecessary costs of around 30–80 billion USD are generated each year that could be avoided through better coordination between the various actors in the healthcare system [5]. In addition, the high administrative overheads of the American healthcare system lead to more than 250 billion USD in unnecessary costs [6]. And as early as 2012, duplicate tests resulting from a lack of information-sharing generated additional costs of around three billion francs per year in Switzerland [6]. Current estimates are not available – but it is highly probable that the cost inefficiencies have continued to grow over the last 10 years.

Chapter 12

# Precision Medicine: The Therapy Just for Me

*Our key message:*

In the digital era, healthcare systems will move away from standardized treatment guidelines toward personalized treatment plans that are based on the entirety of the data that have been saved about the patient (blood tests, X-ray images, CT and MRI scans, omics data, microbiome, vital signs, etc.). Treatments will constantly be improved, because real-world databases make optimization possible. The care that patients receive will also be personalized by digital coaches who respond to the individual needs of the patient throughout the process and motivate them to adhere to the treatment and modify their behavior.

The Digital Pill: What Everyone Should Know about the Future of
Our Healthcare System, 163–166
Copyright © 2021 by Emerald Publishing Limited
All rights of reproduction in any form reserved
doi:10.1108/978-1-78756-675-020211012

Personalized medicine will be one of the most significant developments in the healthcare system of the future. The era of "one size fits all" is clearly over – standard treatments are becoming a thing of the past. In the future, therapies will be based on all the data collected on a patient as well as the global store of medical knowledge; this will allow treatments to be tailored to each patient. Three developments are making this possible: first, the sequencing of human DNA and the resulting knowledge about a person's genetic "fingerprint" and how it impacts on their health. Thanks to the digital support provided by ever-improving processors, the genome can be decoded faster and more cost-effectively than ever. In conjunction with advances in knowledge in the field of molecular biology, this scientific progress is allowing treatments to be tailored ever more precisely to specific patient groups.

Second, the information collected in databases (from genome to fitness tracker) is making it possible to understand people and their health progressively better and more comprehensively and to answer important questions: Why do different people respond differently to the same treatment? How should treatments be adapted to achieve better results?

We are convinced that the previously standardized treatment guidelines will be overhauled bit by bit. In their place will be increasingly individualized treatment guidelines that can be tailored to different patients and types of disease. This more individualized treatment has a better chance of success, both in terms of healing and of cost-effectiveness.

Third, the developments in artificial intelligence and the exponential growth in the processing power of computers are an important driver of personalized medicine. Increasingly intelligent algorithms are helping identify and interpret data patterns in real-world databases. In the future, the success of pharmaceutical companies will depend not only on having the best biologists and chemists, but also the best software engineers and access to the best health database.

How will we benefit from personalized health care? First and foremost, through better treatment for every individual. In cancer therapy, tumors are already increasingly being analyzed at the molecular level to determine which treatment they are most likely to respond to. Second, personalized medicine is also bringing about efficiency gains. Currently, many drugs are administered on a large scale. Under the principle of trial and error, they are also prescribed to people for whom they don't work at all. The better personalized medicine becomes, the faster drugs and treatments can be applied in a targeted manner. The personalization of medications will dramatically improve their efficacy and minimize side effects. This can boost cost-efficiency and prevent human suffering.

The digital coach is another aspect of personalized medicine, one that caters to each patient's individual needs, just as a personal trainer would. But digital coaches have the advantage of being scalable, and therefore affordable – and they are making personalized medicine available in less economically developed countries as well. Examples include the diabetes app mySugr; Meru Heath, a digital coach that helps with mental disorders; and Kaia Health, an app that suggests individually tailored exercises for back pain and uses a video camera to check whether they are being performed correctly. In the healthcare system of tomorrow, many people will have a digital personal coach at their side.

But personalized medicine is also leading to significant challenges. Approval requirements for medicines and reimbursement systems need to be reformed, that is to say adapted to preventive and therapeutic measures tailored to ever smaller patient groups. Digital diagnostic devices require new regulations. Data privacy and patients' individual liberties again come into play here. How do we handle all the data about diseases that is collected and systematically analyzed? How do we handle patients who have genetic testing done for a specific diagnostic purpose, and in the process accidentally discover that they are carriers of a serious hereditary disease? How do we protect the right of not wanting to know?

In tomorrow's world of health care, genetic testing and other methods of medical profiling will become diagnostic standards, just like blood tests are today. One important principle could be that genetic testing must always be supervised by a doctor. Governments will need to establish clear rules and quality standards for DIY genetic testing. Genetic tests are complex procedures, and the answers they give to medical questions are often not black or white, but come in many shades of gray. For example, how should a woman handle the knowledge, revealed through a DNA test, that she – like actor Angelina Jolie – carries a mutation of the *BRCA 1* gene and therefore has a much higher risk of developing breast cancer? Besides the radical solution of a double mastectomy chosen by Jolie, thorough and frequent check-ups might also be an option. So a doctor should be involved in interpreting the test results. At present, not every online DNA test offers this sort of medical consultation, so many of these services should be viewed with a critical eye. A teleconsultation with a physician would also be an option. What's most important is that the individual not be left alone. In addition, lawmakers must play a role in regulating the quality of service providers of genetic and other complex tests. As more and more companies push into this market, minimum quality standards must be applied and compliance monitored.

The economic dimension of personalized, or precision, medicine also should not be forgotten. It is increasingly becoming an issue of location. The larger the database, the more comprehensive and higher quality the data, the greater the opportunities for medical insights and potential economic benefits. China and the United States are leading this global race and are well on the way to dominate this new and promising field of medicine. Since the decision by US President Obama to fund precision medicine, one million human genomes have been sequenced in the United States and compiled in a database. More than 200 million USD of public funds have been invested [1]. China is at least as engaged in the development of precision medicine. The country hopes this will help it finally become a leading center of the pharmaceutical and medical industry. To this end, it plans to invest more than 9 billion USD by 2030. In addition, the People's Republic has the world's largest genetic laboratory as well as the largest storage facility for human genetic material. One advantage that China has is the sheer size of its population and its considerable competence in the field of artificial intelligence. And although it may sound cynical, a somewhat different understanding of data privacy is helpful in the development of this field [2, 3]. In the EU, the ICPerMed consortium – in which Switzerland and Canada are also involved – was set up in 2016. ICPerMed brings together more than 30 European and international non-profits as well as ministries and funding agencies of the European Commission to jointly research and share information on approaches to personalized medicine [4]. The goal is to counteract the fragmentation of the European market and develop scalable solutions and partnerships so that Europe can also assume a leading role in the new, innovative field of precision medicine.

Personalized medicine, as we have seen, leads to an entirely new mindset in the healthcare system. Medicine is becoming increasingly driven by data and evidence. We are now moving toward a learning system, one that gets a bit smarter and more capable every day in the fight against disease. Scientific findings, high-quality databases, the comprehensive introduction of electronic medical records, and collaboration between physicians and digital assistants are all prerequisites for making personalized medicine a reality. This can only happen through partnership between health agencies, insurance companies, manufacturers, doctors, hospitals, and patient organizations.

Chapter 13

# Focus on Results and Transparency: Payment on Delivery

*Our key message:*
In the digital age, compensation in healthcare systems will be based on transparency and the delivery of results. In the future, instead of payment for individual services rendered, solutions will be remunerated. Only when a positive result is delivered will payment be made. The groundwork for this is being laid by the increased transparency that is made possible by the digital and networked collection of patient data.

Most services are based on the fact that we know in advance what they will cost. Whether at a restaurant, salon, or auto repair shop, we know what we will be required to pay. When it comes to our health, however, we often do not know the price of a doctor's visit or the different elements of our treatment. In many healthcare systems, for instance in Germany and the United States, the insured parties often never even see their medical bills. Of course this makes it difficult to keep an eye on the costs.

**The Digital Pill: What Everyone Should Know about the Future of**
**Our Healthcare System, 167–169**
Copyright © 2021 by Emerald Publishing Limited
All rights of reproduction in any form reserved
doi:10.1108/978-1-78756-675-020211013

Digitalization will now lead to more transparency. We will know in advance what the service providers in the healthcare system put on the invoice and can react accordingly. Pay-for-performance models for the use of modern cancer medications as well as examples from Oscar Health and Collective Health in the United States show how digitalization can be used to build cost-effective health networks, which center around incentives for providing patients with the best possible treatment. Digitalization is also helpful in exposing the black sheep in the healthcare sector. In the future, things will be difficult for those who cannot deliver quality. This will go so far that health insurance companies will be able to remove doctors from their healthcare network if their treatments deliver poor results, if they are assessed very negatively by patients, or if the costs of treatment are significantly above average for no reason.

New systems of incentives will lead to better and more streamlined medicine. The existing incentive system encourages the players to conduct as many examinations as possible on a patient, even if these are not urgently required. In many cases, after all, it is the health insurance provider who pays. A system that usually prescribes its patients everything that it can, but not necessarily what each individual actually needs, leads to enormous inefficiencies with limited success in terms of health outcomes. In the future, physicians and hospitals will be helped by digital assistants who suggest treatment plans based on the medical state of the art. This will ensure that services are provided based on scientific evidence. In the United States alone, unnecessary treatments and tests generate extra costs amounting to 600 billion USD; in Switzerland, the amount is two billion Swiss francs [1, 2]. On top of this come the costs of tests that are conducted multiple times due to the poor networking of the actors in the healthcare system. Today, these are also reimbursed without objection.

So we need a new system of compensation that focuses on preventive medicine and the maintenance of good health. Instead of paying doctors according to the sheer volume of tests, available medical equipment, and treatments, they should be rewarded for curing patients as quickly as possible and keeping them healthy. In addition to the medical services provided, in the future the success of the treatment will play an important role in remuneration.

When we see that billions are spent on the treatment of diabetes, but that despite this, more than half of all diabetics have elevated blood sugar levels, one thing should be clear to us – we can do better [3]. The same message is delivered by the statistic that half of all medications are taken in the wrong amounts and at the wrong times [4]. This is why we are calling for the compensation received by doctors, hospitals, and pharmaceutical companies to be tied to the success of the treatment whenever possible. Otherwise society will have to keep paying more and more money for the healthcare system without people benefiting significantly from it in terms of their health.

### *Technological Solutions*

Clearly, the digital transformation of the healthcare world offers enormous opportunities. The question is, who will profit, and who will potentially pay the price? Digitalization can help us master the challenges currently facing our healthcare system. Value-based digital compensation systems can help reduce healthcare costs without sacrificing quality. Real-world data will open up completely new possibilities in medical research, and efficient clinical trials will accelerate medical progress. Digital assistants will help people live healthy lives, becoming an effective weapon in the battle against the epidemic of non-communicable diseases. Telemedicine and digital tracking of vital signs suggest an affordable solution to the increased need for care in an aging society by providing seamless care and diagnostic monitoring at relatively low labor costs. For example, digital tools can recognize if an older person has fallen and send out an automated call for help, or they can monitor whether senior citizens are taking their medications at the right times and in the correct dosage.

And it is not just the patients in developed countries who will benefit. Access to medical care can be expanded through the digitalization of the healthcare sector, especially in poor or remote regions. Developing countries, in particular, could benefit from the digital health revolution. Diagnosis and treatment recommendations based on artificial intelligence represent an important building block in granting access to acceptable health care to the 3.4 billion people who earn less than 5.50 USD per day. In the near future, unstaffed mini-clinics (see Chapter 5) will be found in shopping malls and other public locations in developing countries. They will offer many people the potential to receive decent medical care at modest prices.

In Kenya, 83% of the population use the internet; in Senegal, 58% [3]. This is an opportunity not to be missed. Telemedicine is an affordable way to bring medical care to areas where there are no medical specialists. This was described most impressively by the newspaper *Die Welt* in a report on telemedicine in Tanzania, where telecytology was used to help correctly analyze a tissue sample from a young man. In telecytology, the images of tissue taken with a microscope are transmitted by WiFi to a pathologist. There are only 30 pathologists in all of Tanzania, so pathologists from around the world, including Germany, volunteer to help them in their spare time. Without telemedicine, in many cases it would be impossible to distinguish between benign and malignant tumors. Telemedicine saves lives every day, not just in Tanzania, but in many other countries across the globe [4]. In the healthcare world of tomorrow, there may soon already be more digital doctor's visits than analog ones. The digitalization of the world of health care goes hand in hand with a promise to facilitate better care for a more extensive group of patients at affordable costs.

But digitalization also brings major challenges that need to be tackled. Our society needs to hold a debate about solidarity and responsibility in the healthcare sector. What risks must be borne by the individual, and what risks will society carry? In the digital world of health care, the patient will become transparent. If their data fall into the wrong hands, the danger might be great. It is the task of everyone involved to prevent this. Above all, we must prevent the solidarity of the healthcare system from being undermined. Patients must not experience discrimination, because their genetic profile shows they are at higher risk of being more frequently ill than others, or of having higher medical bills than their peers.

Chapter 14

# Preventive Medicine: Prevention is Better than Cure

*Our key message:*
In the digital age, healthcare systems will undergo a massive shift toward the logic of prevention. They will rely on screening and prophylaxis, including diagnostic monitoring, instead of focusing on healing after an illness has developed, and manage their investments based on this principle. They will take the effects of health literacy seriously, and place great emphasis on health education at all levels, especially in schools.

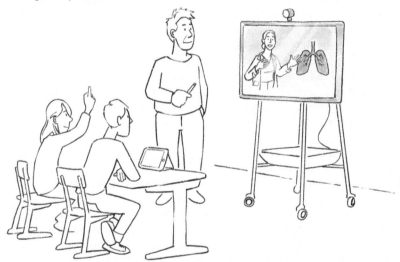

Digitalization is an important key to restructuring our healthcare system and assigning greater importance to prevention. Because as everyone agrees, prevention is the best medicine. Preventive medicine and diagnostic monitoring are of particular importance in the field of non-communicable diseases (NCD). To date, not much is set aside by way of funding for prevention – it represents only 3% of

The Digital Pill: What Everyone Should Know about the Future of
Our Healthcare System, 171–175
Copyright © 2021 by Emerald Publishing Limited
All rights of reproduction in any form reserved
doi:10.1108/978-1-78756-675-020211014

healthcare costs. The inadequate appreciation and remuneration of preventive medicine has also meant that we have fewer and fewer young doctors embarking on careers in general medicine. Becoming a medical specialist is much better paid and more prestigious; preventive medicine has a comparatively low status in the current system. Doctors have little time for prevention, not least because of their busy schedules.

The digital healthcare world will give doctors back the valuable time that they need for preventive medicine. In the future, digital coaches will lighten physicians' load by taking the lead in the management of chronic illnesses, for instance. In addition, digital trackers will help continuously record patients' vital signs. Through diagnostic monitoring, for the first time it will become possible to speak with patients about preventive health based on all the facts of their case. In the new digital world, doctors will be paid to assume the role of a behavioral coach in their conversations with patients.

Furthermore, there is bound to be a shift in our perspective on health and disease. There will no longer be only the two alternatives of healthy or ill, black or white. Instead, there will be more of a continuum of different shades of gray. And we will all be able to affect where we fall on this spectrum. In the healthcare system of tomorrow, we will not wait until the symptoms of a disease appear, but through our preventive behavior try to stay as healthy as possible, day by day. We will move away from snapshot medicine that only looks at the patient's current state at the moment of the examination. What we need is to continuously observe our own health as part of our daily routine. Through automated sensors, systematic screenings, and regular check-ups, the warning signs of a disease can be caught earlier, preventive medical services for patients can be improved, and costs can be cut.

Medical research will also shift its perspective due to digitalization. It will turn more to the origins of diseases, and thereby to prevention. In researching diseases like Alzheimer's, formerly we could only collect patient data from the time of diagnosis onward. Thanks to electronic medical records that are aggregated in databases, it will now be possible to look at the past as well. So researchers can better understand what factors affect the development of diseases and how we can prevent them. In the area of mental illness in particular, data series can be used to develop new preventive therapies. They will hopefully contribute to the long-awaited breakthrough in the fight against Alzheimer's disease.

The major challenge in working with patients will be motivating them to adopt preventive behaviors. People are often reluctant to believe in statistics and probabilities that link a specific behavior to a specific disease – certainly not when it comes to their own personal habits. The best example of this remains the use of tobacco. Almost one in three Swiss citizens smoke; in China, it is one in two – despite credible scientific findings and a widespread public information campaign explaining the harmful effects. Fitness trackers and apps could help motivate people to make a lasting shift to healthier lifestyles by guiding and helping them to develop healthy daily routines. Digital coaches can also play a role here. Let's take advantage of these opportunities and transform our healthcare system into a preventive system.

There are many examples that show that such a transformation of our healthcare system to one of preventive medicine would lower both costs and human suffering. In partnership with the renowned London School of Economics, Public Health England set up several prevention programs and examined them for their return on investment, in this case the savings which the initiatives achieved by eliminating certain healthcare costs. All of the examined programs were aimed at preventing mental health problems. In the UK, more than 100 billion GBP in costs are incurred in the treatment of mental illnesses. The results of the study speak for themselves: For every pound that was invested in one of the eight preventive programs, up to five pounds were saved in healthcare costs in the following three years [1].

In the United States as well, there is evidence that preventive medicine reduces the strain on the healthcare system. A team from the *Harvard Business Review* spent years observing the CareMore healthcare chain, which specializes in primary care medicine. In contrast to most doctor's offices, the physicians of CareMore try to see their patients as often as possible. Instead of once a quarter, diabetes patients at CareMore are asked to come in almost once a week. This helps provide the patients with more intensive care, to motivate them, and thus prevent critical situations from developing. CareMore patients visit emergency rooms 20% less frequently than comparable patient groups. If they do have to go the hospital, their stay is more than 10% shorter. It is conceivable that this type of tight-knit care could achieve even greater cost reductions if it were also supported digitally. For example, digital technology would make monitoring of the blood sugar levels of diabetics more seamless, preventing expensive follow-on conditions such as leg ulcers and eye problems. At CareMore, up to 35% of the doctor's remuneration is based on patient satisfaction and positive health outcomes. CareMore shows how the healthcare system of tomorrow could work [2].

Worldwide, NCD cost us more than 6,000 billion USD every year. Half of these costs could be avoided through prevention. This is why a greater focus must be placed on how preventive medical programs can be implemented for lasting success. Only when such initiatives are easily and affordably scalable will the majority of the population enjoy the benefits of prevention. We are convinced that digital tools will play a decisive role here.

### Health: A Required Class

People can only be healthy when they are able to take control of factors that affect their health. And to achieve this, they first and foremost need knowledge about health and illness. Teaching health literacy to as many segments of the population as possible is an important goal. It is also the best method for preventing NCD. Studies show that people with higher levels of health literacy are healthier. All efforts to spread knowledge about prevention to the general public will pay off, especially in an era of rising healthcare costs.

So we urgently call on governments to require the teaching of health in schools. Preventive health should start as early as possible. The more established the habits, the more difficult it is to change the behavior. Up till now, health has only received a brief mention in the general school curriculum. Making heath a school subject could help turn children into empowered actors within the healthcare system. In health class, children could learn that they can have an effect on their own health, and how that works. This would not just include the "greatest hits" such as the harmful effects of active and passive smoking, drugs, and excessive alcohol consumption. Instead, schools could lay the foundations for an understanding of healthy nutrition. What are healthy foods? Why shouldn't I consume more than 5 grams of salt per day? What foods contain salt? School cafeterias could also play a role by offering healthy, balanced meals. The fact that fries with ketchup are also served there from time to time is of course one of life's little pleasures.

But healthy eating alone is not enough. Young people must also be encouraged to get more exercise. This topic has received far too little attention in school life so far. Physical activity has been proven to lower the risk of contracting breast cancer, diabetes, and cardiovascular diseases. Our mental health is also better if we do not spend all our time just sitting around. However, teachers and parents often find it annoying when children and young people run and play around them. How absurd! Instead of preventing this active play, it should be encouraged. How can we accept the fact that 80% of schoolchildren worldwide do not get enough exercise [3]? The effect of physical activity on health has been clearly documented, with the statistics of the World Health Organization (WHO) delivering an unequivocal message.

And still we do nothing. We make the students sit at their desks from morning to evening and do not seem to be capable of integrating exercise into their instruction. Furthermore, we overload young people with all sorts of details about biology, chemistry, and physics. But only very few of them have learned to pay attention to their body, to listen to its signals, to find a good balance between nutrition, enjoyment, and exercise. These missed chances lead to significant extra costs for our over-extended healthcare systems in the medium- to long-term. It would also be possible to save young people from numerous NCD in their later lives.

It would be so easy; it would not take much to instill a necessary awareness of healthy lifestyles in our schools. A first measure could be placing a higher priority on physical education. Schools should follow the WHO's recommendation of 60 minutes of exercise per day for children [3]. This applies in particular to schools that are in session all day. Why isn't is possible to make sure that every child gets an hour of exercise each day at school? To achieve this, we could easily forego a few minutes of class time in all the other subjects. Let's foster the health literacy of our children. Applying this knowledge will spare them a lot of suffering down the road. And it would relieve our society of an enormous burden.

But health needs to move toward the center of our public discourse outside of schools as well. Many of the innovations that digital medicine brings will trigger such discussions, because they will require us to make decisions about our society's values. How do we want to handle the huge amounts of data and the possibilities they open up to us? To what extent should prevention be the focus of our healthcare system? Do we want genetic screening for everyone, for instance so we can counteract the genetic risk factors for cancer? Or would we rather know nothing about the risk factors and enjoy a more carefree existence? None of these questions have a right or a wrong answer. It is about balancing the values, responsibility, and freedom of our society. All of us, not just politicians and healthcare companies, need to engage in this debate.

Even if the transition to a modern, digitalized healthcare system brings us new questions, we are convinced that only a forward-looking system based on the five pillars described above can meet demographic challenge and cope with diseases. The "digital pill" goes hand-in-hand with a promise to make healthcare better, more accessible, and more affordable. We advocate seizing these opportunities in a spirit of optimism.

# Glossary and Abbreviations

| | |
|---|---|
| App | An app (short for application software) is a computer program that can perform a range of functions. Apps are normally installed on mobile devices such as smartphones or tablets and expand the functionality of these devices. Apps may be paid or unpaid (= free) and are usually downloaded from an app store. |
| Artificial Intelligence (AI) | Artificial intelligence is a branch of computer science concerned with replicating human cognitive functions and having them performed by computers and algorithms. The idea is to enable computers to solve problems without human intervention, thereby simulating intelligent behavior. |
| Augmented reality | Computer-based enhancement of the real-world environment, for example, by augmenting reality with virtual elements that are projected onto smartglasses or a headset, for example. |
| Biotech | Short for biotechnology, an interdisciplinary science concerned with using living organisms or molecules (enzymes, cells, bacteria, etc.) in technical applications, for example, to produce new active ingredients for medicines. |
| Blog | A blog (short for weblog) is an electronic diary posted on the internet. In this diary, the author of the blog (the blogger) composes items on a variety of topics that can then be commented on by their readers (known as followers). Blogs normally reflect the personal views of the blogger and are not subject to the same standards of journalism as online articles in newspapers or magazines. |
| *BRCA1/BRCA2* | Human genes which, as mutations, lead to a dramatic increase in breast cancer risk. |
| Cardiovascular diseases | Diseases affecting the heart or blood vessels, such as heart attack or high blood pressure. |
| Chatbot | A computer program that enables text-based online dialog with a virtual assistant. Written exchanges with chatbots are so similar to those between humans that it is often hard for the user to tell that they are not in contact with another human, and that the conversation is in fact being managed by algorithms. |

| | |
|---|---|
| Compliance | Adherence to the therapy prescribed by a physician (e.g., medication) during a course of treatment. |
| Computer tomography (CT) | Computer tomography is an imaging process used in much the same way as ultrasound scans or X-rays to help with medical diagnoses. |
| Contact tracing app | Smartphone apps that are used to trace contacts in the context of epidemics or pandemics. The apps identify persons who have been in the vicinity of a source of infection and may therefore also be infected. Contact tracing apps are a means of breaking the chain of infection. |
| Cyberchondria | A mental disorder due to the anxiety-amplifying effects of searching the internet for healthcare information, leading to fear of being seriously ill without any founded diagnosis to this effect. |
| Diseasome | A measure of an individual's genetic predisposition or risk for developing various diseases in the future. |
| DNA | DNA stands for deoxyribonucleic acid. DNA is a molecule that contains our genetic code with all the instructions that cells need to build and maintain an organism. |
| Electrocardiogram (ECG) | An electrocardiogram records the electrical activity of all the heart muscles. An ECG provides a means of monitoring multiple aspects of the state of health of the heart. |
| Environmentome | A measure of the impact of the external environment and the capability of an individual to process toxins. |
| Epigenome | A multitude of chemical compounds that can tell the genome what to do. The epigenome comprises all the chemical compounds and proteins that attach to DNA and can turn genes on or off and regulate the production of proteins in certain cells. |
| ETH Zurich | Eidgenössische Technische Hochschule Zurich, Switzerland. |
| Exacerbation | In a medical context, this is when a disease becomes worse, its symptoms increase, or it flares up again. |
| Generation Z | Generation Z describes young people born in or after 1995, although the exact years in which Generation Z is deemed to begin and end are disputed and vary from one source to the next. One key descriptor used for Generation Z is "digital natives," referring to their familiarity with and fluency in using digital media and the internet as a result of growing up with this technology. |

| | |
|---|---|
| Genomics | A field of molecular biology that deals with the structure, function, evolution, and mapping of genomes. |
| Gigabyte | A byte is a unit of digital information. One gigabyte equals one billion bytes ($10^9$). |
| Gross domestic product (GDP) | Gross domestic product represents the market value of all finished goods and services produced in a country and is thus a measure of that country's economic output in any given year. |
| HD resolution | HD stands for high definition. |
| Health literacy | The ability of an individual to obtain, understand, evaluate, and use healthcare information in order to make appropriate decisions concerning their health in everyday life. |
| HSG | University of St Gallen, Switzerland. |
| Hypoglycemia | Abnormally low blood sugar levels. |
| Lifestyle reward programs | Bonus programs that reward a healthy lifestyle with financial incentives. |
| Magnetic resonance imaging (MRI) | Magnetic resonance imaging is used in much the same way as ultrasound scans or X-rays to help with medical diagnoses. |
| Machine learning | Machine learning technology teaches computers to perform tasks by automatically learning from large volumes of data, instead of programming them to handle the tasks. |
| Metabolome | Derived from the term metabolism, the metabolome is the complete set of metabolic properties of a cell or organism. |
| Microbiome | The sum total of all microbes (e.g. bacteria, fungi) that live on and in the human body (e.g., in the gut, on the skin, etc.). |
| Non-communicable diseases (NCDs) | Also referred to as non-communicable chronic diseases, these include diabetes, cancer, and dementia, for example. |
| OECD | Organisation for Economic Co-operation and Development |
| Off-label use | Use of medication other than for the purpose for which it is approved. |

| | |
|---|---|
| Omics data | Data from various fields of biology, all of which end in -omics, including genomics and proteomics, for instance. |
| Online forum | Online forums are virtual platforms that facilitate the exchange, dissemination, and archiving of opinions, knowledge, and personal experience of a specific topic. The knowledge can be compiled or commented on by the users of the forum. Online forums permit asynchronous communication, that is platform users do not have to communicate in real time and can still read items that were posted years ago. |
| Orthosomnia | An unhealthy preoccupation with improving sleep habits and/or sleep data recorded by a sleep tracker device. |
| Pay-for-performance | Pay for performance is a compensation system, in which payment only becomes due if a treatment delivers the desired results. Also referred to as "outcome-based pricing." |
| Peer group | A group of similar or like-minded people, for example, people with a similar socio-demographic profile. In the field of medicine, a peer group will often be a group of patients with the same disease. |
| PHQ-9 score | A measure of the severity of depression, developed by the American Psychiatric Association. |
| Public-private partnership | Collaboration between a government agency and a private-sector company within a contractually governed special purpose vehicle. |
| Proteome | The full set of proteins in an organism (e.g., a human being) under defined conditions at a given time. |
| Proteomics | The study of the proteome, that is, the full set of proteins in an organism. |
| Quantified self | Self-tracking. The tendency to collect more and more data about one's own life and analyze it (e.g., vital signs, activity, and nutrition). |
| Real-world data | Data acquired outside controlled clinical studies. |
| Renminbi (RMB or CNY) | The currency of the People's Republic of China. The official abbreviation is CNY, although RMB is often used in China. Another common name for renminbi is yuan. On March 30, 2020, one renminbi was worth approximately 0.13 euros. |

| | |
|---|---|
| RNA | RNA stands for ribonucleic acid. RNA is a macromolecule that can carry genetic information and is essential to the production of proteins. |
| Swiss franc (CHF) | The currency of Switzerland and the Principality of Liechtenstein. One franc equals 100 Rappen. On March 30, 2020, one Swiss franc was worth approximately 0.94 euros. |
| Terabyte | A byte is a unit of digital information. One terabyte equals 1 trillion bytes ($10^{12}$). |
| Transcriptome | The set of all genetic sequences transcribed from DNA to RNA in a cell at any given time; that is to say, the sum total of all RNA molecules created in a cell. |
| US dollar (USD) | The currency of the United States of America. On March 30, 2020, 1 USD was worth approximately 0.91 euros. |
| Value-based medicine, outcome-based medicine | A perspective that focuses primarily on the benefits and success of the treatment. |
| Venture capitalist | An investor who provides capital to a company with high growth potential in return for a stake in that company. |
| Vital signs | The key indicators of vital functions. The four most important vital signs are heart rate, respiratory rate, blood pressure, and body temperature. Another vital sign frequently measured in intensive care medicine is oxygen saturation. |
| World Economic Forum (WEF) | The World Economic Forum is a foundation created by economist and philanthropist Klaus Schwab which stages an annual conference in Davos, Switzerland. The WEF attracts leading figures from the worlds of politics, business, and society. |
| World Health Organization (WHO) | The World Health Organization is the agency of the United Nations responsible for coordinating activities in respect of international public health. |
| YLD | Years of life disabled or years lost due to disability is a societal measure of the disease or disability burden in populations |
| Yottabyte | A byte is a unit of digital information. One yottabyte equals one septillion bytes ($10^{24}$). |
| Zettabyte | A byte is a unit of digital information. One zettabyte equals one sextillion bytes ($10^{21}$). |

# Bibliography

## Chapter 1

[1]  Riley, J. C. (2005). Estimates of regional and global life expectancy, 1800–2001. *Population and Development Review, 31*(3), 537–543.

[2]  Zijdeman, R., & Ribeira da Silva, F. (2015). Life expectancy at birth (total). Amsterdam: IISH Dataverse. Retrieved from https://hdl.handle.net/10622/LKYT53

[3]  Field, M. J., & Behrman, R. E. (2003). Assessing health-related quality of life in end-of-life care for children and adolescents. In M. J. Field & R. E. Behrman (Eds.), *When children die: Improving palliative and end-of-life care for children and their families* (p. 41). Washington, DC: National Academies Press.

[4]  Tan, S. Y., & Tatsumura, Y. (2015). Alexander Fleming (1881–1955): Discoverer of penicillin. *Singapore Medical Journal, 56*(7), 366.

[5]  World Health Organization. (2010). *Statue commemorates smallpox eradication.* Geneva. Retrieved from https://www.who.int/mediacentre/news/notes/2010/smallpox_20100517/en/.

[6]  Morgan, A. J., & Parker, S. (2007). Translational Mini-Review Series on Vaccines: The Edward Jenner Museum and the history of vaccination. *Clinical & Experimental Immunology, 147*(3), 389–394.

[7]  Statistisches Bundesamt. (2019). Vdek – Basisdaten des Gesundheitswesen 2018/2019. Retrieved from https://www.vdek.com/presse/daten.html

[8]  Crimmins, E. M., & Beltrán-Sánchez, H. (2011). Mortality and morbidity trends: Is there compression of morbidity? *Journals of Gerontology Series B: Psychological Sciences and Social Sciences, 66*(1), 75–86.

[9]  World Health Organization. (n.d.). Health statistics and information systems. Retrieved from https://www.who.int/healthinfo/global_burden_disease/metrics_daly/en/. Accessed on January 28, 2020.

[10]  Ärztezeitung. (2014). Dialyse: Ein Lebensrettendes Minusgeschäft? Retrieved from https://www.aerztezeitung.de/Politik/Ein-lebensrettendes-Minusgeschaeft-241433.html. Accessed on January 28, 2020.

[11]  World Economic Forum. (2019). Thailand gave healthcare to its entire population and the results were dramatic. Retrieved from https://www.weforum.org/agenda/2019/04/thailand-gave-healthcare-to-its-entire-population-and-the-results-were-dramatic/. Accessed on January 8, 2019.

[12]  The Guardian. (2019). It's a godsend: The healthcare scheme bringing hope to India's sick. Retrieved from https://www.theguardian.com/global-development/2019/mar/21/godsend-healthcare-scheme-bringing-hope-india-sick-ayushman-bharat. Accessed on January 8, 2020.

[13]  CNBC. (2018). Why Medical Bills in the US are so expensive. Retrieved from https://www.youtube.com/watch?v=3NvnOUcG-ZI. Accessed on January 27, 2020.

[14]  The Guardian. (2017). The Americans dying because they can't afford medical care. Retrieved from https://www.theguardian.com/us-news/2020/jan/07/americans-healthcare-medical-costs. Accessed on October 1, 2020.

[15]  CNBC. (2019). This is the real reason most Americans file for bankruptcy. Retrieved from https://www.cnbc.com/2019/02/11/this-is-the-real-reason-most-americans-file-for-bankruptcy.html. Accessed on January 29, 2020.

[16]   Yip, W., Fu, H., Chen, A. T., Zhai, T., Jian, W., Xu, R., Mao, W. (2019). 10 years of health-care reform in China: progress and gaps in Universal Health Coverage. *The Lancet, 394*(10204), 1192–1204.

[17]   Tham, T. Y., Tran, T. L., Prueksaritanond, S., Isidro, J. S., Setia, S., & Welluppillai, V. (2018). Integrated health care systems in Asia: An urgent necessity. *Clinical Interventions in Aging, 13*, 2527.

[18]   US Department of Health & Human Services. (2016). MEPS Data. Retrieved from https://www.registerednursing.org/healthcare-costs-by-age/. Accessed on January 29, 2020.

# Chapter 2

[1]   Kasumov, A. (2018). Soaring health-care costs forced this family to choose who can stay insured. Retrieved from https://www.bloomberg.com/graphics/2018-risking-it-uninsured-family/. Accessed on March 17, 2020.

[2]   The World Bank. (2019). 2017 Life expectancy at birth, total (years). Retrieved from https://data.worldbank.org/indicator/SP.DYN.LE00.IN?locations=US&name_desc=true. Accessed on March 17, 2020.

[3]   Interpharma. (2019). Grosse Zufriedenheit mit dem Gesundheitswesen. Retrieved from https://www.interpharma.ch/fakten-statistiken/1830-grosse-zufriedenheit-mit-dem-gesundheitswesen. Accessed on March 17, 2020.

[4]   AOK Die Gesundheitskasse. (2019). Umfrage belegt Zufriedenheit der Deutschen mit Gesundheitswesen. Retrieved from https://www.aok-bv.de/presse/dpa-ticker/index_22727.html. Accessed on March 17, 2020.

[5]   Gallup. (2019). Healthcare System A to Z. Retrieved from https://news.gallup.com/poll/4708/healthcare-system.aspx. Accessed on March 17, 2020.

[6]   Xu, K., Soucat, A., Kutzin, J., Brindley, C., Maele, N. V., Toure, H., Cherilova, V. (2018). *Public spending on health: A closer look at global trends*. Geneva: World Health Organization.

[7]   World Health Organization. (2015). Current health expenditure as a percentage of gross domestic product (GDP). Retrieved from https://www.who.int/data/gho/data/indicators/indicator-details/GHO/current-health-expenditure-(che)-as-percentage-of-gross-domestic-product-(gdp)-(-). Accessed on March 28, 2019.

[8]   Neue Zürcher Zeitung. (2018). Krankenkasse: Prämien kosten bis zu einen Fünftel des Einkommens. Retrieved from https://nzzas.nzz.ch/wirtschaft/krankenkasse-praemien-kosten-fuenftel-einkommen-ld.1447205. Accessed on June 20, 2018.

[9]   Swissinfo. (2017). Health insurance costs keep on rising. Retrieved from https://www.swissinfo.ch/eng/expensive-coverage_health-insurance-costs-keep-on-rising/43553132. Accessed on July 17, 2019.

[10]  Statistisches Bundesamt. (2019). Statistisches Jahrbuch 2019 – Kapitel 4 Gesundheit. Retrieved from https://www.destatis.de/DE/Themen/Querschnitt/Jahrbuch/jb-gesundheit.pdf?__blob=publicationFile. Accessed on March 17, 2020.

[11]  Tozzi, J. (2018). Employees' share of health costs continues rising faster than wages. *Insurance Journal*. Retrieved from https://www.insurancejournal.com/news/national/2018/10/08/503575.htm. Accessed on October 1, 2020.

[12]  Witters, D. (2019). U.S. Uninsured rate rises to four-year high. Retrieved from https://news.gallup.com/poll/246134/uninsured-rate-rises-four-year-high.aspx. Accessed on July 17, 2019.

[13]  Dezan Shira & Associates. (2018). China's healthcare reforms underscore market growth. Retrieved from https://www.china-briefing.com/news/healthcare-reforms-underscore-market-growth-china/. Accessed on March 3, 2019.

[14]  Fu, W., Zhao, S., Zhang, Y., Chai, P., & Goss, J. (2018). Research in health policy making in China: Out-of-pocket payments in Healthy China 2030. *BMJ, 360*, k234. https://doi.org/10.1136/BMJ.K234

[15]   OECD. (2018). Asia Pacific should reduce inequalities in access to care for the most marginalised groups. Retrieved from https://www.oecd.org/health/asia-pacific-should-reduce-inequalities-in-access-to-care-for-the-most-marginalised-groups.htm. Accessed on January 10, 2020.

[16]   Koopman, R. J., Mainous, A. G., Diaz, V. A., & Geesey, M. E. (2005). Changes in age at diagnosis of type 2 diabetes mellitus in the United States, 1988 to 2000. *Annals of Family Medicine, 3*(1), 60–63.

[17]   Bundesamt für Öffentliche Gesundheit. (2016). *Faktenblatt Nichtübertragbare Krankheiten.* Bern: Eidgenössisches Departement des Innern.

[18]   Cigna Health Insurance. (2015). From sick care to health care: Building a sustainable system. Retrieved from https://3blmedia.com/News/Cignas-Second-Annual-CR-Report-Highlights-Cignas-Leadership-Helping-Build-Sustainable-Health. Accessed on March 25, 2019.

[19]   Bloom, D. E., Cafiero, E., Jané-Llopis, E., Abrahams-Gessel, S., Bloom, L. R., Fathima, S., O'Farrell, D. (2012). *The global economic burden of noncommunicable diseases.* Working Paper No. 8712. Program on the Global Demography of Aging.

[20]   Institute for Health Metrics and Evaluation. (2017). *Global Burden of Disease Study 2016 (GBD 2016) Results.* Seattle, WA: Institute for Health Metrics and Evaluation.

[21]   Suliman, A. (2016). Paging all the doctors: The looming public health crises threatening to take down China's health care system. Retrieved from https://qz.com/756585/diabetes-is-chinas-next-public-health-crises/. Accessed on March 25, 2019.

[22]   Wang, F. (2017). China's Diabetes Problem: From 1% to 10% in 36 years. *The Wall Street Journal.* Retrieved from https://blogs.wsj.com/chinarealtime/2016/11/14/chinas-diabetes-problem-from-1-to-10-in-36-years/. Accessed on March 9, 2019.

[23]   OECD. (2015). *Health at a Glance 2015: OECD Indicators.* Paris: OECD Publishing. http://dx.doi.org/10.1787/health_glance-2015-en.

[24]   López-Olmedo, N., Popkin, B. M., Smith Taillie, L., & Taillie, L. S. (2018). The socioeconomic disparities in intakes and purchases of less-healthy foods and beverages have changed over time in Urban Mexico. *Journal of Nutrition, 148*(1), 109–116.

[25]   Watson, K., & Treanor, S. (2016). The Mexicans dying for a fizzy drink. *BBC News.* Retrieved from https://www.bbc.com/news/magazine-35461270. Accessed on September 3, 2019.

[26]   Gagnon-Arpin, I., Verdejo, J., Sutherland, G., Dobrescu, A., Villa, G., Habib, M., Suarez, S. (2017). Modelling the burden of cardiovascular disease in Mexico and the impact of reducing modifiable risk factors. *Value in Health, 20*(2017), A399–A811.

[27]   OECD. (2016). OECD Reviews of Health Systems: Mexico Report. Retrieved from https://www.oecd-ilibrary.org/docserver/9789264230491-en.pdf?expires=1553518870&id=id&accname=ocid195658&checksum=A5A96C71B36E03434ED65B048493D21D. Accessed on March 25, 2019.

[28]   Lorenzoni, G., Azzolina, D., Gafare, C. E., Gregori, D., & Lobjeois, E. (2017). Eating patterns in Mexico and obesity in children: Results from the NutriRun project. *Archivos Latinoamericanos de Nutrición,* 67. Retrieved from https://search.proquest.com/docview/2076974624?accountid=28962

# Chapter 3

[1]   Neue Züricher Zeitung. (2018). Krankenkasse: Prämien kosten bis zu einem Fünftel des Einkommens. Retrieved from https://nzzas.nzz.ch/wirtschaft/krankenkasse-praemien-kosten-fuenftel-einkommen-ld.1447205. Accessed on June 20, 2019.

[2]   Yun, Y., Rhee, Y. S., Kang, I. O., Lee, J. S., Bang, S. M., Lee, W. S., Hong, Y. S. (2005). Economic burden and quality of life of family caregivers of cancer patients. *Oncology, 68*(2–3), 107–114.

[3] World Health Organisation. (2018). Key Facts Sheet Cancer. Retrieved from https:// www.who.int/en/news-room/fact-sheets/detail/cancer. Accessed on March 21, 2018.

[4] Drewnowski, A., & Popkin, B. M. (1997). The nutrition transition: New trends in the global diet. *Nutrition Reviews, 55*, 31–43.

[5] World Health Organization. (2010). *Global status report on noncommunicable diseases 2010*. Geneva: World Health Organization.

[6] Burger, M., Bröstrup, A., & Pietrzik, K. (2000). Abschlussbericht zum Forschungsvorhaben Alkoholkonsum und Krankheiten. Im *Auftrag des Bundesministeriums für Gesundheit. Schriftenreihe des Bundesministeriums für Gesundheit* (Vol. 134). Baden-Baden: Nomos.

[7] World Health Organization. (2014). *Global Status Report on NCDs*. Geneva: World Health Organization.

[8] World Health Organization. (2017). *Noncommunicable Diseases Progress Monitor*. Geneva: World Health Organization

[9] Gmeinder, M., Morgan, D., & Mueller, M. (2017). *How much do OECD countries spend on prevention?* OECD Health Working Papers No. 101. OECD Publishing, Paris. https://doi.org/10.1787/f19e803c-en

[10] Ärzteblatt. (2018). Männer weiter Vorsorgemuffel. Retrieved from https://www. aerzteblatt.de/nachrichten/98922/Maenner-weiter-Vorsorgemuffel. Accessed on March 9, 2019.

[11] Cheng-Tek Tai, M. (2012). Medical Ethics: An oriental understanding of health, *Tzu Chi Medical Journal, 24*, 92e95. https://doi.org/10.1016/j.tcmj.2012.02.010

[12] Naik, A. (2017). Paying the doctors as long as they keep you healthy. Retrieved from http://ashwinnaik.com/blog/2017/03/03/paying-the-doctors-as-long-as-they-keep-you-healthy/. Accessed on March 26, 2019.

[13] European Commission. (2019). Sweden Healthcare. Retrieved from https://ec. europa.eu/social/main.jsp?catId=1130&langId=en&intPageId=4809. Accessed on July 18, 2019.

[14] Nordenram, G. (2012). Dental health – Health in Sweden: The National Public Health Report 2012. Chapter 16. *Scandinavian Journal of Public Health, 40*(Suppl 9), 281–286.

[15] Health Promotion Board. (2019). Annual Report 2018/2019. Retrieved from https://www.hpb.gov.sg/docs/default-source/annual-reports/hpb-annual-report-2018_2019.pdf?sfvrsn=df71c372_0. Accessed on January 20, 2019.

[16] Phan, T. P., Alkema, L., Tai, E. S., Tan, K. H., Yang, Q., Lim, W. Y., Chia, K. S. (2014). Forecasting the burden of type 2 diabetes in Singapore using a demographic epidemiological model of Singapore. *BMJ Open Diabetes Research and Care, 2*(1), e000012.

[17] Bloomberg. (2019). These are the worlds' healthiest nations. Retrieved from https:// www.bloomberg.com/news/articles/2019-02-24/spain-tops-italy-as-world-s-healthiest-nation-while-u-s-slips. Accessed on December 16, 2019.

[18] Lawrence, D., Shah, A. K., Lee, E. K., Conway, S. J., Ramkumar, M. K., James, H. J., Ashar, B. H. (2018). Primary care provider preferences for communication with inpatient teams: One size does not fit all. *Journal of Hospital Medicine, 13*(3), 177.

[19] European Commission. (2012). *Study on enhancing procurement of ICT solutions for healthcare*. Belfast/Bonn: European Commission.

[20] New England Healthcare Institute. (2010). A matter of urgency: Reducing emergency department overuse. Retrieved from https://www.nehi.net/writable/publication_files/file/nehi_ed_overuse_issue_brief_032610finaledits.pdf. Accessed on March 28, 2019.

[21] Truven Health Analytics. (2013). *Preventing* unnecessary ER visits to reduce health care costs. Retrieved from http://truvenhealth.com/media-room/press-releases/detail/prid/113/Study-Finds-Most-Emergency-Room-Visits-Made-by-Privately-Insured-Patients-Avoidable. Accessed on March 28, 2019.

[22] Caldwell, N., Srebotnjak, T., Wang, T., & Hsia, R. (2013). How much will I get charged for this? Patient charges for top ten diagnoses in the Emergency Department. *PLOS ONE, 8*(2), e55491. https://doi.org/10.1371/journal.pone.0055491

[23] Hawkins, M. (2017). Survey of physician appointment wait times. Retrieved from https://www.merritthawkins.com/uploadedFiles/MerrittHawkins/Content/Pdf/mha2017 waittimesurveyPDF.pdf?source=post_page. Accessed on July 25, 2019.

[24] Irving, G., Neves, A. L., Dambha-Miller, H., Oishi, A., Tagashira, H., Verho, A., & Holden, J. (2017). International variations in primary care physician consultation time: a systematic review of 67 countries. *BMJ Open, 7*(10), e017902.

[25] Medinside. (2017). Assistenzärzte: 90 Minuten am Patientenbett. Retrieved from https://www.medinside.ch/de/post/assistenzaerzte-90-minuten-am-patientenbett. Accessed on June 15, 2020.[26] Woolhandler, S., & Himmelstein, D. U. (2014). Administrative work consumes one-sixth of US physicians' working hours and lowers their career satisfaction. *International Journal of Health Services, 44*(4), 635–642.

[27] Netflix. (2019). 2018 Annual Report. Retrieved from https://s22.q4cdn.com/959853165/files/doc_financials/annual_reports/2018/Form-10K_Q418_Filed.pdf. Accessed on January 1, 2020.

[28] Densen, P. (2011). Challenges and opportunities facing medical education. *Transactions of the American Clinical and Climatological Association, 122*, 48.

[29] Bloom, D. E., Cafiero, E., Jané-Llopis, E., Abrahams-Gessel, S., Bloom, L. R., Fathima, S., O'Farrell, D. (2012). *The global economic burden of noncommunicable diseases*. Working Paper No. 8712. Program on the Global Demography of Aging.

# Chapter 4

[1] Bertelsmann Stiftung. (2018). *Das Internet: Auch Ihr Ratgeber für Gesundheitsfragen? Bevölkerungsumfrage zur Suche von Gesundheitsinformationen im Internet und zur Reaktion der Ärzte.* Gütersloh: Bertelsmann Stiftung.

[2] Doherty-Torstrick, E. R., Walton, K. E., & Fallon, B. A. (2016). Cyberchondria: Parsing health anxiety from online behavior. *Psychosomatics, 57*(4), 390–400.

[3] Mitteldeutscher Rundfunk. (2018). Was "DR. GOOGLE" mit uns macht. Retrieved from https://www.mdr.de/wissen/dr_google_macht_uns_krank-100.html. Accessed on January 15, 2020.

[4] World Health Organization. (2013). *The solid facts: Health literacy.* Geneva: World Health Organization.

[5] Babylon Health. (2013). NHS 111 powered by Babylon Outcomes evaluation. Retrieved from https://assets.babylonhealth.com/nhs/NHS-111-Evaluation-of-outcomes.pdf. Accessed on January 16, 2020.

[6] Topol, E. (2019). Why doctors should organize. *The New Yorker.* Retrieved from https://www.newyorker.com/culture/annals-of-inquiry/why-doctors-should-organize. Accessed on March 1, 2020.

[7] Wicks, P., Massagli, M., Frost, J., Brownstein, C., Okun, S., Vaughan, T., Heywood, J. (2010). Sharing health data for better outcomes on PatientsLikeMe. *Journal of Medical Internet Research, 12*(2), e19.

[8] Alivecor. (2020). Clinicians. Retrieved from https://clinicians.alivecor.com/. Accessed on January 16, 2020.

[9] Medpage Today. (2018). Apple Watch 'should not mean a wearable physician'. Retrieved from https://www.medpagetoday.com/cardiology/arrhythmias/75650. Accessed on January 16, 2020.

[10] Forbes. (2019). Healthy.io raises $60 million Series C and receives FDA clearance for smartphone-based diagnostic test. Retrieved from https://www.forbes.com/sites/james-somauroo/2019/09/12/healthyio-raises-60m-series-c-and-receives-fda-clearance-for-smartphone-based-diagnostic-test/#101139c028b1. Accessed on January 16, 2020.

[11] Roberts, J. S., Gornick, M. C., Carere, D. A., Uhlmann, W. R., Ruffin, M. T., & Green, R. C. (2017). Direct-to-consumer genetic testing: user motivations, decision making, and perceived utility of results. *Public Health Genomics, 20*(1), 36–45.
[12] Pitkin, F., Watson, L. A., & Foster, R. (2017). Direct to consumer laboratory testing: A review. *Annals of Clinical and Laboratory Research, 5*, 2.
[13] Ioannidis, J. P. (2016). Stealth research and Theranos: Reflections and update 1 year later. *JAMA, 316*(4), 389–390.
[14] Wiggins, A., & Wilbanks, J. (2019). The rise of citizen science in health and biomedical research. *The American Journal of Bioethics, 19*(8), 3–14.

## Chapter 5

[1] Hellin, T. (2002). The physician–patient relationship: Recent developments and changes. *Haemophilia, 8*(3), 450–454.
[2] Hao, H. (2015). The development of online doctor reviews in China: An analysis of the largest online doctor review website in China. *Journal of Medical Internet Research, 17*(6), e134.
[3] Practo. (2019). Your home for health. Retrieved from https://www.practo.com/company/about. Accessed on January 20, 2020.
[4] Docplanner. (2019). Making the healthcare experience more human. Retrieved from https://www.docplanner.com/about-us. Accessed on January 20, 2020.
[5] MobiHealthNews. (2018). 95 Prozent of Americans find online doctor reviews reliable, survey suggests. Retrieved from https://www.mobihealthnews.com/content/95-americans-find-online-doctor-reviews-reliable-survey-suggests. Accessed on January 20, 2020.
[6] Globe and Mail. (2018). Doctors can pay to hide negative reviews on websites like RateMDs.com. Should we use them? Retrieved from https://www.theglobeandmail.com/life/health-and-fitness/article-doctors-can-pay-to-hide-negative-reviews-on-websites-like-ratemdscom/. Accessed on January 20, 2020.
[7] Hong, Y. A., Liang, C., Radcliff, T. A., Wigfall, L. T., & Street, R. L. (2019). What do patients say about doctors online? A systematic review of studies on patient online reviews. *Journal of Medical Internet Research, 21*(4), e12521.
[8] Sweeney, V. (2015). Doctor on demand review. *Youtube 13.02.2015.* Retrieved from https://www.youtube.com/watch?v=sxP5EahPQuE. Accessed on January 20, 2020.
[9] Singh, A. P., Joshi, H. S., Singh, A., Agarwal, M., & Kaur, P. (2018). Online medical consultation: A review. *International Journal of Community Medicine and Public Health, 5*(4), 1230–1232.
[10] Harvard Business School Forum. (2015). Yisheng, C. China's DoctorOnDemand app. Retrieved from https://www.hbs.edu/openforum/openforum.hbs.org/goto/challenge/understand-digital-transformation-of-business/chunyu-yisheng-china-s-doctorondemand-app.html. Accessed on January 20, 2020.
[11] BBC. (2019). Would you be happy to see your doctor online? Retrieved from https://www.bbc.com/news/business-47196286. Accessed on January 20, 2020.
[12] Forbes. (2019). AI will not replace doctors, but it may drastically change their jobs. Retrieved from https://www.forbes.com/sites/forbestechcouncil/2019/03/15/ai-will-not-replace-doctors-but-it-may-drastically-change-their-jobs/#140a576f636a. Accessed on January 20, 2020.
[13] Brady, A. P. (2017). Error and discrepancy in radiology: Inevitable or avoidable? *Insights into Imaging, 8*(1), 171–182.
[14] Technode. (2016). AliHealth invests $34m in Medical Imaging Services Company Wlycloud. Retrieved from https://technode.com/2016/03/30/alihealth-invests-wlycloud/. Accessed on January 20, 2020.

[15]  World Bank. (2018). Nearly half the world lives on less than $5.50 a day. Retrieved from https://www.worldbank.org/en/news/press-release/2018/10/17/nearly-half-the-world-lives-on-less-than-550-a-day. Accessed on May 1, 2020.

[16]  Muse, E. D., Godino, J. G., Netting, J. F., Alexander, J. F., Moran, H. J., & Topol, E. J. (2018). From second to hundredth opinion in medicine: A global consultation platform for physicians. *NPJ Digital Medicine*, *1*(1), 55.

[17]  Zion Market Research. (2018). *Global E-Pharmacy market will reach USD 107.53 billion by 2025*. Retrieved from https://www.zionmarketresearch.com/news/compounding-pharmacies-market. Accessed on January 20, 2020.

[18]  Swissmedic. (2019). Swissmedic Leitfaden Arzneimittel aus dem Internet. Retrieved from https://www.swissmedic.ch/swissmedic/de/home/humanarzneimittel/marktueberwachung/arzneimittel-aus-dem-internet/leitfaden-arzneimittel-aus-dem-internet.html. Accessed on April 20, 2020.

[19]  U.S. Food and Drug Administration. (2019). Internet pharmacy warning letters. Retrieved from https://www.fda.gov/drugs/drug-supply-chain-integrity/internet-pharmacy-warning-letters. Accessed on April 20, 2020.

[20]  Zhang, L., Zakharyan, A., Stockl, K. M., Harada, A. S., Curtis, B. S., & Solow, B. K. (2011). Mail-order pharmacy use and medication adherence among Medicare Part D beneficiaries with diabetes. *Journal of Medical Economics*, *14*(5), 562–567.

[21]  Fernandez, E. V., McDaniel, J. A., & Carroll, N. V. (2016). Examination of the link between medication adherence and use of mail-order pharmacies in chronic disease states. *Journal of Managed Care & Specialty Pharmacy*, *22*(11), 1247–1259.

[22]  Schmittdiel, J. A., Karter, A. J., Dyer, W., Parker, M., Uratsu, C., Chan, J., & Duru, O. K. (2011). The comparative effectiveness of mail order pharmacy use vs. local pharmacy use on LDL-C control in new statin users. *Journal of General Internal Medicine*, *26*(12), 1396–1402.

[23]  Waddington, C., & Egger, D. (2008), "Integrated Health Services – What and why?" WHO Department of Health System Governance and Service Group, Technical Brief No. 1, May 2008. World Health Organization, Geneva.

[24]  MobiHealthNews. (2019). Ping An Good Doctor launches commercial operation of One-minute Clinics in China. Retrieved from https://www.mobihealthnews.com/news/asia-pacific/ping-good-doctor-launches-commercial-operation-one-minute-clinics-china. Accessed on January 21, 2020.

[25]  Frost & Sullivan. (2016). 2016 China Hospital Outlook. Retrieved from https://cds.frost.com/p/44959#!/ppt/c?id=P827-01-00-00-00. Accessed on January 21, 2020.

# Chapter 6

[1]  eMarketer. (2019). Digital Ad Spending 2019. Retrieved from https://www.emarketer.com/content/global-digital-ad-spending-2019. Accessed on January 21, 2020.

[2]  Meru Health. (2020). Testimonials. Retrieved from https://www.meruhealth.com/testimonials-all. Accessed on January 21, 2020.

[3]  Dascal, J., Reid, M., IsHak, W. W., Spiegel, B., Recacho, J., Rosen, B., & Danovitch, I. (2017). Virtual reality and medical inpatients: A systematic review of randomized, controlled trials. *Innovations in Clinical Neuroscience*, *14*(1–2), 14.

[4]  Maples-Keller, J. L., Bunnell, B. E., Kim, S. J., & Rothbaum, B. O. (2017). The use of virtual reality technology in the treatment of anxiety and other psychiatric disorders. *Harvard Review of Psychiatry*, *25*(3), 103.

[5]  Cnet. (2018). VR could be your next painkiller. Retrieved from https://www.cnet.com/news/virtual-reality-at-hospitals-could-be-your-next-painkiller/. Accessed on January 21, 2020.

[6]  Mindmaze. (2020). Empowering the human brain to heal. Retrieved from https://www.mindmaze.com/mindmotion/. Accessed on January 21, 2020.

[7]  Nicholl, B. I., Sandal, L. F., Stochkendahl, M. J., McCallum, M., Suresh, N., Vasseljen, O., Mair, F. S. (2017). Digital support interventions for the self-management of low back pain: A systematic review. *Journal of Medical Internet Research, 19*(5), e179.

[8]  Dobson, R., Whittaker, R., Pfaeffli Dale, L., & Maddison, R. (2017). The effectiveness of text message-based self-management interventions for poorly-controlled diabetes: A systematic review. *Digital Health, 3*, 2055207617740315.

[9]  Rose, T., Barker, M., Jacob, C. M., Morrison, L., Lawrence, W., Strömmer, S., Baird, J. (2017). A systematic review of digital interventions for improving the diet and physical activity behaviors of adolescents. *Journal of Adolescent Health, 61*(6), 669–677.

[10]  Wahle, F., Bollhalder, L., Kowatsch, T., & Fleisch, E. (2017). Toward the design of evidence-based mental health information systems for people with depression: A systematic literature review and meta-analysis. *Journal of Medical Internet Research, 19*(5), e191.

[11]  Morrison, D., Wyke, S., Agur, K., Cameron, E. J., Docking, R. I., MacKenzie, A. M., Mair, F. S. (2014). Digital asthma self-management interventions: A systematic review. *Journal of Medical Internet Research, 16*(2), e51.

[12]  Unni, E., Gabriel, S., & Ariely, R. (2018). A review of the use and effectiveness of digital health technologies in patients with asthma. *Annals of Allergy, Asthma & Immunology, 121*(6), 680–691.

[13]  Ma, T., Sharifi, H., & Chattopadhyay, D. (2019). Virtual humans in health-related interventions: A meta-analysis. In *Extended Abstracts of the 2019 CHI conference on human factors in computing systems*, Glasgow, Scotland (pp. 1–6).

[14]  Waltz, E. (2018). Pear approval signals FDA readiness for digital treatments. *Nature Biotechnology, 36*, 481–482. doi:10.1038/nbt0618-481

[15]  MobiHealthNews. (2019). Fragmentation, regulations pose unique challenges for Europe's digital health market. Retrieved from https://www.mobihealthnews.com/news/fragmentation-regulations-pose-unique-challenges-europes-digital-health-market. Accessed on January 21, 2020.

[16]  European Comission. (2018). Privacy Code of Conduct on mobile health apps. Retrieved from https://ec.europa.eu/digital-single-market/en/privacy-code-conduct-mobile-health-apps. Accepted on January 21, 2020.

[17]  World Health Organization. (2003). *Adherance to long term therapies: Evidence for action.* Geneva: World Health Organization.

[18]  Watanabe, J. H., McInnis, T., & Hirsch, J. D. (2018). Cost of prescription drug-related morbidity and mortality. *Annals of Pharmacotherapy, 52*(9), 829–837.

[19]  Proteus Digital Health. (2019). Proteus Digital Health® DigiMeds Data Demonstrates 99Prozent of Hepatitis C Patients at High Risk for Nonadherence Achieved a Cure. Retrieved from https://www.proteus.com/press-releases/proteus-digital-health-digimeds-data-demonstrates-99-of-hepatitis-c-patients-at-high-risk-for-nonadherence-achieved-a-cure/. Accessed on January 22, 2020.

[20]  Thompson, D. (2019). Interview during CB Future of Digital Health Conference, New York.

# Chapter 7

[1]  Frieden, T. R. (2017). Evidence for health decision making: Beyond randomized, controlled trials. *New England Journal of Medicine, 377*(5), 465–475.

[2]  Kassell, L., Hawkins, M., Ralley, R., & Young, J. (2019). *History of medical records: A critical introduction to the casebooks of Simon Forman and Richard Napier*, 1596–1634.

Retrieved from https://casebooks.lib.cam.ac.uk/astrological-medicine/history-of-medical-records. Accessed on December 9, 2019.

[3]   Opentext. (2017). The history of Heath Information Management: From then to now. Retrieved from https://blogs.opentext.com/history-heath-information-management-now/. Accessed on January 22, 2020.

[4]   Aravind. (2019). *Evolution of Medical Records, development and its importance.* Retrieved from http://old.aurosiksha.org/ebook/medical_records_chapter1.html. Accessed on January 22, 2020.

[5]   Swan, M. (2013). The quantified self: Fundamental disruption in big data science and biological discovery. *Big Data, 1*(2), 85–99.

[6]   Siemens Healthineers. (2015). Smart use of Big Data: The key to the future. Retrieved from https://www.siemens-healthineers.com/en-be/news/mso-big-data-and-healthcare-2.html. Accessed on January 22, 2020.

[7]   Andreu-Perez, J., Poon, C. C., Merrifield, R. D., Wong, S. T., & Yang, G. Z. (2015). Big data for health. *IEEE Journal of Biomedical and Health Informatics, 19*(4), 1193–1208.

[8]   Fortune. (2016). Here's how IBM Watson Health is transforming the Health Care Industry. Retrieved from https://fortune.com/longform/ibm-watson-health-business-strategy/. Accessed on January 22, 2020.

[9]   Quintero, D., & Lee, F. (2019). *IBM reference architecture for high performance data and AI in healthcare and life sciences.* Armonk: IBM Corporation.

[10]  Dinov, I. D. (2016). Volume and value of big healthcare data. *Journal of Medical Statistics and Informatics, 4*, 1–7.

[11]  Nature. (2019). The future of electronic health records. Retriebed from https://www.nature.com/articles/d41586-019-02876-y. Accessed on January 22, 2020.

[12]  Arndt, B. G., Beasley, J. W., Watkinson, M. D., Temte, J. L., Tuan, W. J., Sinsky, C. A., & Gilchrist, V. J. (2017). Tethered to the EHR: Primary care physician workload assessment using EHR event log data and time-motion observations. *The Annals of Family Medicine, 15*(5), 419–426.

[13]  Spil, T., & Klein, R. (2014). Personal health records success: Why Google Health failed and what does that mean for Microsoft Health Vault? In *47th Hawaii international conference on system sciences*, Hawaii (pp. 2818–2827).

[14]  Safran, C., Bloomrosen, M., Hammond, W. E., Labkoff, S., Markel-Fox, S., Tang, P. C., & Detmer, D. E. (2007). Toward a national framework for the secondary use of health data: An American Medical Informatics Association White Paper. *Journal of the American Medical Informatics Association, 14*(1), 1–9.

[15]  Koczkodaj, W. W., Mazurek, M., Strzałka, D., Wolny-Dominiak, A., & Woodbury-Smith, M. (2019). Electronic health record breaches as social indicators. *Social Indicators Research, 141*(2), 861–871.

[16]  Domas, S. (2016). Protecting medical devices from Cyberharm. *TEDx Columbus.* Retrieved from https://www.youtube.com/watch?v=EyqwUFJKZo0, 5.12. 2016. Accessed on January 22, 2020.

[17]  Herbert, T. (2018). Was ist der Unterschied zwischen Privatsphäre und Sicherheit? Retrieved from https://www.globalsign.com/de-de/blog/was-ist-der-unterschied-zwischen-privatsphaere-und-sicherheit/. Accessed on January 22, 2020.

[18]  Murgia, M. (2017). How data brokers sold my identity. *TEDxExeter.* Retrieved from https://www.youtube.com/watch?v=AU66C6HePfg. Accessed on January 22, 2020.

[19]  Barth-Jones, D. (2012, July). The 're-identification' of Governor William Weld's medical information: A critical re-examination of health data identification risks and privacy protections, then and now. *Then and Now.* Retrieved from https://ssrn.com/abstract=2076397 or http://dx.doi.org/10.2139/ssrn.2076397.

[20]  Beauchamp, T. L., & James F. C. (2001). *Principles of biomedical ethics.* Oxford: Oxford University Press.

[21] Sim, I. (2019). Mobile devices and health. *New England Journal of Medicine*, *381*(10), 956–968.
[22] Pentland, A. (2009). *Reality mining of mobile communications: Toward a new deal on data*. In *Social computing and behavioral modeling* (p. 1). Boston, MA: Springer.

# Chapter 8

[1] Immelt, J. (2019). *CB insights future of health conference*, February 10, Fireside Chat with Jeff Immelt, New York.
[2] Comparis. (2019). *Jeder neunte Patient erhält vom Arzt keine Rechnung*. Retrieved from https://www.comparis.ch/comparis/press/medienmitteilungen/artikel/2013/krankenkasse/arztrechnung/patienten-rechnung. Accessed on November 22, 2019.
[3] Health Care Cost Institute. (2019). Healthy Marketplace Index. Retrieved from https://www.healthcostinstitute.org/blog/entry/hmi-2019-service-prices. Accessed on November 22, 2019.
[4] New England Healthcare Institute. (2010). A matter of urgency: Reducing emergency department overuse. Retrieved from https://www.nehi.net/writable/publication_files/file/nehi_ed_overuse_issue_brief_032610finaledits.pdf. Accessed on March 28, 2019.
[5] New England Healthcare. (2008). Waste and inefficiency in the U.S. Health Care System. Retrieved from https://media.washingtonpost.com/wp-srv/nation/pdf/healthreport_092909.pdf. Accessed on March 28, 2019.
[6] Pratt, M., Macera, C. A., & Wang, G. (2000). Higher direct medical costs associated with physical inactivity. *The Physician and Sports Medicine*, *28*(10), 63–70.
[7] Etkin, J. (2016). The hidden cost of personal quantification. *Journal of Consumer Research*, *42*(6), 967–984.
[8] Neue Züricher Zeitung. (2016). *Dank der Immuntherapie lässt sich das Leben vieler Menschen mit bösartigen Tumoren verlängern*. Retrieved from https://www.nzz.ch/nzzas/nzz-am-sonntag/neue-krebstherapien-immuntherapie-patienten-leben-deutlich-laenger-ld.117887. Accessed on November 22, 2019.

# Chapter 9

[1] The Nobel Prize. (2019). All Nobel Prizes in Physiology or Medicine. Retrieved from https://www.nobelprize.org/prizes/lists/all-nobel-laureates-in-physiology-or-medicine. Accessed on November 12, 2019.
[2] Neuman, K. (2019). When my mother forgot me. *New York Times*. Retrieved from https://www.nytimes.com/2019/06/21/well/family/when-my-mother-forgot-me.html. Accessed on June 21, 2019.
[3] Gorgan, D. (2018). *The impact of digital health companies on cancer treatments: A qualitative analysis*. Ph.D. thesis, Bachelorarbeit Universität St. Gallen, Switzerland. Retrieved from Katalog EDOK HSG (14611875101). Accessed on March 27, 2020.
[4] Sigrist, S., Bornstein, N., Lesmono, K., Dür, A., & Folkers, G. (2015). *Hacking Healthcare*. Zurich, CH: NZZ Libro.
[5] Markarian, J. (2018). *Robotic automation finds use in the Pharma Lab, Pharmtech*. Equipment and Processing Report, Volume 11, Issue 11.
[6] WATRMC 18. (2018). Abraham Heifets, CEO at Atomwise. Retrieved from https://www.youtube.com/watch?v=TyRuN0PPV8g. Accessed on May 17, 2019.
[7] Williams, K., Bilsland, E., Sparkes, A., Aubrey, W., Young, M., Soldatova, L. N., … Oliver, S. G. (2015). Cheaper faster drug development validated by the repositioning of drugs against neglected tropical diseases. *Journal of the Royal Society Interface*, *12*(104), 20141289.

[8]  Novartis. (2017). Bringing virtual reality to the lab. Retrieved from https://www.novartis.com/stories/from-our-labs/bringing-virtual-reality-lab. Accessed on March 26, 2020.

[9]  MIT Industrial Liaison Program (ILP). (2019). Andrew A. Radin & Andrew M. Radin, twoXAR (Video 1–4). Retrieved from https://www.youtube.com/watch?v=nQy_B1Ddf00. Accessed on May 5, 2019.

[10] Pfizer. (2019). Wie künstliche Intelligenz bei der Medikamentenentwicklung hilft. Retrieved from https://www.pfizer.at/get-science/wie-kuenstliche-intelligenz-bei-der-medikamentenentwicklung-hilft/. Accessed on January 22, 2020.

[11] Bookbinder, M. (2017). The Intelligent Trial: AI comes to clinical trials. *Clinical Informatics News*. Retrieved from http://www.clinicalinformaticsnews.com/2017/09/29/the-intelligent-trial-ai-comes-to-clinical-trials.aspx. Accessed on November 4, 2019.

[12] Harris Interactive. (2001). Misconceptions and lack of awareness greatly reduce recruitment for cancer clinical trials. *Health Care News*, *1*(3), 3.

[13] Antidote. (2019). A year in review: An Interview with Antidote CEO, Laurent Schockmel. Retrieved from https://www.antidote.me/blog/a-year-in-review-an-interview-with-antidote-ceo-laurent-schockmel. Accessed on January 22, 2020.

[14] Antidote. (2019). Clinical trial patient recruitment case studies: The value of saving time. Retrieved from https://www.antidote.me/blog/clinical-trial-patient-recruitment-case-studies-the-value-of-saving-time. Accessed on January 22, 2020.

[15] Haddad, T. C., Helgeson, J., Pomerleau, K., Makey, M., Lombardo, P., Coverdill, S., ... LaRusso, N. (2018). *Impact of a cognitive computing clinical trial matching system in an ambulatory oncology practice*. *Journal of Clinical Oncology*, *36*(15), 6550–6550.

[16] Feiner, L. (2019). Apple CEO Tim Cook speaks with CNBC's Jim Cramer: Full transcript. Retrieved from https://www.cnbc.com/2019/01/08/apple-ceo-tim-cook-interview-cnbc-jim-cramer-transcript.html. Accessed on January 22, 2020.

[17] Bot, B., Suver, C., Neto, E., Kellen, M., Klein, A., Bare, C., Trister, A. D. (2016). The mPower study, Parkinson disease mobile data collected using ResearchKit. *Science Data*, *3*, 160011. doi:10.1038/sdata.2016.11

[18] F. Hoffmann-La Roche AG. (2019). *Roche's position on access to & use of real world data*. Basel, CH: F. Hoffmann-La Roche AG.

[19] McKinsey & Company. (2018). *Real-world evidence: Driving a new drug development paradigm in oncology*. Boston, MA: McKinsey & Company.

[20] Amgen Inc. (2017). How real-world data is transforming drug development. Retrieved from https://www.amgenscience.com/features/how-real-world-data-is-transforming-drug-development/. Accessed on January 22, 2020.

[21] Die ZEIT. (2013). Prof. Dr. med. Zufall. Retrieved from https://www.zeit.de/2013/30/entdeckungen-medizin-geschichte-zufall/seite-3. Accessed on January 22, 2020.

[22] Martin, L., Hutchens, M., Hawkins, C., & Radnov, A. (2017). How much do clinical trials cost? *Nature Reviews Drug Discovery*, *16*(6), 381–382. doi:10.1038/nrd.2017.70.

[23] Westdeutscher Rundfunk. (2016). Die stolze Schwerstarbeiterin. Retrieved from https://www1.wdr.de/archiv/contergan/contergan158.html. Accessed on January 22, 2020.

[24] Rassen, J. (2019, October 2–3). Digital Health 150: Aetion [Conference presentation]. CB Insights Future of Health Conference. New York, NY..

[25] All of Us Research Program. (2015). President Obama speaks on the Precision Medicine Initiative. Retrieved from https://www.youtube.com/watch?v=05gkYTBoRLo&t=3s. Accessed on January 22, 2020.

[26] Lunshof, J. E., Bobe, J., Aach, J., Angrist, M., Thakuria, J. V., Vorhaus, D. B., Church, G. M. (2010). Personal genomes in progress: From the human genome project to the personal genome project. *Dialogues in Clinical Neuroscience*, *12*(1), 47.

[27] Molteni, M. (2018). With Medicare Support, genetic cancer testing goes mainstream. *Wired*. Retrieved from https://www.wired.com/story/with-medicare-support-geneticcancer-testing-goes-mainstream. Accessed on January 22, 2020.

## Chapter 10

[1]   Topol, E. (2015). *The patient will see you now: The future of medicine is in your hands*. New York, NY: Basic Books.

## Chapter 11

[1]   Woolhandler, S., & Himmelstein, D. U. (2014). Administrative work consumes one-sixth of US physicians' working hours and lowers their career satisfaction. *International Journal of Health Services, 44*(4), 635–642.
[2]   Gfs.Bern. (2017). *Verändertes Arbeitsumfeld und Einstellung zu neuen Finanzierungsmodellen: Auswirkungen Leistungsorientierung im Gesundheitswesen erkennbar.* Accompanying study commissioned by FMH 2017. Retrieved from https://www.fmh.ch/files/pdf20/2018_02_15_Begleitforschung_Kurzversion_FMH_WIK.pdf. Accessed on June 2, 2020.
[3]   VSAO. (2020). *Arbeitssituation der Assistenz- und Oberärztinnen und-ärzte: Mitgliederbefragung 2020.* Retrieved from https://vsao.ch/wp-content/uploads/2020/05/FL_Auswertung_Grafiken-und-Tabellen_DE_20200511_V01.00.pdf. Accessed on June 2, 2020,
[4]   Spahn, J., Müschenich, M., & Debatin, J. F. (2016). *App vom Arzt: Bessere Gesundheit durch digitale Medizin*. Freiburg: Verlag Herder GmbH.
[5]   Shrank, W. H., Rogstad, T. L., & Parekh, N. (2019). Waste in the US health care system: Estimated costs and potential for savings. *JAMA, 322*(15), 1501–1509.
[6]   Iten, R. (2012, December 4). Inefficiencies in the Swiss Healthcare system – Improvement areas [Conference presentation]. Swiss Academies of Arts and Sciences, Bern.

## Chapter 12

[1]   All of Us Research Program. (2015). President Obama speaks on the Precision Medicine Initiative. Retrieved from https://www.youtube.com/watch?v=05gkYTBoRLo&t=3s. Accessed on December 19, 2019.
[2]   Nature. (2016). China embraces precision medicine on a massive scale. Retrieved from https://www.nature.com/news/china-embraces-precision-medicine-on-a-massive-scale-1.19108. Accessed on December 19, 2019.
[3]   The Innovator. (2019). China leaps ahead in precision medicine. Retrieved from https://innovator.news/china-leaps-ahead-in-precision-medicine-72cfc469df3d. Accessed on December 19, 2019.
[4]   ICPerMed. (2020). About ICPerMed. Retrieved from https://www.icpermed.eu/en/icpermed-about.php. Accessed on March 25, 2020.

## Chapter 13

[1]   Nature. (2016). China embraces precision medicine on a massive scale. Retrieved from https://www.nature.com/news/china-embraces-precision-medicine-on-a-massive-scale-1.19108. Accessed on December 19, 2019.
[2]   The Innovator. (2019). China leaps ahead in precision medicine. Retrieved from https://innovator.news/china-leaps-ahead-in-precision-medicine-72cfc469df3d. Accessed on December 19, 2019.
[3]   Internet World Stats. (2019). Schätzung zum Anteil der Internetnutzer an der Bevölkerung in ausgewählten Ländern in Afrika im Jahr 2019. In *Statista*. Retrieved from https://de.statista.com/statistik/daten/studie/233368/umfrage/anteil-der-internet-nutzer-in-afrika-im-jahresvergleichnach-laendern/. Accessed on July 31, 2019.

[4] Die Welt. (2018). Wo Ärzte über das Internet Leben retten. Retrieved form https://www.welt.de/gesundheit/article180710664/So-funktioniert-die-Telemedizin-in-Tansania.html. Accessed on December 19, 2019.

# Chapter 14

[1] Public Health England. (2017). PHE highlights 8 ways for local areas to prevent mental ill health. Retrieved from https://www.gov.uk/government/news/phe-highlights-8-ways-for-local-areas-to-prevent-mental-ill-health. Accessed on February 12, 2020.

[2] Garg, V., Molosky, A., Palakodeti, S., & Jain, S. (2018). Rethinking how Medicaid patients receive care. Retrieved from https://hbr.org/2018/10/rethinking-how-medicaid-patients-receive-care. Accessed on February 12, 2020.

[3] Guthold, R., Stevens, G. A., Riley, L. M., & Bull, F. C. (2020). Global trends in insufficient physical activity among adolescents: A pooled analysis of 298 population-based surveys with 1.6 million participants. *The Lancet Child & Adolescent Health*, 4(1), 23–35.

# Index